Become the Primary Teacher Everyone Wants to Have

D1141610

No matter how much you want to teach and no matter how well prepared you are, beginning teaching is tough. A teacher's work is never done; even when you work hard, there is always something more you could do. *Become the Primary Teacher Everyone Wants to Have* tells you what teaching is really like.

As you set out on your teaching career, this book offers thoughtful and sensible support from an experienced and sympathetic teacher. Whether you read the book through from cover to cover or dip into sections you need at particular times, each page has suggestions and ideas to help you lay a solid foundation for a fruitful and fulfilling career in teaching. Chapters cover:

- Getting ready for teaching;
- Teaching to reach all children;
- Assessing learning and teaching;
- Communicating with parents and guardians about teaching;
- Relating with colleagues when teaching;
- Integrating life, teaching and learning.

This book will be an invaluable guide for newly qualified and experienced teachers alike who want to develop their practice and thrive in teaching.

Seán Delaney spent 11 years teaching in primary schools in Ireland before completing a PhD in Teaching and Teacher Education at the University of Michigan, USA, in 2008. Since then he has held positions as Senior Lecturer (teaching and learning and mathematics education) and Registrar at the Marino Institute of Education, Dublin, Ireland. He presents a weekly radio programme about education on community radio station 103.2 Dublin City FM and blogs at seandelaney.com.

Become the Primary Teacher Everyone Wants to Have

A guide to career success

Seán Delaney

Routledge
Taylor & Francis Group

LONDON AND NEW YORK

First published 2017
by Routledge
2 Park Square, Milton Park, Abingdon, Oxon OX14 4RN

and by Routledge
711 Third Avenue, New York, NY 10017

Routledge is an imprint of the Taylor & Francis Group, an informa business

British Library Cataloguing in Publication Data
A catalogue record for this book is available from the British Library

Library of Congress Cataloging in Publication Data
Names: Delaney, Seán (Seán Felim), author.
Title: Become the primary teacher everyone wants to have : a guide
to career success / Seán Delaney.
Description: Abingdon, Oxon ; New York, NY : Routledge, 2017. |
Includes bibliographical references.
Identifiers: LCCN 2016011971| ISBN 9781138675629 (hardback) |
ISBN 9781138675636 (pbk.) | ISBN 9781315560571 (ebook)
Subjects: LCSH: Primary school teaching. | Elementary school
teaching. | First year teachers.
Classification: LCC LB1555 .D435 2017 | DDC 372.1102—dc23LC
record available at https://lccn.loc.gov/2016011971

ISBN: 978-1-138-67562-9 (hbk)
ISBN: 978-1-138-67563-6 (pbk)
ISBN: 978-1-315-56057-1 (ebk)

Typeset in Bembo
by Book Now Ltd, London

Printed and bound by CPI Group (UK) Ltd, Croydon, CR0 4YY

To my parents, John and Martha Delaney,
who always appreciated the importance of teaching

Contents

Author

Seán Delaney is a teacher educator and registrar at the Marino Institute of Education, an associated college of Trinity College Dublin, the University of Dublin. He spent eleven years as a primary school teacher before being awarded a Fulbright scholarship to study technology in education at Harvard University. Subsequently he completed a PhD in Teaching and Teacher Education at the University of Michigan, where his supervisor was Professor Deborah Ball. He presents a weekly radio programme about education on community radio station, 103.2 Dublin City FM, and blogs at seandelaney.com.

Preface

On their first day in college, a group of prospective primary school teachers was asked what they hoped to learn on their teacher preparation course. The student teacher who responded first wanted to become really good at teaching reading. The second aspired to supporting children with special educational needs. The third looked forward to gaining insights from psychology into how children think, learn and behave. Another student teacher anticipated becoming strong in communicating with children and keeping their attention. The fifth student teacher's wish was to 'become the primary teacher everyone wants to have'.

The final student's wish is one to which many novice teachers aspire and it encapsulates their optimism and enthusiasm. Affirmation from children, their parents and the principal matters as you find your feet in a new role. It is satisfying for a young teacher near the end of a school year when a child declares, 'We hope you'll be teaching us again next year'. A teacher walks on air when a parent states 'My child and I are glad you're teaching him or her this year'. And most teachers appreciate the implied trust of a principal who confides 'I know you'll do a good job with that class'.

When you are the teacher everyone wants to have, children look forward to entering your classroom because they realise their voice will be heard and they will be respected; lessons will be interesting, tasks will be suitably challenging, and effort will be rewarded. Parents believe that their child is in safe hands with such a teacher and that the teacher is approachable. The principal is confident the teacher will be reliable and conscientious.

Children and parents may like a particular teacher for many reasons, some of which may be beyond the teacher's control: he's good at music; she does lots of physical education; he's young; she's friendly; he's patient; she's funny. But to be intrinsically satisfied that you have become the teacher *everyone* wants to have, you need to know that your teaching is the best it can be.

Such teaching takes deliberate and sustained effort. By getting a teaching qualification you take an important step in that direction. But even with a qualification, learning teaching takes time, possibly over 10,000 hours.[1]

In this book, I want to share some of what I learned during many years of teaching and studying teaching to help you become the teacher everyone wants to have. I hope that what I've learned about teaching will resonate with you, challenge you or inspire you. Above all, I hope it will provide you with ideas to contemplate, to discuss with others and to vivify your teaching.

When you begin working as a teacher your day-to-day teaching is an immediate priority. Achieving a consistently high level of teaching over time is built on a foundation of competence and confidence. In order to commit to a career in teaching you need to experience success, both personal fulfilment and recognition from your colleagues. In representing the complex work of teaching, this book was written to help you become the primary teacher everyone wants to have and to offer you a guide to career success.

Note

1 This is the number of hours needed to achieve expertise in any field according to Gladwell (2008).

Reference

Gladwell, M. (2008). *Outliers: The story of success*. London: Allen Lane (Penguin Group).

Acknowledgements

I was waiting for many years to write this book about teaching. The impetus that made it possible was receiving a Naughton fellowship to spend a semester at the University of Notre Dame in Indiana in the United States. For that I am particularly grateful to Carmel and Martin Naughton who established and funded the fellowship and to Fr Tim Scully and to Fr Seán McGraw and their team in the Alliance for Catholic Education at the University of Notre Dame, where I was offered the space and supports I needed to get started on the book.

Colleagues in Marino Institute of Education offered inspiration and encouragement in bringing this book to fruition. The Governing Body of Marino Institute of Education enabled me to take leave from my position as registrar to begin work on the book. I express particular gratitude to Professor Anne O'Gara, who supported my fellowship application and showed interest in the project along the way; her support included reading an early draft of the manuscript and offering helpful feedback.

Thanks to Gene Mehigan who made suggestions that improved the appendix on teaching reading. Thanks to Shauna Cassidy, Claire Dunne, Joan Kiely, Michael Flannery, Yvonne Higgins, Gerry O'Connell, Julie Uí Choistealbha, Bríd Ní Chualáin, Mai Ralph, Máirín Ní Chonghaile, Miriam Lambe, Valerie O'Dowd and Patricia Slevin for their helpful contributions. I acknowledge colleagues who worked with me on developing and teaching the Teaching and Learning modules in Marino Institute of Education, helping me clarify ideas about teaching; the colleagues included Karin Bacon, Barbara O'Toole, Anne McMorrough, Suzy Macken, Gene Dalton, Tom McGann, Siobhán Cahillane McGovern, Damien Burke, Sinéad O'Reilly and Mary McDonald.

I learned much from the children I taught in primary school; I am grateful to every one of them. The best learning about teaching comes from teaching in a supportive environment and I was privileged to have taught in such primary school settings in Kilkenny, Dublin and Abbeyleix and I thank the principals and colleagues I worked with in the Kilkenny School Project National School, the North Dublin National School Project and Scoil Mhuire, Abbeyleix; they contributed substantially to my learning as a teacher. In my probationary year as a teacher I learned much from Emer Egan who inspected my work on behalf of the Department of Education.

Later I learned a lot through questions and feedback from students on mathematics education modules I taught in Marino Institute of Education; I learned about the difficulties student teachers have in beginning teaching through their work in teaching and learning modules and through school placement. I thank in particular one of those students, Amy Cooke, who inspired the book's title.

I owe a particular debt of gratitude to the Fulbright Commission in Ireland, who awarded me a scholarship in 1998 which enabled me to study at Harvard University. To this day I appreciate the leap of faith the interview panel – chaired by the late Professor Brian Farrell – took in awarding me the scholarship which opened up so many subsequent opportunities for me.

Later, my studies in the United States brought me to the University of Michigan where I learned so much about teaching from many people, especially from Deborah Loewenberg Ball, Magdalene Lampert and Mark Hoover.

I was privileged to have had many wonderful teachers in my own primary and secondary education. I acknowledge in particular Sr Mary Minehan, Sheelagh Garrahy, Joe Lynch (RIP), Mary Fitzgerald and Róisín Feehan.

Thanks to the guests who have agreed to be interviewed on my radio programme, *Inside Education*; I have learned so much about teaching from my conversations with each one. I also acknowledge Professor Eugene Wall from Mary Immaculate College, who helped me clarify some ideas.

The professional illustrations are by Emer O'Boyle. The children's illustrations are by Rebecca Delaney, Grace Delaney, Laura Vesey and Sarah Vesey. Thanks to Maya Delaney, Kai Delaney and Sarah Vesey who appear in the photographs.

I thank the team at Routledge who had confidence in the project and who have provided immeasurable support in bringing it to fruition. In particular I thank Bruce Roberts, Sarah Richardson and Katharine Atherton. I also acknowledge the work of Richard Cook and Jef Boys from Book Now. It is a better book because of their contributions.

Thanks to Richard Hennessy who made several suggestions that improved the book. Annie Ó Breacháin conceived of and planned joint writing retreats which helped accelerate progress on the book in concentrated periods of time. For this and for her reading manuscript drafts aloud and offering feedback on them, I am deeply grateful.

My mentor as a teacher for thirty years now, since I was placed as a student teacher in his class, has been my close friend John Doyle. John read the earliest drafts of the chapters of this book and I could not have asked for a better reader. Indeed his thoughtful, written responses to my early drafts make a fascinating read in themselves. John offered criticism, affirmation and inspiration in roughly equal amounts. I have learned so much about teaching from my discussions and interactions with John that I am forever indebted to him for how he helped me understand teaching; his fingerprints are all over this book.

Thanks to The Random House Group Ltd., for permission to reproduce an extract from *Zen and the Art of Motorcycle Maintenance* published by Bodley Head. Thanks to the National Council of Supervisors of Mathematics for permission to reproduce material from the *Journal of Mathematics Education Leadership*.

Many people have contributed to whatever merits this book has and I am grateful for each person's contribution. Nevertheless, I accept all responsibility for any shortcomings or errors.

Finally, I want to thank my family. My siblings, Declan, Ethna and Dominic, nieces, Rebecca, Grace, Laura, Sarah and Maya, and nephews, David, Mark, Kai and Ken, are a wonderful source of support and inspiration and a constant reminder of how respect for teaching is a driving force in our family. My parents, John and Martha Delaney, always placed a high value on education and made sacrifices so that I could have the best education possible; for that reason, this book is dedicated to them.

Introduction

Although you may not realise its significance at the time, when you close the classroom door on your first school day, you are opening the door on your career as a teacher. You now have substantial responsibility for the education these children will receive in the coming year. Unlike college teaching practice or school placement, you are now being paid for the work you do. You can make more choices than you could make on school placement from the layout of the classroom, to the displays on the wall; from the classroom norms you'll inculcate, to the routines and procedures you put in place. You are more independent and have been entrusted with educating this group of children. Although your work will continue to be inspected, the scrutiny your work receives will differ to the intense grading and analysis you received as a student teacher. It will come from different sources – the children, the parents, the principal, your colleagues, a mentor, perhaps an inspector, and the wider community.

You have much to contend with in these beginning days as a teacher. Indeed teaching is one job where the responsibility you have on day one, is similar to the responsibility of a teacher with many years of service.[1]

You are likely to be concerned with matters of behaviour. Yes, you were given strategies for classroom management in college and they will work with many children. But sooner or later you may encounter children whose behaviour will challenge you in ways you had not envisaged before. Although some such behaviour may be explained by a child's special educational needs, that does not lessen the impact of such behaviour on you or on other members of the class.[2]

You may be overwhelmed by the workload you face and the time constraints under which you must operate. You're not the only one who finds it difficult to balance activities such as handling ad hoc meetings with parents, checking children's work, preparing for the next day's class, recording assessment findings and meeting other paperwork demands. Getting time to reflect on your day's teaching is almost impossible.[3] Communicating with parents, through notes, visits or phone calls is another demand – especially if some level of conflict is involved.[4] Such communication may range from concerns about homework to worries about academic progress or to allegations of one child bullying another.

Despite the demands and difficulties, a beginning teacher today has more supports than ever before. Your colleagues and the school principal may empathise with your situation and offer support that is readily accessible. Or you may have access to a mentor in your own school or elsewhere who can listen to you, then respond, advise and even challenge you on a range of matters. Your college friends, other friends and your family may also offer support. Apart from the people on whose encouragement you can rely, solutions to problems and inspiration may be found in your college notes, online discussion boards and websites. Depending on where you're living, you may have access to continuing professional development, some of which may be geared towards novice teaching.

And despite everything – your years in school as a student in an 'apprenticeship of observation',[5] all your school placement experiences, what you learned in college, and the level of responsibility you have – it is good to remember that you are a novice in teaching. Novice teachers and expert teachers differ in how they conduct various classroom activities from explaining[6] to using representations.[7] But the transition from novice to expert is neither fast nor inevitable. You could move through up to five stages in the transition:[8] novice, advanced beginner, competent teacher, proficient teacher, expert teacher. So there is little doubt that much of teaching is learned on the job.

And yet, you want to do the best you can for every child in your current class. While you are learning teaching, the children are experiencing a year of their education, an education which shapes many of the opportunities they will have in life. This book was written to assist you as you settle into the work of teaching, to help you move from novice towards advanced beginner, competent teacher and beyond. Teaching is a job where learning for your students and for you is never complete. Enjoy the journey.

How to read this book

This book lends itself to being read in different ways. Each chapter was written to stand by itself and the chapters can be read in any order, depending on your interests. Subsequently, you may revisit particular sections and read them in more detail in order to meet a need you have at a particular time in your teaching career – especially in the early years. You may agree with some of the content and disagree with more. Indeed, a good way to use the book would be in a reading/discussion group with peers or colleagues where you can discuss its content in light of your own experiences. Whatever way you choose to use the book, I hope you find it useful in your development as a teacher, either in its own right or as a way of leading you towards the many helpful sources and resources for teaching mentioned in the notes throughout the book.

Notes

1 Fantilli & McDougall (2009).
2 Meister & Melnick (2003).
3 Meister & Melnick (2003).
4 Meister & Melnick (2003).
5 This is the time identified by Lortie (1975/2002) that you spend in a classroom observing your own teachers while a student; it is, however, a limited apprenticeship.
6 Leinhardt (1989).
7 Stylianou & Silver (2004).
8 Berliner (1988).

References

Berliner, D. C. (1988). *The development of expertise in pedagogy*. Paper presented at the American Association of Colleges for Teacher Education, New Orleans.

Fantilli, R. D. & McDougall, D. E. (2009). A study of novice teachers: Challenges and supports in the first years. *Teaching and Teacher Education, 25*, 814–825.

Leinhardt, G. (1989). Math lessons: A contrast of novice and expert competence. *Journal for Research in Mathematics Education, 20*(1), 52–75.

Lortie, D. C. (1975/2002). *Schoolteacher* (2nd ed.). Chicago: The University of Chicago Press.

Meister, D. G. & Melnick, S. A. (2003). National new teacher study: Beginning teachers' concerns. *Action in Teacher Education, 24*(4), 87–94.

Stylianou, D. A. & Silver, E. A. (2004). The role of visual representations in advanced mathematical problem solving: An examination of expert-novice similarities and differences. *Mathematical Thinking and Learning, 6*(4), 353–387.

1

Getting ready for teaching

Where your teaching is going

A newly qualified teaching friend of mine, working as a substitute teacher for three months, was visited in a city school by an inspector as part of her induction programme. The inspector asked to see the beginning teacher's long-term written planning. 'I don't have it', she said, 'I usually just plan my work from day to day'. The inspector, who was nearing retirement, made no comment and continued with the visit looking through the notes she had. He observed her teaching and generally seemed quite pleased with how she was doing. He got up to leave, shook her hand and wished her well. As he was leaving the classroom, the inspector turned to my friend and asked, 'By the way, I'm heading to C_____ from here, naming a city about 200 km away. What's the best way to get there?'.

'When you leave the school grounds, turn right and go to the end of that road and turn left at the T-junction', she began. 'Then continue straight ahead until you come to the third set of traffic lights and turn right. Oh, no, that may be a one-way street. Actually, I'm not exactly sure; I'd need to take a few minutes to think it through', she continued.

'That's what long-term planning is like', he said. 'It helps keep you on the right road as you travel towards your destination'. He smiled and headed off having imparted a lesson to the teacher that she remembers almost thirty years later.

When teaching a class, your destination could be the final day of the school year. Or your target might be to complete the last page of every text-book. Or maybe your destination is reached when all children have achieved a set of specified objectives. More important perhaps than the destination is the journey you undertake with the children over the course of a school year together. Children don't think about where their education is leading them; their primary concern is about the experiences they are having now.

As the teacher, your job is to navigate. Although the destination is unclear or unknown at the start of the year, you have resources to guide you: a curriculum, textbooks, a school plan, other school policy documents, your knowledge of education, your beliefs about how children learn, the goals you want to achieve and your ideas about creating worthwhile experiences for the children.

Covering the curriculum

'But don't I just have to cover the curriculum?' you might ask, and to some extent that is the case. Nevertheless, although variations and limitations exist from country to country, teachers typically have flexibility to make judicious choices about what topics to cover. Your teaching may be influenced by factors such as events in the world around you, the school location, the school type, the circumstances of the children, the class size and the class level(s) you're teaching. When teaching geography, for example, you will want to develop children's geographical thinking but the specific content you use to do this will be influenced by geographical features specific to the area in which you teach. Other subjects, such as mathematics, may require a more comprehensive, sequential approach.

Your written notes are a record of how you intend to mediate the curriculum for your students across all subjects. A well-written plan of work won't guarantee that you teach well, but it gives direction to your work.

Planning as problem solving

Although most teacher preparation programmes encourage teachers to begin their planning with aims and objectives, many teachers plan their teaching in a less linear way.[1] Most teachers focus on activities they will use in the classroom with the children and this leads them to engage in identifying problems, solving problems, implementing solutions, and evaluating solutions.[2]

The kind of problem to be solved may be how to explain to children in science class what a fungus is and how it grows. Or it may be how to use the available materials to help the children practise throwing and catching in physical education. When trying to solve these problems of teaching, you will draw on your knowledge of the children, the curriculum, the resources

TABLE 1.1 Options for content of long-term and short-term planning

	Planning	
	Long-term	Short-term
Option A	Identify teaching problems	Identify detailed solutions to teaching problems
Option B	Identify detailed solutions to teaching problems	Identify problems of teaching and refer to solutions contained in the long-term plans

available and the classroom setting. The solution to such problems is the plan you devise to teach a particular idea to the children in your class. When you implement the plan, you try to monitor how well it's working; maybe you'll use it again, maybe you won't, or maybe you'll modify it.

The level of detail you place in your long-term and short-term planning for teaching will depend on how you like to plan. You might begin your long term plan by identifying teaching 'problems' to be solved later – simply listing topics you would like to teach the children – such as the Bronze Age, skills of tennis, long multiplication or how to write a story (Option A in Table 1.1).

Alternatively, your long-term plan may record detailed solutions to problems of teaching, which identify how chosen topics will be taught: stating what you expect children to already know, the amount of content to be introduced, the teaching sequence of the content, the teaching methods to be employed, the materials to use and the tasks to set (Option B in Table 1.1). Whether your long-term plan identifies only the topics you'll teach ('problems' of teaching) or the detailed specifications of how you'll teach them (solutions to the problems) will depend on how far in advance you like to plan. At the outset of your career, long-term plans may identify planning problems and short-term plans propose solutions.

Planning as composing

Another perspective on planning compares teaching to the creative arts. Seen in this way, teaching is a composing process and planning is its first step. Before writing a first draft, a writer generates and organises ideas. This is the prewriting stage.[3] It equates to the planning stage in teaching. The actual teaching is the first draft of the composition, and subsequently it may be revised.[4]

Templates for planning

When we set about planning, many of us dislike being faced with a blank page to fill; therefore templates can be helpful as a way to scaffold your preparation. You can choose from many templates when planning your teaching[5] or you may use one you found helpful in college. A standard template may make your planning easier for other people to read, such as mentors, principals or assessors. If using a template supports you in generating ideas, then use the template.

But as you gain experience, you may prefer the freedom to plan on a blank page, in a more idiosyncratic way; that should be acceptable too. Standardised templates risk constraining or homogenising how teachers think about their planning. And constrained planning could lead to constrained teaching – teaching that is flat, lifeless or without personality.

No matter how a scheme is written, the reason for writing it is to focus your thoughts and remind you afterwards of key points. The real plan is not the one on a page but the one in your head. That is what counts when you and the children interact with each other. Your planning is the prelude for such interaction because whether you see teaching as problem solving or composition, planning helps you generate ideas for teaching.

Planning versus preparation

The idea of planning leads some people to assume that you can predict precisely what will happen in the classroom between you, the children and the content in your classroom setting. But teaching is rarely predictable. You need to be prepared for teaching but also ready to respond to unexpected or random occurrences in class. A child might be sick. A child may ask questions you cannot answer. A child may know a song, a story or a website that reinforces a key point in a lesson. Such events can unsettle or enhance your planning. Although the terms planning and preparation are used interchangeably, they are not necessarily the same; planning comes from a rational, objectives model, whereas preparation is about getting ready for action.[6]

Preparation is sensitive to where the teaching is happening and responsive to children in the class. When you are prepared for teaching, your subsequent classroom performance resembles disciplined improvisation[7] – like actors performing improvisational theatre or jazz musicians playing at a concert. You respond to what is happening in the classroom, in a way that is informed by your knowledge of the subject, of the curriculum, of children and of teaching, and by your experience to date. Your experience equips you with patterns you can draw on to inform how you think and act in a new situation[8] and as you gain experience, your repertoire grows.

The preparation and improvisation are accompanied by contemplation, where you give yourself time and space to consider the possibilities of what happened in practice in this place.[9] Contemplation differs from reflection in that reflection tends to be an outside, detached view of what happened and contemplation is a view from inside, and more holistic.[10] The origins of the words give clues as to their meanings. Contemplation happened in a dedicated, consecrated place where you looked at something and considered it with a view to the future. The origins of reflection have to do with bending back or turning back one's thoughts.[11]

When you prepare for teaching the children in a particular class, you will probably consult a variety of books, including textbooks, which are available to you. Textbooks and the associated teacher manuals can provide structure and stimuli to support your preparation. They offer question prompts, recommend sources to consult, and present tasks for children to complete. Although textbooks are written specifically for use with children in a classroom setting and their language is age-appropriate, the information they contain is often dry, sketchy and simplistic.

History textbooks, for example, rarely show how historians disagree on the interpretation of events and the challenge of tasks in most textbooks is set at a low level. That's why it's helpful to draw on additional sources such as your college notes, books for a general readership, reliable websites and the curriculum to select possible activities and materials to use. Such sources are a great help for planning schemes of work tailored to your teaching strengths, your class, your materials and your interests.

Long- and short-term planning

Most teachers write two kinds of scheme of work. A long-term scheme of work offers a way to think about and express the work you will do with your class in the coming year or the coming term. A short-term scheme of work does the same for the coming fortnight or week. I generally prepared two long-term schemes of work each year, one from September to December, and one from January to the end of the school year. For short-term planning I preferred fortnightly schemes of work to weekly ones because in addition to halving the number of schemes I had to write, one week is quite short for exploring topics in depth in most curriculum areas.

Another choice to make is whether to write detailed long-term schemes of work and summary short-term schemes of work, or to write long-term schemes of work in summary form and flesh out the detail week by week or fortnight by fortnight (see Table 1.1). In other words, do you try and solve as many teaching problems as you can at the start of the year and term, or do you prefer to identify the problems at the start and solve them weekly or fortnightly throughout the year? This decision depends on how you like to work.

You can put in a lot of work at the start of the year or the start of the term, when your energy level is high, and research several topics in great detail. Then your short-term preparation will refer to the detail in your long-term scheme, meaning that every week or fortnight only minor adaptations to your planning are needed. Alternatively, if you plan the detailed content every week or fortnight, that content may be fresher in your mind when it comes to teaching it and it can be more responsive to children's interests and ideas.

You could show short-term schemes of work to the children. Perhaps your draft schemes could be projected on the whiteboard and discussed with children in older classes. Would you write the scheme differently if you knew the children were going to see it? In some settings children can use a textbook to predict what topics are coming up in a subject but in other settings or subjects, the topics may be new. It would provide the children with a different perspective on their school work and they may offer some useful feedback on the content of the scheme.

A step further would be to involve the children in preparing the scheme with you. Take twenty minutes at the end of the fortnight to discuss what they have learned over the previous two weeks and what they know about upcoming topics. They may even have suggestions about teaching strategies and they may be able to locate some suitable resources. At the end of lessons I regularly ask children to write down questions they have about the lesson content and to identify topics they would like to work on in future lessons. I do this to make them aware of their own learning and to reinforce it.

When Magdalene Lampert prepares short-term plans and daily lessons, she is both preparing to teach the lesson and to learn from what happens in the lesson so that she can teach future lessons better.[12] This is a useful way to think about preparation for teaching. Preparing is not an activity that ends when a lesson is taught. Preparing and teaching are parts of the practice of teaching that continue in a repeating cycle throughout the week, the term, the year. Preparation informs teaching and teaching informs preparation.

Preparation is informed by the children's interests, their attitude to work, their prior achievement and by your own knowledge of the subject. The subsequent teaching is enhanced and informed by experience, knowledge, preparation and contemplation; in turn the act of teaching extends your ability to prepare subsequent lessons because you learn new things about children from what they do, how they work, the questions they ask and what they understand. What you learn formally and informally from teaching informs the next phase of preparation and the cycle of preparing and teaching continues.

Commercial schemes of work

Some teacher manuals lay out content in the form of an annual scheme of work and you need to decide how much, if any, of such material you'll use. Cast a critical eye over the content of such schemes of work and consider to what extent they identify problems you need to solve as a teacher. You may adapt a published programme as your annual scheme of work or reflect it in your short-term planning. As with all decisions about preparing for teaching, you need to decide how best to use the time available for preparation so as to maximise your efforts to support children's learning.

Collaborating with other teachers for planning purposes

Teachers can easily share schemes of work with other teachers – known or not known to them – using the internet. Such cooperation can be helpful for sharing subject information, teaching methods and helpful resources you hadn't thought of for topics you'll soon be teaching. But sharing schemes of work can lead to producing or reproducing notes you have little ownership of and that are geared towards children in a different setting. Acquired schemes may be a solution to someone else's teaching problems but not to yours.

Your written preparation needs to take into account the interests, prior achievements and difficulties of the particular group of children in your classroom at this time; it must also reflect the location and type of school you teach in, the materials available to you, and your knowledge of and interest in the topics to be taught. Finding the right balance between drawing on ideas in other teachers' schemes and tailoring content and approaches to your own class is part of planning for teaching today.

Working with other teachers need not be limited to e-mailing and downloading schemes. As well as cooperating with colleagues in your own school, you can use online forums to team up with teachers in other locations. Collaboration on schemes of work could enable the exchange and discussion of ideas so that the finished scheme of work leads to more creative teaching than any one person could achieve working alone.

A possible model for this is Japanese lesson study. Lesson study began in Japan and it involves several teachers planning a single lesson together; when one or two teachers teach a lesson using the plan, all the teachers observe children's learning; and subsequently, the lesson is collaboratively revised.[13] Many differences exist between lesson study and preparing schemes of work; it is the collaboration among teachers from different schools that I want to highlight. However, collaboration takes time and however desirable it might be, a teacher needs to manage time carefully.

Written planning and preparation for teaching take time, time that could be spent doing work that is more visible to children, such as reading and responding to children's work, setting up experiments, creating attractive classroom displays, and so on. Although planning and preparation are important, you have to prioritise aspects that directly affect the children's experience. A neat, attractive folder may be impressive, even satisfying, but it cannot be an end in itself. Part of the work of teaching is to prioritise interactions with children and to avoid being overwhelmed by paperwork. Although it is helpful to plan ahead for teaching, and some aspects of teaching can be anticipated in advance, time spent on planning needs to be balanced with time spent preparing for interacting with and being responsive to the spontaneity of children and their ideas.

Being accountable

Your principal may ask you to submit monthly reports summarising the topics the children worked on in the various subjects in a particular month. This is a way for the school to be accountable for the work teachers do. The idea is that by listing where you've been, the principal can understand how your journey with the children is progressing. But it is difficult to do justice to the work you do with children over a month in a short written report prepared as a record for yourself and for the principal at the end of the month.

Although such monthly reports may be required by the principal, keeping records of content you work on together in class is useful for you, especially for revising what children learned and assessing it. It reassures you that you have made progress with the children in a given week or month. Such records may take the form of a class portfolio containing annotated photos or samples of children's work, photos of children engaged in activities, notes from parents, photos of wall charts and so on.

At various times throughout the year, schools who make up the Coalition for Essential Schools[14] in the United States exhibit work done by children in school to children in other classes and to parents.[15] The work that is exhibited varies by the children's ages; children in infant classes read for older children, children in junior classes make presentations for parents and use technology to display their achievements. Older children exhibit their work and put on a mini-conference showcasing their work. In some instances the parents are given criteria to assess some of the children's work. Exhibiting children's work in this way is a fitting tribute to the hard work done during a particular time period by children and teachers. It acknowledges the work in a deeper way than what a written monthly report stored in the principal's office can record.

Big ideas

The content of your scheme of work cannot be comprehensive, and that's a good thing. You don't want paperwork that is so rigid or complete that no light or air can enter. Nevertheless, it's good to be aware of what is not included in written plans. Most templates for schemes of work don't require you to state *why* you're teaching a particular topic. Nor do schemes encourage you to connect a topic you're teaching to a big idea[16] – something the children can learn about life through engaging with a topic. However, it is good from time to time to ask yourself why you're teaching a topic and where it fits in a child's developing knowledge of the world. Important as it is, sometimes it can be difficult to relate what's done in school to broader themes of life.

I studied the play *Romeo and Juliet* in post-primary school but never thought much about it beyond its being a tragic love story. Twenty years later I visited a school in Massachusetts and the children were studying the idea of conflict. They explored the topic by studying both *Romeo and Juliet* and the history of Northern Ireland. Suddenly Romeo was a Protestant and Juliet was a Catholic. A historical event and a piece of literature were used to help children understand different manifestations of conflict. By exploring conflict, something we all experience from time to time, the US teacher connected aspects of history and literature that I had not connected before. The big ideas behind the topics you teach could relate to conflict, but they could also relate to beauty, trust, love, adventure, exploration, discovery, creativity, endeavour, communication, honesty, perseverance and so on. Anything that captures the children's imaginations and that you find interesting will work.

Schools that belong to the Coalition of Essential Schools plan much of their work around what they call 'essential questions'. These are questions about aspects of life that are important and that have either no easy solution or no solution at all. Answering them requires children to conduct research, to reflect on the questions and to pose additional questions of their own. Primary school children work on questions such as: What makes a good friend? Why do you suppose some people break their promises? If there was no electricity, how would our lives be different? What are the traits of a good leader? How would our town survive if a natural disaster struck?[17]

A good question is one that captures the curiosity of the children – they constantly return to it and try to look for new ways to answer it. Although the essential questions given above are roughly ordered by age from younger to older, some questions can be explored at different levels by children of different ages. These questions are typically explored across many school subjects.

Children often link ideas from subjects in ways we don't expect. Recently a teacher I know was asked by one of her fourth-class children if Adam and Eve lived at the time of the Stone Age. The question took the teacher by surprise and she wasn't sure how to answer it. Although the teacher hadn't thought about it before, the boy was simply making connections between work done in history and religion class.

Cross-curricular integration

For many years teachers have been encouraged to make connections among curriculum subjects.[18] Yet, as a beginning teacher I often found that difficult to do. Even teachers with lots of experience find subject integration difficult, which is not surprising given how our education system is organised. You probably attended schools where, at post-primary level at least, subjects were taught as discrete disciplines.[19]

Primary curricula too are usually laid out subject by subject. In college, student teachers are typically taught subject by subject. Textbooks are published by subject discipline. Consequently, few models for sustained integration of subjects exist to inspire teachers to make substantial connections across disciplines. As a reminder to look for connections across subject disciplines, a space for integration on a scheme template is useful. But filling the space where no deep connections are apparent, does little to achieve the kind of meaningful integration that many experts describe.

What appears to be integrated teaching can sometimes be superficial. Integrating drama and history must advance children's thinking in both drama and history. Teachers can use drama to create spaces where children's understanding of the historical society, group, person or event being explored can lead to a deep exploration. To do this effectively, teachers need to understand drama and be knowledgeable about the historical event being dramatised.

For example, it's not enough for children to dress up in horned helmets and swords to act out being Vikings. A teacher needs to construct a Viking space in the classroom, to try and have the children experience the society the Vikings lived in with the choices they had, the views of the world they held and the relationships with each other that they might have had.[20] Each subject discipline taught in school is associated with distinctive practices for thinking or creating. Integration is about interweaving these practices with particular topics as part of planning for teaching.

Daily plans

Another helpful form of planning or preparation, not usually required by principals or inspectors, is a daily plan. When you get more experience, such a plan may not even be written down, though a list can be useful as a reminder of things to do: equipment to prepare or borrow, or a poster to acquire, materials to be photocopied. These plans can reflect last-minute changes that are required, or decisions taken about specific activities that had not been finalised in a scheme.

Short-term planning notes may include decisions about how the room will be laid out for certain activities, or reminders to confirm that the hall, computer room or school library is available at a particular time if necessary. This short-term planning will allow you to respond to the children's interest shown in the topic to date.[21] Such planning usually won't take much time, but can help the day flow smoothly.

Professional judgement

One drawback of schemes of work is that they can be inflexible. Events happen in a classroom that were not anticipated when schemes were prepared. If a major news story breaks, or an interesting visitor calls to the school, it may not be mentioned in your notes. For example, a child may bring in her pet tortoise for the class to see. Another child may bring in memorabilia from when his grandfather served abroad as a soldier with the United Nations. Perhaps you find out about a case of serious bullying among children in the class. Or a particular topic you're teaching may take off among the children, and their enthusiasm, interest and curiosity surpass anything you expected when you initiated the topic. It is difficult to cut short a topic when the children are so captivated by it.

Planning needs to be flexible enough to take advantage of and respond to such moments. Sometimes, though, you may decide that what you have planned in your scheme of work takes precedence over matters that arise informally or casually. Such decisions are difficult because you are trying to weigh up the benefits of spending the limited time you have with the children on something that may inspire them and stay in their memory, versus something that you have put thought into preparing for them. At such times, it is worth remembering that a scheme of work should serve your teaching and not dictate it.

Making a decision about whether to deviate from a plan or to continue requires professional judgement. The term 'professional' is widely used today to describe someone who has expertise in an area such as teaching, and it describes the kind of behaviour or performance that is expected of someone who is conscientious and responsible in doing their work. In teaching, you work in an environment where sometimes no clear unambiguous outcome can be predicted in advance. Instead informed judgement is required of someone who can be trusted to make such a judgement.

You enter a classroom and your students care little about your schemes, lesson plans or objectives. Depending on their age and disposition, they may want to share with you some news from home, tell a joke, chat with friends, finish homework, play a game, make a jigsaw, ask a question, revisit a topic previously taught or simply relax. They are open to learning but what they want to discuss may be different to what you have in mind. You may want to talk about an event from history or about care for the environment, while your students are more preoccupied by a local house fire, a big news story, some celebrity gossip or the result of a football match.

Do you continue with your planned topic knowing that the children's minds may be elsewhere, or do you spend time responding to their interests, even though they are unrelated to what you had planned to teach? Ignoring their concerns is possible but for some children at least, their interests may simmer below the surface, interfering with what you're teaching. Or you could judiciously select one of the children's concerns and explore it.

Such exploration about an unanticipated topic may include trying to learn more about what happened, where it happened, when it happened, how it happened, why it happened, what effects it had and its likely consequences for the future. Resources such as maps, dictionaries, library books and the internet could be helpful guides. Such an approach could lead you into ideas that are new to you, ones where you are learning alongside the children, where you encounter ideas from multiple curriculum subjects and where you depart from what you had planned for part of the day.

Early in your career, deciding to depart from your plan to pursue a topic of interest to the children is not a decision to take lightly. You need to weigh up the benefits for the children's education of going on such a tangent. How you make the choice raises questions about how children learn (e.g. when they are ready, interested and motivated to do so or in a logical sequential way?), what education is for (e.g. completing particular textbooks and materials or better understanding the world around them?) and about the role of the teacher (e.g. an expert on many topics or a learner?).

You see, a teacher is in a trusted position. Within certain limits and in most settings, a teacher has a good deal of autonomy about what topics to teach, when to teach them and how to teach them. In practice, this autonomy is often ceded, in part at least, to the textbooks. Notwithstanding this, the optimal topics, timing and methods may differ from one child to another. Your challenge is to make the best decisions you can for all the children in your class.

In making difficult decisions where multiple options are possible, teachers are not alone. One researcher who looked at how medical doctors worked, noted the following:

> The plain fact is that many decisions made by physicians appear to be arbitrary – highly variable, with no obvious explanation. The very disturbing implication is that this arbitrariness represents, for at least some patients, suboptimal or even harmful care.[22]

If random decisions are made by practitioners of what is considered to be a profession based on rigorous science and where life and death are at stake, we should not be surprised if it happens in teaching.

Many decisions that teachers take about what to teach and how to teach are based on best guesses and tradition rather than on solid evidence. Even though the situations that require such decisions have been responded to by countless teachers prior to now, teachers have few forums and little time in which to share and analyse decisions made and actions taken by their peers and predecessors.

So when you have difficult decisions to make, you may need to draw on whatever wisdom is available to you in making those decisions. Such wisdom can be informed by your own beliefs and may be sourced in your knowledge of education disciplines, in your knowledge of educational research, in the curriculum, in the ethos of the school in which you teach or in a combination of these sources.

As part of your teacher preparation you have probably studied philosophy of education, psychology of education, history of education and sociology of education. Although you may have studied them at an abstract or theoretical level, these disciplines can help you answer critical questions in the classroom. What do children need to learn? Why do they need to learn it? How do children learn? Why is this subject on the curriculum? What is it like to be a child of a linguistic or ethnic minority in this class? What is it like to have parents who are economically poor in this class? The disciplines can help you analyse any classroom situation in which you find yourself and help you make judgements about what to teach and when.

Educational research may also be useful for guiding decisions. The problem with research is that it can be difficult to access when needed. The available research is rarely accessible to teachers in distilled form and it is frequently written in language that is impenetrable for practising teachers. Findings of individual studies can be contradictory or so nuanced as to be difficult to apply in a given situation. And too often research and opinion are mixed together at all levels of the education system from teacher education to policy documents.[23]

Another source of guidance in decision making is the relevant curriculum, which identifies priorities for learning. Although curricula provide details about what children are expected to learn in each curriculum area, they usually articulate a set of aims, principles and features that can give direction to your work. For example, one curriculum prioritises the following aims for children:

- to enable the child to live a full life as a child and to realise his or her potential as a unique individual;
- to enable the child to develop as a social being through living and cooperating with others and so contribute to the good of society; and
- to prepare the child for further education and lifelong learning.[24]

Such overarching aims provide another source of guidance for teachers in their work. They are challenging because they seem quite simple and obvious and yet, amidst the hustle and bustle of a classroom with lively children, several textbooks, and daily demands, they can seem quite remote or unachievable. But they provide the backdrop against which teaching and learning is intended to happen.

The school's ethos may also help inform your judgement in teaching. Sometimes schools express their ethos in a mission statement, some take inspiration from the person or group who established the school or from a local person or historical figure of note, and other schools may have a more implicit ethos. The ethos helps prioritise what is valued in your school and may guide how you respond to situations from a child arriving in class hungry to how you deal with an incident of money stolen from someone in the classroom.

Not every decision you make in the classroom can or will be considered through disciplinary lenses, research lenses and so on. Such lenses indicate possible sources of guidance for you as you begin to teach. And some problems and decisions are worth considering from multiple perspectives. Over time you will be able to make such decisions almost by instinct but initially, more deliberation is required. Of course a teacher cannot deliberate over every decision. That would be exhausting. In order to reduce the number of decisions that have to be made daily, teachers create classroom routines.

Routines

Much of your teaching will be based around routines that you establish early in the year. A routine is something that is done regularly in the class by the teacher or by the children so that it becomes almost automatic. Picture a teacher announcing to the children that it is time for the class to go to the computer room. Without further instruction, every child stands up, puts their bag on their chair, pushes the chair under the table and waits for the teacher to announce which table is to line up first. That is a routine.

Think of a child reading aloud for the class a story he has just written. When he finishes, several children respond by making one positive comment and posing one question for the author. That is a routine.

Imagine a teacher putting a mathematics calculation on the board for the class to solve. One child is asked for her answer. Regardless of whether the answer is correct or incorrect, the teacher asks, 'And how did you figure that out?'. That is a routine. It is something that happens regularly, almost without thinking, so that the teacher and children can focus their efforts on learning new content rather than inventing everything afresh each day.

Such routines may or may not be described in your scheme but they are essential to the smooth running of the classroom. You may even take some routines for granted because they are ones you learned from teachers on school placement or even from teachers who taught you. Routines can be set up to cover teaching decisions (such as what materials to use, when to use group work, how long to spend on an activity), teaching styles and strategies, and classroom management.[25] They are activities done so regularly that after a while neither you nor the children are conscious that you are following a routine. But at the start of the year it is worth investing time in planning and implementing them.

Once routines are known by you and the children, they create thinking time for you and reduce confusion for children because fewer lengthy, daily explanations are required. Specific routines include decisions such as how desks and chairs will be laid out in the classroom, where a lesson takes place (e.g. computer room, gym, part of classroom), the typical structure and sequence of a lesson (e.g. first check homework, then present task, then discuss work done on task), who will be involved (whole class, one group at a time, individual child), what behaviour is expected, how children's achievement and behaviour are monitored, how instructions are given, how materials are distributed to the class, how copies are to be laid out, the writing style to be used, instruments that can be used for writing and colouring, what to do when finished work early, transitions between lessons, tidying up the room, where to store books during the day and overnight, entering and leaving the room, and going to the toilet. Once established, each routine frees time for you to attend to the many novel issues that arise as you and the children interact with each other and with the subject matter in the busy environment of the classroom.

Checklists

Atul Gawande writes that a big problem confronting professionals across many fields today is not that we don't have enough information to do our work. It is that we are overwhelmed with ideas and information.[26] The difficulty is getting the information you need when you need it. A teacher teaching several subjects has much to know and recall: key teaching points, productive tasks for children, useful teaching strategies, examples and representations of content, probing questions, fruitful connections across topics, which content is difficult and which is easy for children, which children will find particular content easy or difficult, and typical prior knowledge and misconceptions held by children.

In the atmosphere of a busy classroom it is easy to forget or omit some key teaching points or to miss opportunities for cross-curricular links with other subjects or topics. Gawande notes that the work of airline pilots and surgeons has been made safer by using specially designed checklists to follow when implementing difficult aspects of their work. Gawande advocates checklists as a way to routinely check that something important has been done when it should be done. Checklists take many different formats and are developed in different ways.

Although several checklists for teachers are available on the World Wide Web, I am not aware of their widespread use in teaching. Yet it seems as if checklists could help teachers prepare for many aspects of teaching from teaching specific topics to conducting a parent–teacher meeting, and from writing a class test to equipping a classroom. Usable checklists have several features including clarity, efficiency, precision, practicality, brevity and having been tested in the real world.[27] It seems as if identifying the potential of such checklists and developing them would be a worthwhile professional activity and a way to promote teamwork among teachers.

Timetable

You will probably follow a timetable. A few teachers I know use alternative approaches to timetables, where they plan their work around activity centres or they structure the day around questions and topics raised by the children which are interrogated in great depth, leading from one topic or question of interest to another. Such approaches require experience and substantial teacher subject knowledge to work effectively.

I find that using a timetable helps ensure that I allocate sufficient time to every subject – especially those I find more difficult to teach. I usually shared a copy of the timetable with children in older classes I taught because they like knowing what is coming up and it encouraged me to follow it as much as possible.

Following the timetable precisely is not always possible. Teaching and learning don't happen in neat slots on a timetable. Sometimes a poem I was teaching fell flat; it just didn't work with the class and I finished the lesson early. More often, when the time for a lesson was up, we still had plenty to do and, perceiving that the children were working productively or on the verge of grasping a new idea, I would let the lesson overrun into the next subject's time. That would have a domino effect on other lessons until the bell rang, when it was no longer possible to extend the time. Break times are sacrosanct for the children, if not for the teacher.

When I drew up a timetable for the first class I taught, I tried to vary what I was doing at different times, to make the days interesting for the children. One day we'd start with mathematics, another day with English, another day with history and so on. A mentor suggested that children like routine and they like to have the same subjects at the same time of the day. From then on I made my timetables more predictable in format and they generally worked well.

Another teacher I know talks about the temperature of the class and the importance of evaluating the temperature to know what content and what kind of activity to do at particular times of the day. Some classroom activities raise the temperature of the class; children become more boisterous, more active and more vocal at these times. Visual art lessons, drama, music, class discussions, group work and physical education may raise the class temperature because of children's excitement or just the physical activity involved. Other activities lower the classroom temperature: writing, reading, individual work, and thinking time are examples. The idea is to be conscious of that fact and to vary activities throughout the day. In general it makes sense to follow an activity that raises the classroom temperature with one that lowers it.

I used to teach art lessons to senior classes on Friday afternoons. Children were excited at the prospect of the weekend and consequently, they found it difficult to focus on the visual arts lesson, which led sometimes to quite boisterous behaviour. Applying the principle of regulating the classroom 'temperature', I eventually learned to timetable writing lessons for last class on a Friday afternoon and visual arts lessons for first class on a Monday morning. When I made this change, the children looked forward to coming to school and having visual arts on Monday mornings. Their behaviour on Friday afternoons improved too.

Students' interest and attention

So your schemes of work are ready and the timetable is in place; it might seem as if the teaching is now the easy bit. Not quite. Written preparation neither captures all that happens in your class nor guarantees that your teaching will be animated. The schemes or work are prepared at home, or in the classroom before or after class. Now you have to win over the children's interest and attention.

Depending on the class level and the time of year, their minds could be preoccupied with how their team is doing in the league, who is doing well in some reality TV contest, the sports they'll play at lunchtime, how they'll surpass the highest score on their computer game, where they're going with their Granny on Saturday, the row they had with their best friend, how they can impress the boy or girl they fancy in the class, concerns about their parents constantly arguing at home, and so on. Your job is to get the children to put aside these concerns for long enough to focus on what you have prepared to teach them. For some children, that will take little effort, for others it will take a lot.

In order to get the children interested in learning, a teacher can tap into some inherent drives we all have – to satisfy curiosity, to be competent and to belong to a community of learning.[28] Posing questions that will be answered during a lesson may help you to tap into children's curiosity. You could ask, for example, 'Have you ever wondered how our town got its name?' or 'What game, which is now played all over the world, was invented because snowy, cold weather prevented children in one school from playing outdoor games?'[29] You could announce that you're going to show them how to make sure that they don't get overcharged when they go shopping. You could tap into their curiosity by showing the class a closed box or a suitcase and wonder aloud what could be in it.

The experience of success will also motivate children. When children achieve competence and begin to develop confidence associated with that, they may be inclined to want to learn more. Contributing to a task or a project as a member of a group is another way to interest children in their school work.

However, getting children's attention is just the first step. If children are going to learn, you need to build on their attention. Just knowing how the town got its name may not be enough to create empathy with the people who first settled in an area. Knowing why a game was invented may not be enough to understand the mind-set of someone who had the creativity to invent a game. In order to avoid being overcharged, children may need to spend time estimating the cost of various shopping baskets and trolleys so that they will be able to do it for themselves. And although the suitcase of a soldier containing artefacts from a war may get children's attention, more ambitious and thoughtful teaching will be needed to help children under-stand the cause of the war and the horror of living through it.

Even when you have the children's attention, lessons can go off-track. Children may ask questions you did not anticipate and to which you do not know the answer. A more difficult kind of question to answer is when a child asks in any subject or for any topic 'Why do we have to learn this?'. It's a reasonable question; why shouldn't a student know why something is worth learning? Most topics and subjects are taught for a combination of educa-tional, economic, social and political reasons. You can fob off the question by responding that children have to learn it because it's on the curriculum. Or you can tell children that they'll need it when they're older. Ted Sizer refers to this as the 'castor oil problem' – take it now and you'll feel better later.[30]

How you explain why you're teaching a given topic will vary from class to class and from school to school, depending on children's prior experiences and the experiences of their families. Why do we learn mathematics? Because it helps train your mind to think well. It might help you get a job. You'll be able to estimate the cost of your purchases at the supermarket. All answers are valid but not all will satisfy children who are struggling to complete a page of fraction calculations.

Why do we learn history? It helps us appreciate our heritage. The past has shaped the lives we live today. We may learn lessons from the past that will guide future decisions. Again, various answers are possible but will they motivate a child to empathise with children who were alive in Ancient Rome?

An alternative approach would be to turn the question back to the child and open up the discussion to the class. Why do they think a subject is important or not important? That option won't work for every class but with some classes the question could be discussed in a way that brings to the surface ideas and conceptions the children hold about a subject and why they are learning it. And it is good for learners to think about why they are learning what they are learning, just as it is good for teachers to think about why they are teaching what they are teaching.

Nevertheless, questions from children like 'Why do we have to learn this?' can be disheartening when they are asked because they seem to imply that the student is thinking 'This work is boring' or 'I'm not enjoying what we're doing'. If it's any consolation, most teachers face similar questions from time to time.

Teachers generally work hard to make lesson content as interesting as possible for children, within the constraints imposed by the curriculum, the materials available, the parents' expectations, the classroom environment and the composition of the children in the class. Sometimes when children seem to indicate lack of interest it may prompt you to rethink how you teach and what you can do to make a topic more interesting. But teachers are not entertainers. Learning at all levels requires effort and even some drudgery. The idea of learning as fun is enticing, and sometimes learning really is fun. But often learners need to persevere through difficult terrain before reaching a more hospitable place; the consolation for children is that the teacher is there to help if they get stuck.

A related idea is that education should be relevant to children.[31] The idea of teaching content that is meaningful, interesting and useful to children makes sense. I have used scenarios around lengths of swimming pools to make multiplying and dividing metres relevant and have chosen material for reading lessons based on children's interests. However, teaching for relevance is more than teaching what is immediately relevant.[32] Teaching must introduce children to ideas and insights that are enduring[33] and that help them live well in their village, town, county, country, continent and in the world.

Key points of Chapter 1

1 Schemes of work document how you solve problems of teaching.

2 Planning is done for accountability; preparation is part of teaching and done to directly help children's learning.

3 Try to identify the big ideas that lie behind everything you teach.

4 Professional judgement about teaching decisions is informed by your knowledge of education disciplines, education research, the curriculum, and the school ethos.

5 Routines can make your classroom run more efficiently.

6 Make work interesting where possible and help children learn that although learning is worthwhile, not all learning is fun in the short term.

7 Record and publish work done and work being done for children and their families to observe and for your own satisfaction with progress made.

Notes

1 John (2006); Yinger (1980).
2 Yinger (1980).
3 Rodrigues (1983).
4 Owen (1991).
5 See for example http://www.teacherinduction.ie/planning/planning-primary and http://nccaplanning.ie/.
6 Yinger (1990).
7 Described by Sawyer (2004).
8 Yinger (1990, p. 85).
9 Yinger (1990).
10 Yinger (1990).
11 Barnhardt (1988/2003).
12 Lampert (2001, p. 119).
13 Lenski, Caskey & Anfara (2009).
14 http://www.essentialschools.org/
15 For more see http://www.essentialschools.org/resources/375.

16 See for example, http://www.authenticeducation.org/ae_bigideas/article.lasso?artid=99

17 Questions taken from or inspired by Jamie McKenzie (2005) Chapter 10, 'Essential questions'.

18 This is sometimes referred to as cross-curricular work, curriculum integration, or interdisciplinary work and is closely associated with thematic work (Hayes, 2010). Models of integration have been identified by Fogarty (1991).

19 A process of change is currently in place in relation to the junior cycle in Ireland's post-primary schools. The goal is to organise students' learning around 24 statements of learning rather than around specific subjects. See http://www.juniorcycle.ie/NCCA_JuniorCycle/media/NCCA/Documents/JC-Framework_FINAL_02oct12.pdf for more details.

20 This example is from Fionnuala Waldron, of Dublin City University. Hear a podcast of my interview with her at http://insideeducation.podbean.com/2013/04/21/programme-172-fionnuala-waldron-on-teacher-education-21-4-13/.

21 For more details on this see Yinger (1980).

22 From Eddy, D. (1990), 'The challenge' in *Journal of the American Medical Association*, 263(2), 287–290, cited in Gawande (2002, p. 239).

23 However, some entities have attempted to prepare or synthesise policy-ready research findings. Three such entities are the International Performance Indicators in Primary Schools centre at Durham University (www.cem.org/evidence-based-education), the Centre for Research and Reform in Education at Johns Hopkins University (http://education.jhu.edu/research/crre/), and the Institute of Education Sciences (http://ies.ed.gov/).

24 Government of Ireland (1999, p. 7).

25 The section on routines uses ideas and examples from Yinger (1980).

26 Gawande (2011).

27 Gawande (2011).

28 Bruner (1966).

29 The game is basketball and it was invented by James Naismith: http://en.wikipedia.org/wiki/James_Naismith.

30 Sizer (1992, p. 159).

31 Rogers (1969, p. 137), cited on p. 41 of Furedi (2009).

32 Shane (1971).

33 Furedi (2009).

References

Barnhardt, R. K. (Ed.). (1988/2003). *Chambers dictionary of etymology*. New York: Chambers.

Bruner, J. S. (1966). *Toward a theory of instruction*. Cambridge, MA: Belknap Press of Harvard University Press.

Fogarty, R. (1991). Ten ways to integrate curriculum. *Educational Leadership, 49*(2), 61–65.

Furedi, F. (2009). *Wasted: Why education isn't educating.* London: Continuum.

Gawande, A. (2002). *Complications: A surgeon's notes on an imperfect science.* New York: Picador.

Gawande, A. (2011). *The checklist manifesto: How to get things right.* London: Profile Books.

Government of Ireland. (1999). *Primary school curriculum: Introduction.* Dublin: The Stationery Office.

Hayes, D. (2010). The seductive charms of a cross-curricular approach. *Education 3–13: International Journal of Primary, Elementary and Early Years Education, 38*(4), 3811–3387. doi: 10.1080/03004270903519238

John, P. D. (2006). Lesson planning and the student teacher: Re-thinking the dominant model. *Journal of Curriculum Studies, 38*(4), 483–498.

Lampert, M. (2001). *Teaching problems and the problems of teaching.* New Haven, CT: Yale University Press.

Lenski, S. J., Caskey, M. M. & Anfara, V. A. (2009). Using the lesson study approach to plan for student learning. *Middle School Journal, 40*(3), 50–57.

McKenzie, J. (2005). *Learning to question to wonder to learn.* Bellingham, WA: FNO Press.

Owen, F. (1991). Teaching as a composing process. *The English Journal, 80*(3), 57–62.

Rodrigues, R. J. (1983). Tools for developing prewriting skills. *The English Journal, 72*(2), 58–60.

Sawyer, R. K. (2004). Creative teaching: Collaborative discussion as disciplined improvisation. *Educational Researcher, 33*(2), 12–20.

Shane, H. G. (1971). The rediscovery of purpose in education. *Educational Leadership, 28*(6), 581–584.

Sizer, T. R. (1992). *Horace's compromise: The dilemma of the American high school.* Boston: Mariner Books (A Houghton Mifflin Company).

Yinger, R. J. (1980). A study of teacher planning. *The Elementary School Journal, 80*(3), 107–127.

Yinger, R. J. (1990). The conversation of practice. In R. T. Clift, W. R. Houston & M. C. Pugach (Eds), *Encouraging reflective practice in education: An analysis of issues and programs.* New York: Teachers' College Press.

2

Creating an atmosphere for teaching

Misbehaviour undermines teaching

Beginning teachers often worry about managing children's behaviour in the classroom. Many experienced teachers think about this too but over time most teachers develop at least enough survival skills to ensure that most classroom interactions are focused on academic work.

Student misbehaviour can take various forms. It can be limited to one or two children who frequently disrupt the class with inappropriate comments and actions; or several children or groups of children in a class may exhibit misbehaviour which, though apparently not connected, cumulatively makes teaching the class difficult. Misbehaviour can be occasional, frequent or constant; it can be minor, moderate or serious. It can be directed at the teacher, at classmates, at property or at no-one in particular.

Describing it in this way makes misbehaviour sound abstract, but lies, taunts, interruptions, mumbling, passing notes and throwing objects are very concrete for a teacher who goes home from school upset, who is reluctant or afraid to discuss it with colleagues or the principal and who knows not how to respond to it. Indeed, student misbehaviour is a major cause of job dissatisfaction among teachers, especially early in their careers.[1]

Misbehaviour not only affects the teacher but children too can be upset by it. Quiet children may feel threatened by an unruly environment. Children who want to work and achieve may resent the attention given to noisy peers. Non-participants in creating trouble, who seem to enjoy it when it's happening, may feel conflicted afterwards about observing a classmate or a teacher who is upset. Sometimes even the perpetrators can feel remorse but seem to be caught in a cycle that is difficult to break out of without losing face.

A working classroom needs order, not as an end in itself, but to create the conditions where every child feels safe and is enabled to grow intellectually, emotionally, spiritually, physically and socially. An ordered classroom does not need to be a joyless, austere place; it is an atmosphere where a constructive work ethic is tempered by a respectful sense of goodwill, fun and humour. Mutual respect among children and between the teacher and the children is the oil that keeps the parts of the classroom engine moving smoothly, avoiding unnecessary friction.

Friction in any relationship is draining. Even when teaching goes well, it saps your energy. Teaching in an environment with ongoing friction makes the work exhausting. It is difficult to concentrate on preparing well or teaching well when lessons are constantly being undermined by out-of-place actions and comments. As a result, teachers develop various skills and strategies for having children desist from misbehaving.

Ignore it. Raise the voice. Rule with an iron fist. Impose incentives and sanctions.[2] Reprimand the class. Reiterate the class rules. Isolate and discuss the matter with the main culprit. Seek support from websites or online forums.[3] Use online resources for managing children's behaviour.[4] Send children to a colleague or to the principal. Blame it on the children's home situations. Contact a parent. Some of these strategies may help and may make it possible to teach well.

For substitute teachers, who often do not have the time to establish a relationship with the children, using such measures may be essential. Some of the strategies listed above, however, respond to symptoms rather than to addressing underlying causes of misbehaviour. Furthermore, children learn from how a teacher responds to classroom misbehaviour. Therefore I'd like to discuss some dimensions of children's misbehaviour and ways of preventing, or at least minimising, it.

But let's take a moment first to think about the complexity of classroom behaviour and interactions. At any moment in a classroom, many things are happening. Visualise a scene in a classroom where a teacher, Ms Murphy, is discussing with the class the build-up to World War I. Several children appear to be attending carefully and participating in the discussion.

However, one boy has his hand up to ask a question related to the lesson topic. A girl has her hand up because she wants to go to the toilet. A girl sitting at the back right desk just punctured an ink cartridge with a compass and the ink is flowing onto her desk. The boy sitting beside her is looking for some tissue paper to mop up the ink. One boy is alternatively making sounds and throwing rolled-up balls of paper across the room to attract the attention of another boy, and trying not to attract the teacher's attention. Another boy is resting his head on his hands because he has been feeling unwell since break-time. Then an announcement comes over the classroom intercom from the principal asking children who have paid for school tracksuits to go immediately to the school office. All these incidents are competing for Ms Murphy's attention in addition to the main work of leading the discussion.

Some matters are one-off happenings that can be ignored. Some need to be dealt with immediately and no more thought of them. Others need to be seen as part of a larger pattern of events in the classroom that provide information about some children's application to their work; those are the ones worth recording. When all these things are happening, Ms Murphy is trying to prioritise the main work which is the class discussion about World War I and so she tries to respond to the various actions in a way that minimises any disruption to that. It is only afterwards, when things have settled that a teacher can begin to see things in perspective, to see which actions are part of a bigger pattern and thus are worth noting. Taking time to think back on interactions from the school day is often referred to as reflective practice.[5]

A child in a classroom where such events are taking place may be oblivious to many of them. Each student sees a classroom from their own point of view. A teacher, in contrast, is constantly monitoring what is happening in all parts of the classroom to ensure that children are on task, interested, attending, and that everyone is safe. Teachers respond to interruptions, whether it is a parent delivering a child's forgotten lunch, children delivering milk for break-time, a colleague withdrawing children for a learning support lesson or the principal speaking over the intercom.

Often noise from an adjacent classroom or from the road outside intrudes on a lesson. Some children complain that they are too warm, others are too cold; some children can't find their books when they need them and others need to borrow a pen or a ruler. Teachers are constantly monitoring such activities and this is what drains a teacher's energy in the course of a day, a week, a term, a year. It is work that is invisible to many and runs parallel to teaching, but if such monitoring does not happen, the class won't run smoothly. Another factor that contributes to the smooth flow of teaching is the classroom culture that is created.

Classroom culture

The word 'culture' has come to mean many things but it originates from the Latin word '*cultura*' meaning cultivation.[6] It conveys the idea of careful preparation for something that, with suitable attention and nurturing, will bear fruit over time. The meaning I have in mind relates to the attitudes, values, goals and practices[7] that are cultivated in your classroom and in the school as a whole.

Let's take the classroom first. Whether you recognise or acknowledge it, a culture becomes established in your classroom. It determines matters such as which children's ideas are valued, how safe children feel about expressing opinions or talking through an idea aloud in the class, what is expected from children, how you respond to children's mistakes, the extent to which children are expected to justify their answers or claims and how willing children are to help and learn from one another.

In my own teaching, I try to create a classroom where all children have something to contribute, where all children know that, and where all children can do that without fear of ridicule. I want children to be able to diagnose their own errors or to be able to state why their answer is correct rather than have them become dependent on me to confirm that an answer is correct or not. I try to use errors as a resource for everyone to learn from and usually thank children for highlighting an aspect of a topic that can be problematic for them when learning the topic. I want children to learn from each other and to respond to each other in a thoughtful and respectful way.

Such classroom practices do not emerge by accident. When I began teaching I remember having, by default, classes where it quickly became obvious to other children who among their peers was authoritative on a given topic and who was not. At that time I inadvertently reinforced the idea to children that they needed to rely on me to confirm that a given answer was correct or not.

When a new teacher begins with a class, there is a great opportunity to establish new practices and norms. This can be done through the classroom rules, through actively modelling respectful listening, through welcoming mistakes, seeking contributions from all children and by bedding down valued behaviours from early in the school year. Once a classroom culture has been established, in relation to teaching approaches or discipline, it is difficult to change it during the year.

Discipline as an educational goal

The meaning of the word 'discipline' can refer either to punishment, or to orderly conduct and action arising from training or instruction.[8] Traditionally in schools discipline and punishment were synonymous. If a child misbehaved, the teacher punished the child – often using corporal punishment. The threat and reality of such 'discipline' made the teacher's job possible – and left a legacy of generations of people who despised both school and education.

But discipline has another meaning, which has to do with acting in an orderly way with self-control, the kind of discipline we associate with an athlete who trains in all weathers and at all times of the day to achieve a goal, or with a promising young musician who chooses to practise when friends are having a good time, or with someone on a diet who refuses to sample one of the tasty chocolates being passed among a group of friends.

Learning self-discipline is a goal of all education.[9] If children have self-discipline, they can apply themselves to any project and experience success. They can make short-term sacrifices for longer-term gains. They can see the value of studying now in order to have success later, in an exam, for instance. But when children are taunting each other and making derogatory comments about classmates and being disruptive in class, it is not easy for a teacher to think about developing their self-discipline. A first priority for many teachers is to create an atmosphere in the classroom where children are engaged in school work and misbehaviour is minimised.

Classroom management

Jacob Kounin[10] has documented a well-known and well-respected approach to classroom management. He studied videotapes of many teachers and identified four teacher actions that were associated with having children focused on their school work and minimising misbehaviour. His recommended approach to achieving children's cooperation is to prevent problems before they arise or intervene before they escalate. The best known teacher action is what he calls 'withitness'.

Withitness refers to the ways and the extent to which the teacher demonstrates to children that the teacher's imaginary inbuilt webcam captures everything they do. The teacher may be working with one group of children when misbehaviour is observed elsewhere in the room. In some way – eye contact, a gesture, a comment, for example – the teacher indicates to the perpetrator that the misbehaviour has been noticed.

Alternatively, the teacher may be helping one child when a potential incident brewing in another part of the room is noticed. The teacher communicates – perhaps by moving close to the children or by removing an object being misused – that the action needs to stop thus ensuring that other children do not become involved. This strategy works in part because the teacher notices what is happening, but an equally important part is showing the children that it has been noticed. They get the message that the teacher is 'with it', is aware of what is going on in the classroom all the time.

Other actions associated with increasing student involvement and decreasing misbehaviour are overlapping, group focus and maintaining momentum.[11] Overlapping refers to how well a teacher can multitask – attend to two classroom interactions simultaneously without losing focus on either one. For example, the teacher is listening to Sarah read and Kai presents written work to have it checked; the teacher continues listening to Sarah's reading while responding to Kai and indicating what he should do next, and then compliments an aspect of Sarah's reading.

Group focus refers to how well the teacher minimises student passivity and maximises student engagement in an activity. For example, instead of calling on one child to answer a question, every child in the class has a mini-whiteboard and each writes the answer on the board and raises it for the teacher to check.

Finally, maintaining momentum refers to how fluently and smoothly the work of the classroom moves along. A teacher who does this makes smooth transitions from one lesson to another and rarely interrupts a lesson to discuss behavioural or procedural matters.

Kounin's idea of withitness is particularly helpful as a way of preventing misbehaviour in the classroom and I always try to position myself in a classroom where every child is in view. Some teachers, however, find that an approach like Kounin's is limited if children persistently offend.

Other teachers dislike trying to regulate children's behaviour through rewards and sanctions; they perceive the teacher taking on a policing role, conducting a kind of surveillance of the children. When it works, the children behave well, not necessarily because they should but because they are likely to be caught if they misbehave; if the teacher leaves the room, however, the class could erupt.

One valuable lesson I learned was that children can only learn to obey if they have room to disobey.[12] If the teacher is constantly monitoring the classroom, are children behaving well because they know it's a good thing to do or because they are afraid of being caught? While in the classroom, children may comply with a teacher's request to please the teacher. But they may learn little about the virtues of respectful behaviour. It brings to mind another incident where a teacher tried to force a child to tell the truth.

Classroom incident

The scene is an early years classroom in a Catholic school. At the end of the school day the teacher occasionally presents a sweet treat to the child who behaves 'best' that day. One day, when returning to the classroom after small break, the teacher noticed that the day's treat, a thin cylindrical lollipop with a colourful clown's face on it, was missing. The teacher immediately set about finding out who had stolen the lollipop. She began by asking:

Who stole the lollipop that was here on my desk before break-time?

[*No reply.*]

Now, boys and girls, God will be very disappointed if you don't own up. Who took the lollipop?

[*No reply.*]

Now, I hope that I don't have to phone the police. If the police come along, *they'll* be able to tell who took the lollipop.

[*Some awkward shifting in chairs but still no reply.*]

They'll put powder in your throat and they'll know who ate the lollipop.

One four-year-old visualised a member of the police putting powder down his throat. It sounded much worse than experiencing the teacher's wrath for stealing the lollipop. He raised his hand: 'I took it Teacher', the boy replied, even though he had not taken the lollipop.

I share this incident from my own school experience to illustrate that how a teacher responds to misbehaviour in the classroom is a time of learning for children. A teacher may tell children to be honest and to respect the property of others, but how the teacher responds to such incidents teaches children more about acting morally than anything the teacher says. In the lollipop incident the teacher tried to compel one child to tell the truth, but instead scared another child into telling a lie.

The teacher assumed the lollipop had been taken by someone in the class even though other equally credible scenarios existed. For example, the culprit could have been someone from another classroom who entered the room at break-time and took the lollipop when everyone was in the playground. Even if the offender was in the room, why frighten at least some children with a dishonest threat of calling the police or putting powder down their throats? Instead the teacher could have expressed disappointment at what happened and explained the consequence that there would be no prize that day. The perpetrator could have been asked to return the lollipop or to admit quietly to the teacher what had happened. This would have been easier for a child than admitting to the offence in front of classmates.

An offender needs to be offered a dignified route to atonement. If the child chooses not to admit to what happened, a subsequent feeling of regret or remorse may prompt the child to be more honest in future. The teacher might also review the concept of an award for the 'best in the class'. Are the criteria for the award clear and transparent to the four- and five-year-old children? Are the criteria applied consistently and objectively? Does every child begin the day with an equal chance of winning the award? Perhaps the lollipop was taken by someone who felt they deserved it or by someone who knew they had little chance of ever winning it.

Moral discipline

Teachers need to ensure the safety of children in the classroom. Teachers also want children to learn to behave responsibly whether the teacher is watching them or not. Teaching is about knowing what is going on in the classroom but it is also about deciding what to respond to, how to respond to it and what to ignore. Sometimes a teacher needs to compel children to behave in a particular way, for safety reasons or because a child has obviously transgressed a classroom rule; other times a teacher needs to trust a child, because the teacher does not have all the information or because the teacher wants the child to learn to be honest.

A classroom observer may wonder why a teacher is overruling a child's protest of innocence or why a teacher is allowing a child to lie to her despite evidence that suggests the child is guilty. Unlike policing, teaching is first about educating, including moral education, and when faced with incidents of student misbehaviour a teacher's response to a specific incident is influenced not just by what happened but by what children will learn from that response. A disciplined classroom is needed for learning to take place; by experiencing how discipline is exercised, children learn how to respond to moral questions and dilemmas. Thus, discipline generates conditions for learning and discipline generates learning.

Classrooms provide many opportunities for learning about life. That happens clearly across the various curriculum subjects where children learn to be literate and numerate, to be creative and physically active, and to enquire systematically. Equally important is what they learn about life as part of the hidden curriculum.

As children navigate through a classroom from day to day they learn from classmates and from their teacher about trust, fairness, authority, respect, kindness, honesty, and obedience. Children notice how rules are established in a classroom. When one child trips another child, when money goes missing from the teacher's drawer, when a teacher promises a reward for careful work, when a child copies answers in a test, when a child is sad because a pet dog died, when one child denies calling another child an offensive name, when a child offers to stay in class at break-time to be with a classmate who is unwell, children notice. Children also notice how the teacher responds.

Because the teacher is the figure of authority in the class, the teacher's reaction is a particularly important source of children's learning. Although a teacher can plan for what is learned in various curriculum subjects, handling classroom incidents is often more spontaneous because you typically have little time to plan how you will respond. This so-called hidden curriculum is highly visible to children. Responding to interactions around discipline from a moral development perspective has been referred to as moral discipline[13] or developmental discipline.[14]

From this perspective, how a teacher handles behavioural matters is an opportunity to teach the children about acting morally more than it is about controlling children's behaviour. Controlling behaviour is a short-term, albeit essential, goal, whereas learning to act morally is for life. Indeed, seeing behaviour management from a moral perspective demands a different way of thinking about how the classroom is run. It informs the atmosphere of the class and how the class is organised, as well as how incidents of misbehaviour are handled. Where possible, a democratic approach is taken to making decisions in the class. This may apply to class rules. Children discuss with the teacher at the start of the year what rules would be helpful for the smooth running of the classroom and they are developed based on fairness, kindness, trust and respect. Generally expressed in a positive way, an agreed list might include rules such as:

- I will respect my classmates.
- I will do my best.
- I will listen to the teacher.

- I will be honest.
- I will raise my hand when I want to speak.

When drawing up class rules, I have sometimes included 'rules' that are not so much about how to behave as about how the class works. Such 'rules' include the following:

- You can learn a lot from your classmates.
- If you understand something, help others to understand it.
- It is good to ask questions or say 'I'm not sure' if you don't understand.

Or when adapted for younger children:

- Share your ideas.
- Help each other to learn.
- Ask questions if you don't understand.

These 'rules' are used to promote the idea of class members acting as a community engaged in learning. Each person is expected to act as a resource for other class members' learning. As the year progresses some rules may need to be amended or added. Such decisions may be made at class meetings which are held from time to time to discuss matters relating to moral values and understanding. Meetings with individual children may also be held from time to time to discuss behaviour in light of moral issues.

The goal of the approach is to develop autonomy among the children – that they will learn to act responsibly and respectfully even when no-one is looking. Praise and rewards are used sparingly because they are extrinsic rewards and don't necessarily help children experience the satisfaction of acting morally. Competitions, which set children against one another, run counter to such an atmosphere.

However, many children like competitions and teachers find them useful to motivate children. They are used widely to practise spellings or number facts where you have to answer a set of questions in a limited time. Possibly competing as part of a group would counteract some of the negative aspects of competitions.

Nevertheless the skills tested in competitions are often lower order and class members know in advance who is likely to win; children already know who is good at tables or good at spellings. Another problem with competitions is that the urge to win can override every other concern and it ultimately distracts children from the content the competition was intended to support. Or the children sacrifice thoughtful work in order to complete work quickly – before others in the class.

That is probably why my favourite competition in school was the slow bicycle race on Sports Day. The winner was the person who came last and who showed skill, control, patience and determination to cycle as slowly as possible without putting a foot on the ground. In short, when teachers decide to use competitions in class, they need to take into account the conflicting lessons that children can learn from them.

A teacher adopting a developmental or moral approach to discipline tries to build and maintain a respectful, caring and trusting relationship with children and among children. Although that sounds easy, nurturing a relationship with a child who acts in a challenging or hostile way can be difficult. Indeed, the children who most need to experience such relationships might be the children who are most likely to misbehave in class. It can help to develop 'a view of children as wanting to learn and wanting to have mutually caring relationships but often needing help in doing so'.[15] From a moral development perspective, student misbehaviours are seen as mistakes and a potential source of future learning. Instead of receiving threats from the teacher about the consequences of misbehaviour, children are given reminders about how to act in class.

Nevertheless, sometimes misbehaviour needs to have consequences for children. In such cases, consequences of misbehaviour are matched to a given offence rather than being generic. If a child makes a mess in part of the room, the consequence could be that the child tidies the mess; if a child offends another, the consequence may be to make a sincere apology. Consequences are often related to the number of similar previous offences. Sometimes restitution may be possible where a child replaces a broken or stolen object.[16]

In many cases children can be asked to propose fitting consequences for their actions. This encourages them to develop responsibility and to reflect on how their action may have impacted on another person. In addition, a teacher may apply consequences on a case-by-case basis taking into account extenuating circumstances.

Responsibility for misbehaviour

Early in my teaching career I came across a somewhat similar approach that was based on children being responsible for their behaviour. It came from a book with the clever title, *He Hit Me Back First* by Eva D. Fugitt.

She made the point that a teacher cannot be responsible for the behaviour of the children in her class. Each child makes a choice about how to act and the actions don't always correspond with what the teacher wants. That knotted feeling a teacher gets in their stomach when a class is boisterous, noisy or unsettled comes from a teacher trying to achieve perfection by having children do what the teacher wants. But when a teacher realises that each child is making their own choices about how to behave, it is liberating. The teacher is not responsible for the children's behaviour. Teachers are responsible for their own behaviour and for creating an environment where learners are motivated and challenged to respond in a disciplined way.[17] So how would Fugitt motivate learners to use self-discipline in the classroom?

Fugitt's approach is built around using exercises to make children aware of their will – their deliberation, motivation, decision making, planning and execution – and around setting goals for themselves. The 'will' exercises consist of having the children follow instructions for doing innocuous tasks using their bodies, beginning with simple ones and progressively moving to more difficult ones. However, before they follow the instructions given, the children must state what they are going to do. So, 'I will tap my head with my fingers three times'. Done. 'I will clap my hands five times'. Done. 'I will stand on one leg for 10 seconds'. Done. Additional similar instructions can be made up; the idea is to develop the children's concentration and to develop their will.

A second task recommended by Fugitt is for children to set one daily goal for themselves – easy ones at first. Children require plenty of teacher support to get started doing this. She gives each child a template where they have to write what their goal is, identify four benefits of achieving it, four burdens of not achieving it and their plans to achieve it. At the end of the day they have to say if they achieved their goal and to state why or why not.

So, a child may set a goal to learn a new expression in French. The benefits might be:

■ My teacher will be happy with me.
■ I'll be able to speak more French.
■ I will feel more confident.
■ My homework will be easier.

The burdens of not achieving it might be:

■ My French won't improve.
■ I'll be disappointed with myself.

- I'll find the next test difficult.

- My teacher will be cross.

Plans to achieve it might be:

- I'll find a phrase that I don't understand.

- I'll ask the teacher what it means.

- I'll write down the expression and its meaning in my notebook.

- I'll speak it in a sentence to my mother.

Another idea I found useful in Fugitt's book was to ask a child who misbehaves, 'How does that help you?'. Fugitt describes it as a 'magic question' as long as it is used sincerely and judiciously. I used approaches from the book both with individual children and with the class as a whole; it didn't solve all behavioural problems but it did help. The greatest benefit for me in reading this book was its message that each child is responsible for how they behave; that idea saved me a lot of stress.

Children's classroom identities

Magdalene Lampert writes that classrooms have characteristics that can place social and personal stress on children as well as teachers.[18] Children are trying to establish acceptance among their peers, and trying to establish an identity for themselves, in relationships that are independent of their families. They may adopt or experiment with an identity that is comfortable for them and that helps them to survive in a class where they cannot take for granted the kind of ready acceptance most find in their families. Children may adopt identities in class such as the joker, the quiet one, the sporty one, the socialiser, the loud one, the serious one and so on.

The teacher wants them to become people who take their school work seriously, who apply themselves diligently to their work, and who are prepared to sincerely engage in discussions across all subjects. In other words, the teacher wants each child to take on the identity of a student for at least that part of the day when they are working together. A child who refuses to adopt behaviours that are characteristic of the identity of a student – asking questions, making conjectures and completing tasks – creates tension for a teacher whose goal is for the child to learn.

Tension can be caused for the child too if the identity required by the teacher differs from the identity displayed to the child's peers. A child may know that the right thing is to engage with what the teacher is doing, but doing the right thing may conflict with the child's adopted identity as, say, the class joker, and the child may wonder what their peers will think of them if they start acting out of character. Few children, in older classes at least, want to be called a teacher's pet if losing friends is the price they must pay.

Therefore a teacher walks a fine line between seeking and publicly acknowledging student effort and helping each child maintain credibility among their peers. Achieving this balance means that a teacher needs to be sensitive to children's classroom identities while making every effort to extend and challenge each child to do the best they can across the curriculum. A teacher will usually glean information about children's identities from early in the school year by talking to children before, during and after class, and by observing children in their interactions with classmates.

Teacher–student relationships

When a teacher works with children for a year[19] the teacher builds a relationship with the class as a group. It is an intense relationship because for every day of the school year teacher and children work together in a relatively small space. During the year the teacher's relationship with the children and the children's relationships with each other will change.

Tuckman[20] has identified five stages that groups typically pass through when they work together. Early in the year the relationship is about testing and dependence where members of the class find out what behaviours are acceptable in the class and they look to the teacher for guidance in how to act and on the nature of the work that lies ahead. A strong leader is needed at this stage and the teacher can set the agenda for how the group will work and what kind of work has to be done. The children enter the class with certain expectations based on the previous year or their prior knowledge of the teacher. This is the new teacher's opportunity to orientate the class to a new way of working, which may mark a change from prior expectations or from ways of working in the past.

The second stage is one of conflict among class members and is probably less pronounced among classes where children have mostly worked together before. For new groups, changed groups or new members of a group, there may be feelings of anxiety, threat and perhaps resistance as group members respond emotionally to the demands of the task ahead. If this happens, the teacher needs to know that it is a common, transitory, stage in the process of groups as they adjust to working together.

The third stage is the development of class cohesion, where group-generated norms are established. The fourth stage is the stage you want to reach; it is where children and teacher have functional relationships and they can achieve insight. The fifth stage is separation or termination, and this stage is about disengagement and ending.

In short, these stages of group formation have been summarised respectively as forming, storming, norming, performing and adjourning. Although the stages were devised to refer to all kinds of groups, many of the stages resonate with my experience of teaching. When things are going well, a group gets to the performing stage very quickly. However, some classes find it difficult to move away from the storming phase, especially if members of the class have never bonded or if new members are not helped to integrate well.

Although some teachers might be surprised at including a separation or termination stage, at least one teacher, Magdalene Lampert, discusses at length how she deliberately adjourns her class at the end of the year. She looks back by tying together the strands of work done during the year; she looks ahead by communicating to children how their studies of the subject may develop; she responds to the pre-summer giddiness and timetable unpredictability with alternative activities; and she elicits feedback from the children about their experience of being in her class during the year.[21]

Applying routines and rules

Establishing rules and routines is an important part of successful classroom management.[22] Making decisions on the points above is just one step towards a successful school year. Equally important is to implement the rules and routines consistently. Children need to know what the rules and expectations around behaviour are and that they will be applied. Doing this is important throughout the year, but if it's not done meticulously for the first month, children's behaviour throughout the year can make teaching more difficult.

Consistent application of rules and routines is not easy. As teachers, we like to get down to serious learning early in the year, and in our hurry to get stuck in, we may turn a blind eye to minor deviations from some requirements. That may lead on occasion to being lax about some rules that have been introduced or forgetting to follow up on a sanction that is due. Although deviation from the rules may happen towards the end of the year, the first month is not the time for that.

Children need to know where they stand. One experienced teacher said that in matters of discipline, teachers need to be more stubborn than their students.[23] That's a good way of putting it. It takes a certain stubbornness to insist that every behaviour or action complies with the agreed procedures but if it's done early in the year, it pays dividends later on. I remember one of my teachers on school placement saying that she was particularly fussy about how children spelled words, how they wrote in their copies and so on at the start of the year; if she didn't do that, standards would fall throughout the year.

Student engagement and disengagement

Up to now I have been writing about discipline as if it only involved disruptive or boisterous behaviour by the children. But another category of behaviour exists that is less intrusive on the teacher's day-to-day work but which needs to be mentioned. Peter was a boy I taught in fifth and sixth class. I considered him to be a highly capable student. When I set work for the class, he was usually one of the first to finish. He would ask me to check his work. It was usually fine – enough to satisfy the task requirements but far less than he was capable of. It seemed that he knew what was sufficient to tick the boxes or satisfy the teacher but he was not going to excel to the extent that I believed he could. My fear was that such an approach to work – doing just enough to get over the line – could become for him a habit in other life activities.

Children who are lazy, disengaged or apathetic about their class work or homework provide a challenge for teachers. Primary teachers derive much satisfaction when children appear to be engaged in their work; however, teachers are less likely to complain about disengaged children.[24] That may be because post-primary teachers are more likely than primary teachers to experience children who are disengaged.[25]

Nevertheless, teachers need to respond to children who appear to be lazy or disengaged. Such children are more easily ignored than children who frequently disrupt the class, because they are not disruptive. However, disengagement cannot be ignored because children who are poorly engaged often achieve poorly. For children who are not highly engaged in school work, an important factor is the quality of the teacher–child relationship.

Disengaged or under-engaged children benefit from a warm, empathetic teacher who shows interest in them, provides structure for them and supports their autonomy by giving them choices, and making connections between school work and their interests.[26] The challenge in developing such relationships is that a teacher is trying to build a relationship with thirty children at a time and, as mentioned earlier, the children in most need of a positive relationship with adults are the children who are most likely to resist the teacher's attempts to build one.

Whole school involvement

Everything I have mentioned so far is based on the idea that classroom management is solely the domain of the classroom teacher. Although the teacher has substantial responsibility in that area, the class teacher acts in a larger environment that includes what is done by colleagues, the principal and parents in relation to behaviour. Today whole-school approaches to behaviour management are becoming more widespread.[27] Such approaches involve teaching children the positive behaviours that are expected from them, consistently acknowledging such behaviours when they are observed and consistently applying consequences for problematic behaviour.[28] For such programmes to work, rules and behaviour reinforcement in each class-room need to be consistent with rules and reinforcements in the school overall; the code of positive behaviour in each classroom can be related to the code of positive behaviour in the school as a whole.

Even with strong supports in place to create a constructive learning environment for your students, from time to time a single child in a class will seriously and consistently disrupt what would otherwise be a stable environment. For some teachers this will happen rarely, if at all. Such behaviour may be attributed to a child's underlying condition, diagnosed or undiagnosed. Distinguishing the behaviour of such children from children who exhibit other signs of misbehaviour can be difficult, especially for a beginning teacher. Behaviour of such children can be unsettling both for children and the teacher in a class, especially if there is more than one such child present. Although consistent approaches to discipline in a school may help, they may be insufficient, and additional supports may be needed for such children.

Difficult situations

Engaging constantly with children who are disengaged, misbehaving or testing class structures is difficult. This can be compounded by particular flashpoints from time to time. You ask a child to do something – stand away from their peers or return a book to a shelf, for example – and the child refuses to do so. Confrontation. Silence follows. Tension builds in the room. Other children watch. In this conflict, you can only lose. Therefore, try and defuse the situation as early as possible. Point out to the child that the response was unacceptable and that you will speak to the child at break time. That helps you save face with the rest of the children while showing the class that such an attitude is not acceptable. By break time, the tension will usually have dissipated and it will be easier to have a proper discussion with the child. If that is not possible, the principal can be asked to speak with the child at that stage.

Another difficult moment is when a teacher is upset, frustrated or angry in the classroom. Because teaching involves a sustained relationship in a relatively small space throughout the course of a year, teachers will experience many emotions. Many times these emotions are positive: pride, happiness, satisfaction, caring. Other emotions may be negative:[29] anxiety, guilt, frustration, anger. In the course of a given day, or week it is natural to experience a range of emotions.

The emotions may originate in school (as a result of interactions with colleagues, meeting a parent, the visit of an inspector, a change in conditions or job requirements, damage to personal property, hearing an offensive comment, or through interactions with children) or they may be attributable to or exacerbated by factors not related to school (e.g. tiredness, stress, or relationship matters).[30] Prospective teachers rarely learn about emotions and how to regulate them in teacher preparation programmes.[31]

Yet our emotions can impact on how we do our work and being aware of the integral part our emotions play in teaching is important. It is good for teachers to acknowledge and accept all emotions that are felt before work, when working and after work. It is also worth identifying emotions, reflecting on them and discussing them. After reflecting on a strong emotion, it is better to reappraise the event that triggered the emotion than to suppress an unwelcome emotion. It is also good to adopt several coping strategies.[32]

As part of managing emotions that arise when teaching, it is sometimes necessary to show restraint in expressing emotions in the presence of children. For example,[33] a teacher may feel joy when a student does good work, but expressing the joy publicly may embarrass the child or cause the child to be teased by peers. Potentially more problematic is the display of negative emotions.

Sometimes a teacher pretends to be angry with a child or with the class; but other times the anger a teacher feels is real. The teacher may be provoked by something a student says or does or refuses to do. Such provocation can lead to the teacher feeling angry towards a child or towards a group of children. At such a time, refrain from acting out of anger towards the children. Use whatever strategy is helpful – pause, physically withdraw, breathe deeply, make a joke, have the class do some quiet work, tell a student to see you after class, or use some coping inner 'self-talk'.[34] Avoid any physical contact with a child at such a time, avoid shouting and avoid making comments that may be sarcastic. After the intensity of an emotion has subsided, a teacher may decide to discuss it with the children, informing the children that, for example, 'I was disappointed with what you did earlier/yesterday'.

Safety

Parents and teachers want children to be safe in school and schools have policies in place to ensure that children stay safe. According to Maslow's theory of human motivation, once a person has satisfied their basic physiological needs of food, air and water, the next set of needs to emerge are safety needs. Safety needs include 'security; stability; . . . freedom from fear, from anxiety and chaos; [and a] need for structure'.[35] If a child is to flourish in school, the child needs to feel and be safe, physically and psychologically, and to have a sense of belonging.

Although teachers receive advice about safety in the school in general, I want to mention some precautions teachers can take in order to maximise children's safety in the classroom. Many school accidents happen in the playground[36] and the principal and colleagues can advise on how they can be minimised in a particular school. Several years of my teaching experience were spent sharing a building with a troop of scouts and it was not unusual to arrive in school on a Monday morning to find tents set up in the sports hall or to find the remains of a bonfire in a corner of the playground. That experience may have coloured my views on safety in the classroom.

The suggestions below are far from comprehensive but most relate to situations that colleagues or I experienced in our classrooms. Be mindful that any object can be turned into an object of danger in a classroom, so vigilant observation is always helpful. Nevertheless, I hope that the suggestions below may sharpen your awareness of how you think about and minimise risk to children's safety in your teaching.

Within the physical and resource constraints that exist, you will try to set up your classroom in a way that best matches your approach to teaching and your beliefs about learning. Rarely have classrooms enough wall space and storage space so you need to be careful to avoid compromising safety when you lay out the room. Keep all doors and passageways clear of objects so that they can be easily accessed if an emergency evacuation is required. Avoid storing objects on top of tall presses because they could fall off and hit someone on the head when the door is opened or if the press is shaken.

Be careful that children don't trip on electrical cables or extension leads and look for other potential trip hazards in the room. In an early childhood room, putting covers on unused sockets is advisable so that curious fingers are not tempted to explore. It is also useful to remind children about the risk of hands and fingers getting caught in doors.

Most schools have clear policies on administering children's medication and on children who have allergies that may require an urgent response. If you are on medication yourself, make sure that the medicine is stored somewhere that is inaccessible to children, ideally in a locked drawer or cabinet.

Children's work and class posters shouldn't be placed near heaters, especially storage heaters, because they can be a fire hazard. Some teachers use candles at prayer time or cook food on occasions such as Pancake Tuesday. Check school policies on such practices and take particular precautions to prevent burning or fires. Keep fire extinguishers in a fixed place. Different extinguishers are used for different kinds of fires and knowing how to use a fire extinguisher is useful. Using several plugs in a socket with an adaptor is another fire hazard.

Some subjects have particular hazards. In practical subjects such as the visual arts, I advise children to hold a scissors by the closed blades if walking around the class. Avoid using glass containers for water in visual arts or other lessons – when they fall and break, glass goes everywhere. Sharp objects, such as adult scissors or hobby knives, should be stored safely out of children's reach.

In physical education, have the children warm up at the start of a lesson and never have children run with a wall as the end point – children may not be able to stop themselves and may crash into the wall. A line a few metres before a wall is a better endpoint to use. This point is particularly critical outdoors where children may be running on wet grass or downhill. Children also need to be shown how to use equipment and how to carry it, especially in gymnastics.

Have parents accompany the class on trails or walks. Children can wear reflective yellow bibs when they go for a nature walk to make them more visible to motorists and to a teacher if they get lost. In science class, check out the risks associated with various chemicals that will be used. Children should be advised not to taste any substances in science class.

It would also be good to check if a school policy exists on pets in the classroom. Children can learn a lot from caring for pets. However, it can be difficult to maintain good hygiene standards with pets and they may adversely affect children with asthma and hay fever; in addition some children could be inadvertently cruel in their handling of pets.

Because classrooms and activities will vary, a teacher needs to anticipate possible risks that can occur when a group of children is engaged on a particular activity. I always spared the instruction 'Freeze' for a genuine emergency and I reminded children about it prior to any potentially risky activity, or when leaving the school grounds.

In addition to physical safety, the classroom should be a place the children look forward to coming to. No child should have to live in dread of bullying or harassment for any reason. Sometimes bullying episodes can be difficult for a teacher to identify. 'We were only mock fighting' was often said by an apparent victim of a playground fight when I was supervising children's lunchtime break.

I remember one boy in my class who had a nickname related to his skin colour. When I became aware of it, I spoke to the child about it; he claimed that he didn't mind it. However, it is unacceptable for children to call other children potentially derogatory names, even if an individual child has no objection – possibly a pragmatic decision on his part if he thinks no alternative exists. Those who use such names need to learn that using such terms can be hurtful for others. Most schools have detailed policies about bullying which will provide specific information about how teachers in the school respond to such matters.

The other extreme is where young children love telling tales about everything that goes on in the playground. Given the misery some children experience in school with consequent negative effects on their cognitive and emotional development, it is probably better to act on the cautious side of such events and reports, especially if they occur with any frequency. Good communication among teachers can help to build up a picture of similar repeated events.

I remember once when I was a student teacher asking a girl in a class I taught to read her story aloud for the rest of the class. She declined. I asked her again. She declined. 'Go on', I pleaded, 'I read your story and it's really good'. At this stage the class teacher intervened and said that she would prefer if the girl didn't share her story on this occasion. It was a good call; if a child declines to do something in the class, where there is discretion about doing so, the child's wish should be respected. Children can then learn that they can say 'no' to something and that they can expect their 'no' to be respected in situations where a child's safety may be at risk.

What about the teacher's safety? Teachers can be bullied by children. This can take the form of obscene and inappropriate comments, name-calling, deliberate insolence or mimicking characteristic features.[37] Such behaviour is not acceptable and may impact on a teacher's health and wellbeing as well as on the teacher's work.[38] It is also something that can be eliminated by addressing it directly or by having a colleague or a principal address it, though this can be difficult to do. Just as every child should feel safe in school, every teacher is entitled to do their job free from worrying about offensive behaviour from children.

Traumatic events

Apart from obstacles and difficulties that happen to teachers as they go through life, sometimes the school community can be affected by the occurrence of traumatic events. I remember when I was in second class, a boy in the class died from cystic fibrosis. Prior to his death he had been in and out of hospital quite a bit.

I remember many details of what happened at the time. He died in wintertime, just after the Christmas holidays and I remember the teacher calling to my house with details of plans for the funeral. All children in the class wore white ribbons on our sleeves and followed his coffin to the church. I remember a local tenor singing the song 'Suffer Little Children to Come Unto Me' from *The Mass of Saint Francis of Assisi* by Philip Green. I was asked to do a reading at the mass and I remember how visibly upset the boy's mother was.

The vivid details of the event that remain with me forty years later indicate that it was an intense time in my life. I do not recall experiencing grief at the time, but I do know that my classmates and I felt a sense of loss from the class afterwards.

Traumatic events happen in schools from time to time: accidents, deaths of children or teachers, premature deaths of parents. Often these happen without warning. Most schools now have policies and procedures for dealing with such incidents. Supports, which were not available in the past, are now available to schools for responding to such events.[39]

Nevertheless, they can be traumatic and unsettling for children in your class and for you. Children in your class can be affected in different ways by such events. How particular children are affected can depend on the class level of the student that is traumatised, whether or not the child has siblings in your class, how well they know the student or family affected and so on.

The best advice for dealing with such occasions is to mark the matter in line with the traditions and ethos of the school and give children space and time to talk about them. Children may find consolation in suitable prayers, stories, poetry, music and works of art at this time. Children can also be helped to cope with such events if their routine is maintained or quickly re-established. Dealing with such an event in school can be particularly difficult when the teachers too are upset by the incident. At such a time teachers can give support to each other and look after each other as much as possible.

Although traumatic events may be school events, some events may happen more quietly but may be even more traumatic for the individuals concerned. Unfortunately, children are not immune from the waves and storms of life and they may be affected by their parents' divorce, by an accident, by bullying or by abuse. Sometimes you will be informed about such happenings and sometimes you will have no idea of what a particular child in your class is going through.

I remember questioning a child about sexually explicit pictures and language the child had written on a note. I learned several months afterwards that the child had been a victim of sexual abuse. Although teaching involves more than caring for and about children, a caring disposition is a prerequisite for teaching, and sometimes knowing you care is what a student needs more than anything else.

Traumatic events with no connection to the school may also require sensitive handling in school. For teachers of a given generation, place names such as Dunblane, Beslan, Columbine, Sandy Hook and Peshawar evoke memories of appalling tragedies involving multiple deaths of young children. When such events happen, children may need to mark the events in school in some appropriate way.

School culture

Earlier in the chapter I referred to the idea of a classroom culture. Every school too has its own culture. It determines what kind of behaviours and interactions are acceptable and unacceptable in a school. The culture is evident in many ways, such as how teachers speak to children, how teachers respond to children's behaviour, how children address teachers, how teachers relate to one another, how minority children and their parents are treated, how bullying among children is handled, how school policy decisions are taken, and even in more tangible ways such as notices around the school and how clean, warm and bright the school is kept.

A school culture can make a school a pleasant or an unpleasant place to study, work and visit. As a new teacher in a school, it is difficult to change a school culture but it is good to be aware of it, so that you can appreciate and contribute to a positive culture and you can recognise and change or leave one that is toxic or dysfunctional.

In other areas of society – from the police to care workers and from clergy to media personnel – we hear about unacceptable standards of practice. Often such incidents are made public through the work of whistle-blowers who recognised negative aspects of the cultures in which they worked. Being a whistle-blower is a courageous and principled approach to take but it is an action that can take a toll on the whistle-blower personally and economically. As a result, such an action may not be for everyone. However, to recognise a culture for what it is and not to adopt unethical behaviour, even if it is accepted in the school, is something that any teacher can do.

Teachers' dress

An aspect of teaching life that is influenced by the culture of the school is the clothes teachers wear. You might wonder why the topic of clothing comes up at all in a book about what teachers do. And yet, even though many schools don't even have a written policy on what teachers wear, how we present ourselves to others influences how we are perceived.[40]

In addition to the usual items of clothing, professional dress for teachers can extend to hair, hats, footwear, visible piercings and tattoos, as well as how much of the body is covered and revealed. A teacher's clothing can give rise to comment because of its colour, length, tightness, transparency, fadedness, and its written or pictorial content. Although terms such as 'professional' and 'appropriate' are often used to describe what is expected in a dress sense, many disagree on what is covered by such broad terms.[41]

I enjoy wearing clothes that help me feel both comfortable and confident. The clothes we wear can affect how well we fit in among teachers and parents in a particular school community. Some clothes can be perceived as too formal and others can be perceived as too casual in a particular school or for a particular occasion. Although a principal may dress more formally than other staff members, it is often the principal who sets the tone for what dress is and is not acceptable.

Certain clothes are more practical than others for school activities such as teaching physical education, visual arts or nature walks. The clothes worn may also vary according to the age that is taught. When I taught younger age groups, I tended to wear colourful sweaters but when I taught older children, my dress became more formal.

Clothing is considered to be a form of personal expression. Yet when I am a teacher, not only am I expressing myself, I am representing a profession that enjoys respect from society. Associated with the respect accorded to teachers are expectations that they will dress in a particular way;[42] parents may see me as a role model for children. I may not agree with that and I may rebel against it but if I do that, I need to be aware of why it may generate discussion. After all, my clothing is more visible to parents than my teaching. Other professions have dress codes so that when we observe a butcher, a barrister, a builder, a nurse, a chef or a bank official at work, we have expectations of how they'll dress and present themselves to the public.

My own ironic tale in relation to clothing is that in eleven years of primary teaching I rarely wore jeans to school. However, on one of the few days that I wore blue jeans, a professional photographer arrived in the school to take photographs for a television programme the children were to appear on later in the year. A beautiful photograph of the teaching staff at the time was taken and to this day that photo is still displayed in the school, immortalising my day of dressing down!

Key points of Chapter 2

1 A response to classroom misbehaviour can relate to the symptoms or the underlying cause of the misbehaviour.

2 Early in the year a teacher can shape a positive classroom culture focused on student autonomy and respect.

3 Tried and tested approaches for preventing misbehaviour include 'with-itness', overlapping, group focus and maintaining momentum.

4 Moral discipline considers what children learn from how classroom behaviour is regulated.

5 Children can learn to take responsibility for their behaviour.

6 It is good to develop strategies for managing your own emotions when teaching.

7 Steps can be taken to make your classroom a safe place for everyone.

Notes

1 See, for example, Kitching, Morgan & O'Leary (2009) and Ingersoll & Smith (2003).

2 Some sanctions used include verbal or written notes to parents, extra class work, extra homework, detention, exclusion from sport or other activities, a warning card system, writing of lines, cancellation of a popular lesson and suspension (Growing Up in Ireland, 2009).

3 Examples include http://www.smartclassroommanagement.com/ or http://forum.educationposts.ie/index.php.

4 See for example: http://www.classdojo.com/.

5 In the tradition of Schön (1983).

6 Barnhardt (1988/2003).

7 Mish (1998).

8 *Oxford English Dictionary*. Note that the word disciple, which means pupil or follower, has the same etymology.

9 See, for example, Kamii (1984).

10 Kounin (1970).

11 Kounin (1970).

12 I first heard this idea from the philosopher, Joe Dunne.

13 Lickona (1991).

14 See the article by Watson (2008) for a more detailed overview of this area.

15 Watson (2008, p. 181).

16 Suggestion from DeVries & Zan (1994, pp. 187–188).

17 Fugitt (1983). Eva D. Fugitt bases her ideas on psychosynthesis and in particular two books by Robert Assagioli, *Psychosynthesis* and *The Act of Will*, and the book *What We May Be* by Piero Ferrucci.

18 This is a point made by Lampert (2001, p. 327). In some countries, where class groups are relatively stable over time, the risk of stress is less extreme than in countries, such as the United States, where class groups change frequently and many children may spend only one year with the same classmates.

19 In some schools one teacher may work with a group for two years or more because of size or school policy. In those settings, the stages identified here would need to be modified accordingly.

20 Tuckman (1965); Tuckman & Jensen (1977).

21 See chapter 13, 'Teaching Closure' in Lampert (2001).

22 Yinger (1980).

23 http://insideeducation.podbean.com/2012/12/02/programme-154-reflections-on-school-attendance-discipline-and-suspension-2-12-12/

24 Kitching et al. (2009).

25 Roorda, Koomen, Spilt & Oort (2011, pp. 515–516).

26 Roorda et al. (2011, pp. 494–496).

27 These include PeaceBuilders (http://www.peacebuilders.com/), Providing Alternative Thinking Strategies – PATHS (http://www.pathseducation.com/), Steps to Respect (http://www.cfchildren.org/steps-to-respect.aspx), Caring School Community (http://www.devstu.org/caring-school-community), and School Wide Positive Behavioral Interventions and Supports (http://www.pbis.org), all based in the United States.

28 Osher, Bear, Sprague & Doyle (2010, p. 50).

29 Psychologists use the terms positive and negative not to refer to emotions as good and bad but to refer to their congruence with one's goals (Sutton, 2007).

30 Chang (2009); Sutton & Wheatley (2003).

31 Sutton (2007).

32 The sequence of steps for managing emotions outlined in this paragraph was identified for teacher educators by Chang (2009, pp. 212–213). Coping strategies could include engaging in pleasant or relaxing activities, engaging in exercise, thinking things through, looking at things differently, seeking support from others, or thinking about something else (Totterdell & Parkinson, 1999).

33 Example based on one in Sutton & Wheatley (2003).

34 Sutton (2004).

35 Maslow (1954, 1970, p. 39).

36 Kramer, Lightfoot, Knight, Cazier & Olson (2003); Sheps & Evans (1987).

37 Kauppi & Pörhölä (2012).

38 James et al. (2008); Kauppi & Pörhölä (2012).

39 See, for example Department of Education and Science (2007); Irish National Teachers' Organisation & Ulster Teachers' Union (2000).

40 See for example Goffman (1956).

41 Sternberg (2003).

42 See Dunbar & Segrin (2012) for a discussion of this in relation to college teachers.

References

Barnhardt, R. K. (Ed.). (1988/2003). *Chambers dictionary of etymology*. New York: Chambers.

Chang, M.-L. (2009). An appraisal of teacher burnout: Examining the emotional work of teachers. *Educational Psychology Review, 21*(3), 193–218.

Department of Education and Science. (2007). *Responding to critical incidents: Guidelines for schools*. Dublin: Author.

DeVries, R. & Zan, B. (1994). *Moral classrooms, moral children*. New York: Teachers' College Press.

Dunbar, N. E. & Segrin, C. (2012). Clothing and teacher credibility: An application of expectancy violations theory. *ISRN Education, 2012*. doi: 10.5402/2012/140517

Fugitt, E. D. (1983). *He hit me back first: Creative visualization activities for parenting and teaching*. Rolling Hills Estates, CA: Jalmar Press.

Goffman, E. (1956). *The presentation of self in everyday life.* Edinburgh: University of Edinburgh.

Growing Up in Ireland. (2009). *Growing up in Ireland, Key findings: 9-year olds, No. 3, The education of 9-year olds.* Dublin: Economic and Social Research Institute, Trinity College Dublin, Office of the Minister for Children and Youth Affairs.

Ingersoll, R. M. & Smith, T. M. (2003). The wrong solution to the teacher shortage. *Educational Leadership, 60*(8), 30–33.

Irish National Teachers' Organisation & Ulster Teachers' Union. (2000). *When tragedy strikes: Guidelines for effective critical incident management in schools.* Dublin/Belfast: Author.

James, D. J., Lawlor, M., Courtney, P., Flynn, A., Henry, B. & Murphy, N. (2008). Bullying behaviour in secondary schools: What roles do teachers play? *Child Abuse Review, 17*, 160–173.

Kamii, C. (1984). The aim of education envisioned by Piaget. *The Phi Delta Kappan, 65*(6), 410–415.

Kauppi, T. & Pörhölä, M. (2012). School teachers bullied by their students: Teachers' attributions and how they share their experiences. *Teaching and Teacher Education, 28*, 1059–1068.

Kitching, K., Morgan, M. & O'Leary, M. (2009). It's the little things: exploring the importance of commonplace events for early-career teachers' motivation. *Teachers and Teaching: Theory and Practice, 15*(1), 43–58.

Kounin, J. S. (1970). *Discipline and group management in classrooms.* New York: Holt, Rinehart and Winston.

Kramer, M. D., Lightfoot, A. C., Knight, S., Cazier, C. F. & Olson, L. M. (2003). Classroom injuries in Utah public schools. *Academic Emergency Medicine, 10*(9), 978–984.

Lampert, M. (2001). *Teaching problems and the problems of teaching.* New Haven, CT: Yale University Press.

Lickona, T. (1991). *Educating for character: How our schools can teach respect and responsibility.* New York: Bantam Books.

Maslow, A. H. (1954, 1970). *Motivation and personality* (2nd ed.), W. G. Holtzman & G. Murphy (Eds). New York: Harper & Rowe, Publishers.

Mish, F. C. (Ed.). (1998). *Merriam-Webster's collegiate dictionary* (10th ed.). Springfield, MA: Merriam-Webster.

Osher, D., Bear, G. G., Sprague, J. R. & Doyle, W. (2010). How can we improve school discipline? *Educational Researcher, 39*(1), 48–58. doi: 10.3102/0013189X09357618

Oxford English Dictionary. 'discipline, n.'. Oxford: Oxford University Press.

Roorda, D. L., Koomen, H. M. Y., Spilt, J. L. & Oort, F. J. (2011). The influence of affective teacher–student relationships on students' school engagement and achievement: A meta-analytic approach. *Review of Educational Research, 81*, 493–529.

Schön, D. A. (1983). *The reflective practitioner: How professionals think in action.* New York: Basic Books.

Sheps, S. B. & Evans, G. D. (1987). Epidemiology of school injuries: A 2-year experience in a municipal health department. *Pediatrics, 79*(1), 69–75.

Sternberg, R. E. (2003). Attending to teacher attire. *School Administrator, 60*(2), 38–46.

Sutton, R. E. (2004). Emotional regulation goals and strategies of teachers. *Social Psychology of Education, 7*, 379–398.

Sutton, R. E. (2007). Teachers' anger, frustration, and self-regulation. In P. A. Schutz & R. Pekrun (Eds), *Emotion in education* (pp. 259–274). Burlington, MA: Academic Press (an imprint of Elsevier).

Sutton, R. E. & Wheatley, K. F. (2003). Teachers' emotions and teaching: A review of the literature and directions for future research. *Educational Psychology Review, 15*(4), 327–358.

Totterdell, P. & Parkinson, B. (1999). Use and effectiveness of self-regulation strategies for improving mood in a group of trainee teachers. *Journal of Occupational Health Psychology, 4*(3), 219–232.

Tuckman, B. W. (1965). Developmental sequence in small groups. *Psychological Bulletin, 63*(6), 384–399.

Tuckman, B. W. & Jensen, M. A. C. (1977). Stages of small-group development revisited. *Group and Organization Studies, 2*(4), 419–427.

Watson, M. (2008). Developmental discipline and moral education. In L. P. Nucci & D. Narvaez (Eds), *Handbook of moral and character education*. New York: Routledge.

Yinger, R. J. (1980). A study of teacher planning. *The Elementary School Journal, 80*(3), 107–127.

3

Choosing ways of teaching

Chalk and talk

I asked a group of children to draw a picture of a teacher; two of them drew adults standing in front of chalkboards (Figure 3.1). In one picture the teacher seems to be talking to children who have questions about mathematics; other pictures depict adults addressing audiences that are unseen. Like a stethoscope around a doctor's neck, or a white hat on a chef,[1] a chalkboard behind a teacher sums up teaching for many people.

Even though interactive whiteboards have replaced many chalkboards, and teaching today goes beyond standing up and talking, the traditional image persists. It may have shaped the kind of work you expected to do as a teacher just as it shapes what children and their parents expect from teaching. Traditionally, the expression 'chalk and talk' described a teacher's work. It brings to mind someone whose job involves speaking, and writing or drawing on a chalkboard.

Although 'chalk and talk' is often criticised, chalk is a cost-effective resource and talk can be effective at transmitting information to large groups of people. To appreciate the power of well-chosen words, delivered with conviction, to inform, persuade and teach, just think of people like Churchill, Gandhi, Hitler, Jesus, Lincoln, Mandela or Thatcher. Each of them captivated people through story or rhetoric and thereby showed how powerful language can be to persuade and cajole, inspire and bamboozle, and thrill and misdirect.[2]

Although such people show the potential of talk in teaching, there is an art to choosing what to say, how to arrange it, say it, memorise and deliver it. Rhetoric[3] and storytelling[4] are two ways of communicating through speech.

Figure 3.1 A sample of pictures of teachers drawn by children

However, those of us who have sat through lectures or speeches know that the spoken word can as easily turn off or bore listeners as it can inspire and inform them.

In school and elsewhere material can be presented that fails to connect with the interests and knowledge of the audience. 'Chalk and talk' may work for some children and not for others. Moreover, some ideas cannot be grasped through listening alone. So teachers will sometimes stand at a board and talk to the class. But few teachers, if any, will rely solely on a 'chalk and talk' approach; they will instead use a variety of methods to help particular children learn particular content at a given time.

Methods, approaches, strategies and methodologies

'Teaching method' is a term that is widely used but rarely defined. You'll meet it in articles about teaching, on websites for teachers, and in teacher education settings. Sometimes other terms are used such as approaches, methodologies, procedures, and strategies. One book on education refers to 'pedagogical techniques' and summarises them in this list:

> conditioning (the use of stimulus–response techniques); training; instruction (direct conveyance of information); supervision (learning overseen and regulated); facilitation (providing opportunities and resources for learning), modelling (providing an example for the student to follow); and erotetics (the use of questioning).[5]

The specified techniques can be combined in various ways, depending on what you are teaching, who you are teaching and your beliefs and understanding about teaching and learning.

With so many similar terms – such as approaches, methods, strategies, methodologies and techniques – it is difficult to know what constitutes a 'teaching method'. Some lists of methods include homogeneous grouping, seatwork, praise,[6] practical activity,[7] active learning and using the environment.[8] But homogeneous grouping seems more like a way of organising the class to do a particular activity than a teaching method. And terms like seatwork, practical activity and active learning seem too generic to give direction to any kind of planning; you and I could say we are using 'active learning' but have very different kinds of teaching in mind. That makes it difficult for two teachers to have a meaningful conversation about what methods they use. It also makes it difficult to know if a 'method that works' is being applied the way some teachers or researchers found it to be effective.

Some scholars have attempted to disentangle and define the various terms. A teaching approach has been defined as a theory about a subject and how a subject is learned. Various strategies or methods may be consistent with one approach or theory.[9] A teaching strategy can be thought of as a set of purposeful, sequential actions made by a teacher, taking into account several relevant features of the children and class setting, in order to achieve a desired objective. A teaching method too sets out to achieve a desired objective but is not characterised by a developmental sequence of actions, nor does it consider a wide range of factors about the context in which the teaching and learning take place.[10] Methodology is the field of study of various methods, strategies and approaches that are used in teaching.[11] Although such definitions all have merit, and provide ways to disentangle the terms, the definitions are neither widely used nor consistently applied in articles or websites that refer to approaches, strategies, methods and methodologies.

Sample approaches, strategies and methods

Despite the imprecise way in which the terms have been used, some approaches, strategies and methods have been documented and critiqued by scholars. They include the communicative approach and the audiolingual method in language learning and the problem-solving approach in mathematics. The audiolingual method, which is based on structural linguistics and behaviourist psychology, teaches the skills of listening, speaking, reading and writing in that order, puts emphasis on structure, drill and practice, and is often associated with language laboratories.

Communicative language teaching is more an approach than a method; it emphasises language as a means of communication, learning takes place through communicating, and children work on meaningful tasks to maintain their interest.[12] Using a problem-solving approach to mathematics teaching requires children to work alone and collaboratively on multi-step or open-ended problems with judicious prompts from the teacher. Multiple mathematical topics may arise in solving a single problem, and whole-class discussion of the problem is key.[13]

Choosing approaches, strategies and methods

The choice of approaches, strategies and methods used in teaching is influenced by politics,[14] value systems[15] within the country, and the wider culture,[16] as well as by factors at school and class level. Among the school factors that influence strategies and methods used are the available resources including textbooks, the physical and logistical constraints of the teaching spaces, a teacher's desire to maintain control of a class, the ethos of a school, a teacher's knowledge of a subject[17] and a teacher's knowledge of possible strategies and methods.

Teaching approaches can also be fashionable.[18] You need to use your judgement in selecting methods, so you don't dismiss a useful approach that is not in vogue, or embrace another approach unquestioningly just because it's new. As one researcher put it almost forty years ago, 'the history of education is littered with dogmatic theories that are now largely discredited, although they were in vogue for a long time'.[19]

In addition to such approaches, strategies and methods, teachers frequently use commercial approaches or programmes for teaching various subjects. Since I began teaching, some packages that have proved popular among teachers include *First Steps*, *Letterland*, *Jolly Phonics*, *Reading Recovery* and *Maths Recovery*. These packages typically have readymade materials, which are sequenced and attractive to children and straightforward for teachers to use. Usually such packages are expensive, or some professional development may be required to use them as intended; consequently a whole-school decision will be made to invest in or not invest in such materials for one or more class levels.

Limitations of strategies and methods

What a teaching strategy or method promises can differ from what it delivers. Teaching approaches make assumptions about how children learn, but no strategy or method can determine how children will respond. Constructivist teaching approaches assume that children are actively engaged when working on a task, but such engagement is not guaranteed. In mathematics or science, for instance, children may use manipulative materials mechanically, without engaging in any reflection on what they are doing.[20] Questions in a discussion designed to promote higher-order thinking may yield banal answers from children.[21]

In contrast, direct teaching is often associated with more passive student involvement, but even a lecture can sometimes be captivating and inspiring for children. Transcriptions and dictations may be associated negatively with a didactic approach to education. Yet the Irish writer, Joseph O'Connor, has described how, as a teenager learning to write, he repeatedly transcribed in full the short story 'Sierra Leone' by John McGahern,[22] gradually replacing words by McGahern with his own.[23] And dictations can be varied in many ways in order to make them student-centred and interesting; mutual dictation, for instance, requires a pair of children to compile a full text by giving each child half the text and having them dictate the missing half to the other.[24]

Furthermore, the effectiveness of a given strategy to bring about learning may vary among children. Selecting teaching strategies is closer to bespoke tailoring than 'one size fits all'.

Pedagogy

Rather than thinking of approaches, strategies and methods when I teach, I think about who I am teaching, what I am teaching and how I can best help the children engage with the content. I want the lesson to interest the children and me so that their learning yields insights for me too. The teaching – or pedagogy – is the frame I place around the lesson content. It should draw attention not to itself but to the content.

Although my actions to bring about learning are informed by my own experiences as a learner and as a teacher and by my knowledge of philosophical or psychological approaches to education, these are not foremost in my mind when it comes to planning my teaching. I consider how I can organise the classroom for a particular activity. Or I think about teaching and learning actions. Sometimes the action – explaining, telling, writing, demonstrating and so on – will be done by me as the teacher; other times the action will be done by the children; and sometimes we do them together. The objects or the products of our actions will vary and sometimes no object or product will be necessary.

We may write a book or a story or in a journal; we may research a project, a line of development or a patch study; we may view or create a film clip; we may plan a journey or create a school garden. We may talk or play. The activities will be influenced by the resources available – human, technological, commercial or homemade. Although planning teaching is a messy process going back and forth between ideas, resources and my perception of what will work for most children, Table 3.1 illustrates how I think as I plan possible options. The entries in each column are not intended to be comprehensive.

A list of teaching and learning actions is like a menu that can prompt, inspire or simply remind me of options to use in mediating the curriculum for a class. It's a bit like a tradesperson laying out tools on the floor and deciding which ones to use. The chosen action makes certain demands on a teacher. Some require substantial planning time – a nature walk or a performance for example. Others, such as visits or school gardens, may have cost and logistical implications. Some depend on the availability of other people at a particular time (interviewing a guest speaker, for example). Teaching activities such as experiments or projects may take place over several lessons; others generate material that could be used in several lessons either beforehand, afterwards or both (trails and visits, for example).

If I am teaching children who are really interested in dolphins, and I want them to learn about features related to seas in geography, I could encourage the children to complete projects on aspects of marine life and sea features during the year. This could culminate in a school trip to the seaside or to an aquarium, where children could take a tour to see dolphins and observe other features they learned about in their projects.

If I wanted children to gain an appreciation of the link between reading and writing, I could encourage them all to write a book. They would need to revise it several times and edit it to eliminate grammar and spelling errors. We'd have a formal launch where the children would invite family

TABLE 3.1 Sample ways to teach and learn

Sample philosophical or psychological approaches	Sample formal approaches, strategies and methods	Sample models of class organisation	Sample teaching and learning actions	Sample objects and products	Sample resources
Analytic	*General:*	Collaborative learning	Brainstorm	Book	Balance
Behaviourist	Audiolingual	Cooperative learning	Build	Concept maps	Base ten materials
Child centred	Communicative	Cooperative learning	Collect	maps	materials
Classical	Discovery learning	Co-teaching/cooperative teaching	Conduct	Diary	Bench
Constructivist	Inquiry		Create	Dictation	Camera
Contemplative	Language experience		Debate	Example	Chalkboard
Critical	Montessori	Group work	Demonstrate	Film	Computer
Democratic	Silent way	One-to-one teaching	Describe	Game	Environment
Existential	Total physical response		Design	Garden	Guest speaker
Holistic	Whole language	Peer tutoring	Direct	Idea	Instruments
Humanist		Station teaching	Discuss	Line of development	Magnets
Idealistic		Whole class	Draw		Mat
Perennial	**COMMERCIAL:**		Drill	Model	Puppets
Pragmatic			Exhibit	Patch study	Software
Progressive	First steps		Experiment	Picture	Textbooks
Realist	Letterland		Explain	Podcast	Tool
Romantic	Reading recovery		Hypothesise	Poetry and rhyme	Virtual tour
Scholastic			Interview	Place	Webquest
Scientific			Investigate	Problem	Word processor
Teacher centred			Lecture	Project	
			Make	Puzzle	
			Observe	Quiz	
			Perform	Reflective journal	
			Plan	Result	
			Play	Route	
			Pose	Sample	
			Practise	Sculpture	
			Present	Story	
			Produce	Task	
			Question	Trail	
			Read	Transcription	
			Recall	Visit	
			Recite		
			Record		
			Research		
			Role-play		
			Solve		
			Summarise		
			Survey		
			Talk		
			Tell		
			Test		
			Understand		
			View		
			Walk		
			Write		

members to the school and read extracts from their books, which would be published in hard copy and online.

When teaching during National Tree Week the children and I spent time observing trees in the school grounds, sketching them, displaying them, researching the names of different parts of the tree and learning the names of the trees. By doing this throughout the year the learning could be enhanced by observing how the tree changed during the school year. It helped the children to recognise and identify the parts of a tree and appreciate trees as habitats.

When I wanted to encourage young children to talk about their feelings, one book that stimulated children to do so was Jill Tomlinson's book *The Owl Who Was Afraid of the Dark*. The story is about Plop, an owl who through various life experiences changes from being scared of the dark to finding it super. The children listened to the story, talked about it, drew pictures of it and wrote about it and about times when they were afraid. In short, how you choose to teach will vary depending on the interests of the children in the class and what they need to learn, the subject being taught, the topic, and pragmatic factors, such as what is possible and available at a particular time.

For some teachers working from the textbook is the default action of teaching. A textbook has the benefits of being structured, widely available, related to the curriculum and geared towards the age of the children. However, a textbook can also be predictable, sanitised and monotonous for children. Having a list of possible alternative teaching and learning actions is helpful because those actions can help make teaching more interesting for both children and teacher.

The heart of teaching is how teachers and children interact with one another around the content to be taught. When teaching works well, the effect is magical; but the magic comes from the student–teacher–content interaction and is not built into any particular method or strategy.

Animated interactions with children bring your teaching to life. Strategies or methods may help such interactions, but no teaching strategy in itself is a silver bullet. Just as a professional golfer's clubs look less magical when swung by an amateur, every method depends on a teacher to vivify it in the classroom. A teacher can tell a story but if it lacks life and vigour, it won't captivate or inspire children. A teacher could conduct a class discussion and do most of the talking while seeking, hearing or responding to only the occasional student contribution. Children may spend lots of time playing educational games and learn little if the teacher doesn't connect the games to key ideas in the subject being taught. Like so many things in life, although teaching methods are helpful, how successful they are depends on how they are used (Box 3.1). That is where a teacher's expertise shines through.

> ## Box 3.1 Follow the Fleet
>
> I learned at a young age about a teacher's power to guide a programme to fly or fall. When one of my brothers was in primary school, he and his classmates participated in an educational project called 'Follow the Fleet'. Although the programme has now migrated online (http://www.followthefleet.ie), in pre-internet days classes participating in the programme received regular updates through the postal service about the locations of Irish ships – such as the Irish Oak, the Irish Elm and The Irish Rowan – and each package contained lesson plans for the teacher and teaching materials such as maps, puzzles and educational challenges. All were designed to stimulate children's curiosity about all kinds of maritime matters and to offer learning opportunities in subjects like geography and mathematics. However, in my brother's class the arrival of the monthly package came to be dreaded by the children because the teacher used it as a time to reprimand and punish children for forgetting where the ships had been the previous month, for not knowing the names of various seas and so on. Although the materials provided the basis for a stimulating, exciting and authentic project designed to capture children's imaginations, this purpose was thwarted.

How pedagogy tries to make learning happen

In order to illustrate how pedagogy can be applied to bring about learning, I'd like to describe two hypothetical teachers. Let's call them Ms Doyle and Ms Foyle and imagine that each took a class of children to visit a museum.

Ms Doyle visited the museum a week in advance of the class visit. She decided which exhibits the children would spend most time viewing, made notes about pertinent features of the exhibits and devised questions for the children to answer when they visited the museum. After visiting the museum, Ms Doyle used the internet, relevant books and articles to conduct additional research about the chosen exhibits. She then connected what was in the museum to history and geography content the children were working on that year. On the day of the visit each child was given a clipboard and a set of questions to answer. Answering the questions required close observation of the exhibits, some hypothesising and some use of timelines. The visit and the children's answers to the questions were discussed and referred to in subsequent lessons for weeks after the visit.

In contrast, Ms Foyle was unable to visit the museum or find out much about it in advance. She took the class to the museum and let them wander around the exhibits. Ms Foyle spent the time in the museum looking at various displays, reading about them and discussing them with the children who were near her. Afterwards she and her class spent time in the café and gift shop. Subsequently, the visit was mentioned occasionally in class but the mentions were as likely to centre on the bus trip there or to what the children ate in the café, as it was to the exhibits they saw in the museum.

When you consider these two caricatures, it is clear that Ms Doyle's level of advance preparation may not always be possible and despite Ms Foyle's lack of preparation or follow-up, some children likely learned much from the visit. But the exaggerated differences illustrate how Ms Doyle's teaching tries to bring about learning in contrast to a similar activity by Ms Foyle that has little evidence of pedagogical input.

The hallmark of learning teaching is becoming attuned to potential teaching and learning opportunities[25] – opportunities that arise when a student brings in an old programme from a football game, a collection of seashells or a song they learned at summer camp to 'show and tell', or opportunities for children to ask a simple question in a second language instead of the main language of the class. The opportunities discerned by such teaching are informed by the teacher's subject knowledge – knowing children's typical prior knowledge in a given class, knowing why the subject is important and knowing where a specific topic being taught fits in the subject as a whole and across subjects.

Teaching disciplines

A range of academic disciplines underlies the subjects taught in primary school. Scholars conduct research on history, mathematics, science, first and second languages, linguistics and geography. Artists pursue creative work in the visual arts, music and drama, and athletes seek fitness and bid to excel in sport. Social, personal and health education is grounded in the health sciences, psychology and communications. These disciplines and endeavours – and many others – have evolved, some of them over centuries, as ways to organise human knowledge and to display feats of thinking, endeavour and creativity of which humans are capable. Teachers introduce children to these fields of scholarship and endeavour early in the children's lives. That is why it is helpful for teachers to know about the richness that lies behind each of the subjects, where particular topics fit in the broader subject area and why the topics are worth teaching.

On the surface a history lesson may be about life during World War II, but children are also learning about aggression, conflict resolution, and strategy; they are learning to look for and analyse evidence in order to understand life during the war; they are developing a sense of empathy for children their age who were alive then; they are learning how geography influenced the progress of the war and how the war shaped the country, continent and world in which they live today. To teach is to be mindful of the various dimensions of learning that are going on in a given moment.

A novice teacher is unlikely to have such breadth of knowledge across all curriculum subjects at the outset of a teaching career. Such appreciation for and knowledge of subject disciplines develops over time, through living, reading, questioning and reflecting. Curiosity is a great trait for a teacher to have. When you learn as a teacher, you get a taste of how children experience learning as they are helped to make sense of the world.

I know one teacher, now retired, who chose one subject each year in which to specifically deepen his knowledge and over a teaching career he became accomplished in most of them. I am not sure if such an approach to continuing professional development was planned in advance or not but that is how it transpired. To reflect the disposition of teachers towards the pursuit of knowledge, teaching has been called the 'learning profession'.[26]

Knowledge of the disciplines and fields on which school subjects are based places teachers in a landscape they can gradually explore with, and reveal to, children. The landscape comprises the topics to be taught and learned across all subjects. The visible extent of the landscape is constantly expanding, as a result of new knowledge being developed in various disciplines, the creation of new and innovative artwork, and the surpassing of previous human achievements in sport and other fields. Such developments and achievements can be drawn on to inspire work that is done by teachers and children in the primary classroom.

For example, you could use pictures and approaches of established artists to stimulate children's creativity in the visual arts. Contemporary and historical developments in science and exploration can help children appreciate how great thinkers and creators can influence our lives.[27] Through teaching children are helped to encounter and appreciate great thought, creativity and endeavour.

How the discipline of mathematics informs pedagogy

A good example of the link between a subject discipline and the classroom comes from the story of how Andrew Wiles solved Fermat's Last Theorem. The story is vividly told in book and documentary format by Simon Singh.[28] The mathematical content in the programme is beyond most people's understanding but both book and TV programme yield valuable insights into the work mathematicians do. Many comparisons can be made between Andrew Wiles's efforts to solve one of the most difficult problems in mathematics and how children learn mathematics in school.

Andrew Wiles spent many, many hours working on the proof alone in his study at home. Children too need to spend time working alone at mathematics. As Andrew Wiles came closer to solving the prestigious theorem, he needed to discuss his ideas in detail with his close colleagues without attracting the suspicion of others in the university. To do this he organised a course of college seminars which were supposedly for graduate students where he could share and test some of the advanced and difficult mathematical ideas he was working on with the students and with some close colleagues who attended the seminars. Children too benefit from sharing their ideas with their peers and teacher, and asking each other questions when they are solving mathematics problems.

However, because of the potential hype that could surround someone who appeared to be on the brink of solving the famous theorem, Wiles could not explain to the students present that the ideas being discussed in the course were ideas that could lead to a solution of Fermat's Last Theorem. As a result the mathematical content of the seminars was extremely difficult and seemed irrelevant to most of Wiles's graduate students. As a result, many of them stopped attending the seminar classes during the semester – showing that it is hard to keep working at something that's difficult or if you don't know why you're learning it. Children, too, need to know why they are working on various ideas in mathematics and how the ideas are connected to each other.

Despite being a highly accomplished mathematician, Wiles found the mathematics he was working on difficult. That should comfort children who find mathematics difficult – difficulty is not a reason for giving up. The documentary includes an interview where Goro Shimura speaks about his former working colleague, the late Yukata Taniyama, as someone who 'made mistakes in a good direction'. Isn't it good for children to learn that even when they are wrong about something in mathematics, they can learn from their mistakes?

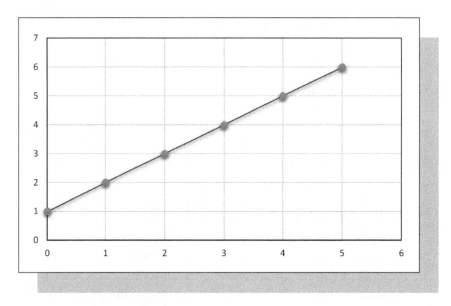

Figure 3.2 A graphical representation of $x + 1$

In constructing his solution to the problem, Wiles connected different areas of mathematics; it is good for children to work on problems where they link ideas in different parts of the subject as well. Sometimes it is useful to know that dividing a whole number by 0.25 is the same as multiplying it by 4, or that 246 is equivalent to two hundreds, three tens and sixteen units, or that $x + 1$ can be represented as shown in Figure 3.2.

The story of Wiles also reminds teachers that new mathematics is still being developed; it is not just a body of facts that was established many years ago that has to be conveyed to children. Finally, the story shows how satisfying it can be to solve a problem in mathematics.

Disciplinary skills and practices

Experts in subject areas constantly try to develop new knowledge in the subject by using various skills.[29] The skills are practices used by scientists, mathematicians, geographers and historians when working in their chosen discipline. Such skills can be replicated in school by children and teachers as they learn and teach content. When children become competent in some of these skills, the skills can help them further their knowledge in those subject areas and can be applied in life generally.

For example, children learn how to use evidence and empathise with people from previous generations in history. They learn how to use maps and question phenomena in geography. In science they learn how to investigate, experiment and evaluate their efforts, and in mathematics they learn how to reason and solve problems. While children are working on specific topics in these disciplines, they can simultaneously develop the underlying skills for building knowledge in the subject.

The disciplinary skills or practices of these subjects can inform teaching strategies for the curriculum subject. In geography and science teaching, strategies could include questioning, observing, predicting, recording and communicating. In mathematics, problem solving, reasoning, understanding and recalling will likely feature prominently. Strategies in history will likely involve using evidence and exploring cause and effect. Skills used in drama are improvising, problem solving, empathising, imagining and hypothesising. So, subject-specific skills and practices are intertwined with teaching strategies.

Although teaching or pedagogy can take many forms, three core practices of teaching are particularly helpful to have in your rucksack as you set out on a career in teaching. Discussion, storytelling and making content explicit can be learned by novice teachers and applied across several curriculum subjects.

Discussion

Most of us are familiar with participating in discussions; they seem so commonplace that little needs to be said about conducting them. Yet, when used as an activity for teaching and learning, discussion can make teaching seem like what Deborah Ball calls an unnatural activity.[30] It seems surprising and a bit counter-intuitive to claim that something as familiar as teaching could be considered unnatural but some examples may help support the claim.

Most teachers would consider themselves to be good at discussing. But leading a class discussion requires doing things that would be considered unnatural in most discussions. Typically in discussions conversation flows freely, any member may ask questions, and participants themselves monitor when they can contribute; pauses or gaps are exceptional; the person who is most enthusiastic at a particular time or about a particular point usually gets the floor; most people look attentively at the person who is speaking; and people usually only ask someone to repeat a point if they don't hear it, don't believe it or don't agree with it.

In contrast, when I conduct a discussion with a class, I usually clarify the topic for discussion at the outset to avoid confusion; I nominate who is to speak next; I often wait several seconds before nominating someone to speak; I'll allow plenty of time for the nominated person, who may be hesitant, to make their contribution; only sometimes do I call on the person who appears most willing to contribute to the discussion; rather than making constant eye-contact with the person who is speaking, I also try to monitor the attention being paid by other discussion participants and non-participants; and I am constantly making decisions about whether to probe a contribution further, ask a contributor to repeat a point, call on someone else to repeat a contributor's point, or move quickly to another contributor.

In addition, the norms of discussion may vary from one subject to another. In visual arts, for example, a discussion may focus on personal ideas, feelings and experiences and the expression of them,[31] whereas in science the focus may be more on predicting, hypothesising and evaluating evidence.

Storytelling

'Who's going to tell us stories now?' That was the question a young boy asked his teacher plaintively when the teacher announced that he was about to retire. What a compliment that was to receive at the end of a career in teaching. A teacher who can captivate children through telling stories will be remembered by children long after they leave the teacher's class. Stories help us learn but more than that, they become part of us, a touchstone by which we live. The appeal of the news, the cinema, and soap operas are all built around humans' inherent love of story. When a teacher tells, rather than reads, a story, children will hang onto every word and follow the teacher into worlds that can be familiar or unfamiliar. This is what gives storytelling its great power as a teaching method.

Ben Okri[32] describes stories as 'shapes we give [children] with which to organise the chaos of existence and of life and of growing up and of time and of psychological experience'. He sees a reciprocal relationship between stories and our lives – the way we shape our lives is a story and the story in turn shapes our lives. Elsewhere he writes that

> a people without stories would be a perfected people, or a forgetful people, or an insane people – which is to say that they are a mythical people, or have ceased to exist, or are on their way to doing so.[33]

As a primary school student I remember one teacher in particular who used to tell us stories – parables from the Bible, mostly. He was a harsh teacher in many ways but if he had a redeeming quality, it was the stories he told. Telling stories creates a kind of magic between storyteller and listener.

The next time I experienced the magic of storytelling was as a student on teaching practice when I was placed with a teacher who used storytelling to vivify his teaching. I remember sitting at the back of his class observing him. It seemed to me as if the teacher was viewing a series of pictures and describing each one vividly as he progressed through the story. I remember the children sitting on the edges of their seats hanging on the teacher's every word. When it was my turn to teach a history lesson, the teacher encouraged me to use story as a means of introducing the children to the Irish Famine.

When I took responsibility for my own class a few years later, I occasionally told stories to the class. The stories I taught were mostly about experiences from my own life. One story I liked to tell was how one of my teachers taught us that wasps only sting when threatened. The incident arose in September when a wasp entered the classroom. Several classmates disrupted the lesson by trying to kill the wasp. Eventually the wasp either left the room or was killed and we thought no more about it. However, coincidentally that afternoon another wasp entered the room and soon after landed on our teacher's nose and stayed there for over a minute. The teacher remained calm and continued with the lesson he was teaching. Years later the teacher revealed to me that at lunchtime he had put jam on the tip of his nose, which attracted the wasp to it. All he had to do was remain calm while the wasp enjoyed the jam!

Despite telling such stories, I doubt if my former students would remember me as a teacher who was a storyteller. A storyteller not only tells stories but also collects stories – looking for stories and identifying them where someone else would miss them. Ben Okri[34] says that stories can come in various forms, including statistics, and that we should continually question the stories we hear. One of my regrets to date as a teacher is that I haven't done a better job of being a storyteller who collected stories. Stories can be found in many places: newspapers, the Bible, history books, myths and legends, heroes and heroines, and life experiences.

According to one teacher friend, every story can be thought about in terms of three phases: (1) Paradise. (2) Paradise lost. (3) Paradise regained but it's not the original paradise; scars or bruises remain to mark the experience. A story begins in a state of balance and happiness. Then something happens to disrupt the happiness. Eventually, happiness returns but a price has been paid for the restored happiness.

Robert McKee[35] says that human desire is at the heart of every story. What does a person desire? What's stopping them from achieving their desire? How does the person react to these obstacles? A storyteller discovers the truth of the character, what they're made of, in the answer to that final question.[36]

These story structures can be applied to many stories. Take 'The Three Little Pigs'. At the start of the story all the pigs are living at home with their mother (paradise). The mother then sends them out to make their way in the world. The first two pigs build houses of straw and wood and each one is knocked down by the wolf who eats the two little pigs (paradise lost). Then the third pig builds a house of brick. The wolf cannot knock down the house and when he decides to enter the house through the chimney, he lands in a cauldron of boiling water and is killed. Paradise is restored because the threat of the wolf has been removed but at a price: two of the pig's siblings are dead and the third pig now knows that the world can be a threatening place.

At the heart of the story is the human desire to make one's way in the world, to move out from home and to be independent. The anthropomorphic pigs must rise to the challenge of finding somewhere to live, where they are protected from life's threats. The third pig learns from the experiences of its siblings that you need to be strong and clever to avoid life's threats.

Making content explicit

A key part of teaching involves making content explicit to children. This can be done through explanations, representations, modelling and examples.[37] Let's consider these one at a time.

Explaining

Explaining is about making something visible to someone or making it understandable. Think of a child looking through a window on a cold morning onto something that is wonderful, beautiful or important. There may be frost or condensation on the window making the object difficult to see. The teacher tries to clear away the mist so that the children can see more clearly, and appreciate or understand what is outside the window. Explaining is about revealing or making clear to children something they have not thought about before or helping them to understand better something they have seen before but have taken little notice of. Often the explanation is linked to something the children already know.[38]

For example, to explain what a pun is, a teacher will likely draw on children's knowledge of homophones, words that sound the same but differ in meaning. Or to explain an electric current, you might begin with children's knowledge of static electricity.[39] Or to explain the conjugation of irregular verbs in a second language, you could begin with a reminder of how regular verbs are conjugated.

Representing

A representation is something that stands for something else. Sometimes children need to learn about something they cannot see directly. It might be a place they cannot visit, like the South Pole or outer space; it might be an idea that is abstract, like photosynthesis in science or the multiplication of fractions; or it might be a process that cannot be observed in the classroom, such as a volcano erupting. In each case a teacher will use something to represent the place or idea or process. It may be an oral or written description, a photograph, a video, a picture, a diagram or sketch, or a 3-D model. The representation is not the place, object, idea or process itself but it gives the children an idea of what it is.

Every representation has some limitations. Looking at a picture of the South Pole gives no idea of how extremely cold and hostile it feels in that environment in the midst of a blizzard. A line drawing of a volcano reveals little of the heat and dust emitted by an eruption. Most maps of the solar system convey little sense of the vast distances involved. A diagram to illustrate multiplication of fractions on its own will rarely help children understand the process.

Using more than one representation of a particular place, concept or process and making connections from one representation to another can provide new perspectives. Teachers can make representations more real, more vivid for children by anticipating the shortcomings of any individual representation and filling the gaps, to breathe life into the representations.

When I was a student teacher, one lecturer played for the class a recording of someone reporting a Gospel story as if it were a report on a radio news bulletin. The lecturer asked what we thought of the news report. 'It made the story seem more real' was a common response. 'But was it more real?' was the lecturer's rhetorical reply. The lecturer was right; the Gospel story was as real in the written format as it was in the more dramatic radio news story format. But the audio representation appeared to be more 'real' to us because it was closer to how we received news at the time. In school some representations may seem to be more real, video for example, but each one has limitations that may be deceptive in making a place, an idea or a process explicit for the learner.

Given the necessity of representations in making content explicit and the limitations inherent in each one, it is helpful if multiple representations can be used to convey important ideas. Furthermore, discussing the limitations of a given representation and making connections from one representation to another help bring distant or abstract content to life for children.

Modelling

Modelling is another way of making content explicit for children. This is where the teacher models or demonstrates ways of thinking or doing.[40] This has an obvious role in practical activities such as doing a forward roll, teaching a dance step, showing how to write cursive script, laying out a copy, making pancakes or mixing paints. A teacher also models thinking processes for children by articulating thoughts on a process at a particular time. This might happen when making the writing process explicit for children.

The teacher might verbalise,

> I want to write a story about an eight-year-old child being lost … I'm trying to think of a setting where a child could actually get lost … It could be a shopping centre or it could be a forest or it could be at the zoo … If I choose the shopping centre, the child would likely approach the centre security staff or an adult and the story could end very quickly … I haven't been to the zoo for a long time so I might find it hard to make it feel real for the reader. A forest could be good because I could decide what trees and animals are in the forest and I could decide how big I want the forest to be – it could be a small forest or a large forest depending on what will happen to the child … With fewer adults around, the child could feel genuinely scared … I'm going to base my story in a forest.

By having the thinking process modelled for them, the children get insights into how a writer thinks about writing a story, considering options and accepting or rejecting them according to how it will unfold.

Examples and non-examples

Another way to make content explicit for children is to use examples. Examples help make abstract ideas concrete. In a music lesson you might be explaining that a semibreve has four beats in 4/4 time, a crotchet has one beat and a quaver has a half beat, and then you want to move on to rest notes. Using an example of a familiar song, such as 'Old MacDonald Had a Farm', where children can hear the different note lengths and some rests, will help reinforce the concepts.

In an English lesson, examples will help to illustrate what a pun is – like the man who was served a bland pastry, which he termed a 'pedestrian croissant'.[41] In physical education, you might ask children to create a sequence in gymnastics. The idea may be new to some children so if you or another child in the class can perform an example, the requirement of the task becomes more explicit.

Examples need to be chosen carefully. If children are learning about prime numbers, '2' is a prime number, but is not a good example to use at first. It is the only prime number that is even and although children need to learn that it is a prime number, it is an atypical example and therefore may be less helpful initially than examples such as 3, 5 or 7. Non-examples too can be helpful in clarifying ideas. Although 9 is an odd number, it is not prime and is a good non-example to use; natural gas and nuclear energy are non-examples of renewable energy sources.

Cognitive challenge

Once you have chosen how you're going to teach a topic to your students, the next step is to pitch the content at a suitable level of challenge. If children are to develop, they need to be extended. We can most easily see this in physical education where children's techniques in throwing and catching and other skills in athletics and gymnastics will only develop if children push on and take on harder challenges as they grow older, stronger and more accomplished.

Similarly, their creative instinct will only develop when they are introduced to the basic techniques in each arts discipline and encouraged to respond creatively to challenging stimuli in arts, drama, music and writing. Children's minds will develop when their thinking is challenged by working on tasks and questions that require sustained and creative thought.

When teachers set children tasks to complete, they vary in the demands they make on children. One way to think about the demands is on a continuum of categories (see Figure 3.3) with tasks that make the least demand on children to the left and tasks that make the greatest demands to the right.

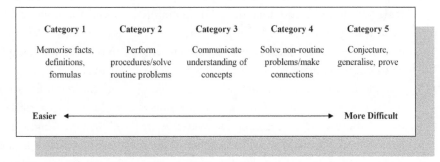

Category 1	Category 2	Category 3	Category 4	Category 5
Memorise facts, definitions, formulas	Perform procedures/solve routine problems	Communicate understanding of concepts	Solve non-routine problems/make connections	Conjecture, generalise, prove

Easier ←————————————————————→ More Difficult

Figure 3.3 Continuum of challenge for students

(Categories taken from Porter, 2002)

In Category 1, children may be required to learn dates of events in history, state when to use a capital letter in writing or know a second-language term for schoolbag. In Category 2, children might be required to punctuate a sentence, perform a forward roll or calculate the answer to 325 × 74. In Category 3, children might be asked to make inferences about a character, compare two materials or organisms or justify an answer to a problem.

Category 4 requires children to complete tasks where no way to do them is immediately apparent, and children need to draw on one or more concepts they already know. In a senior class, children might be asked to plan a school tour, showing the selected route on a map and estimating journey times. Category 5 might involve children developing and proving a mathematical conjecture such as that the sum of two odd numbers is an even number; or they might devise an experiment (or series of experiments) to investigate what plants need in order to grow.

Although there are times when children will engage with tasks from all five categories, it is preferable to have more problems on the right side of the continuum than the left. They need to be challenging, interesting, motivating and accessible to children with different levels of prior knowledge. Ironically, such tasks can be difficult to source; I can never find enough of them[42] but you will find them in various sources, including your college notes, educational websites, textbooks and other commercial sources, and on courses.

A wide range of tasks can be accessed on the World Wide Web. Sometimes I modify such tasks and tailor them for the children in my class. Our expertise as teachers is in selecting tasks that are both relevant to the content and suitable for the children in terms of interest and challenge. A task generally requires children to use certain actions or operations to come up with a product using specific resources.[43] Over time a teacher can build up a bank of tasks that have been successful. Tasks that are available can be considered to make either a low cognitive demand on children – requiring memorisation or routinely using formulas or procedures – or a high cognitive demand or challenge – where children are expected to engage in the relevant discipline or to connect formulas or procedures to concepts or meaning.[44]

Although finding tasks that set good challenges for children is important, it's not enough. Most of us have experienced a child posing a riddle to us and then soon after asking 'Do you give up?' or 'Do you want a hint?'. Knowing the answer, the child cannot understand why we can't figure it out immediately and the child is eager to reveal the answer to us. Even if we demand more time to think through the riddle, children often cannot restrain themselves from telling us the answer.

A teacher, however, must exercise restraint in order to maintain the challenge level of a task as it is worked on. It is good for a student to struggle a bit when doing a task. If the student struggles too little, the task is too easy, if the student struggles too much, frustration may set in. A teacher's expertise is in judging when and how to intervene, when a student is on the tipping point between healthy struggle and unhealthy frustration. When a teacher intervenes, it is easy to give a hint that makes the task so easy that it becomes trivial. The kind of hint given by the teacher needs to be helpful enough to remove any potential frustration but subtle enough to maintain some challenge.

Providing the right nudge means knowing what you want the children to learn, knowing what they have to do in order to complete the task, knowing how they might be thinking about it and knowing what might help them think about it in a more productive way. Even if a teacher had nothing else to do, thinking through those steps for one student is demanding. But doing this for several children while monitoring their engagement in the lesson is something that even with several years' experience behind me, I still find difficult. Nevertheless, maintaining the challenge of a task is still something I try to do.

In addition to giving too big a hint, other factors have been blamed for why the challenges in tasks decline when they are being implemented in the classroom.[45] Sometimes the problem is not suitable for the class – it might not capture the children's interest, they aren't motivated to do it or they don't have the knowledge needed to complete the task. The better the teacher knows the children, the easier it will be to select suitable problems, but even still it can sometimes be difficult matching a task to a class of children.

Another difficulty arises if a teacher emphasises finding the correct answer rather than engaging with the process. When a child answers a mathematics problem, I try to ask 'how did you get that?' in a deadpan way, not indicating if the answer is right or wrong. If children believe that the teacher is only interested in the answer, they will try to get that in the easiest, quickest way possible. The challenge of a task can also be reduced if children are given too much or too little time to work on the task; especially when children rush their work, they are unable to think too deeply about what they are doing.

Although I am advocating challenging children in class, it is difficult when you present a problem to the class and soon everyone is saying, 'It's too difficult' or 'I don't know how to do this' or 'Can you help me, please?'. Saying 'Go on, just give it a go' is easier said than done in that atmosphere.

The easiest thing to do is to compromise and give the children work that will keep them busy but that won't challenge them too much. That is the effect of many tasks in textbooks.

Textbook authors create problems that are relatively manageable, and publishers lay them out in a predictable way. This arrangement minimises complaints of problems being too easy or too difficult, but it also means that the children are learning little new – at best they may be consolidating what they already know. No teacher likes to receive complaints from children – or their parents – that the work is too difficult. The short-term rewards for giving in and providing easy, busy work are huge.[46]

But perseverance is an important trait to develop. In life, children will have more agency over what they do if they are prepared to engage in work that is challenging and innovative over work that is busy and repetitive. On international tests of mathematics, problem solving is one area where many children tend to perform poorly. That may be because in school children rarely get to practise genuine problem solving in mathematics. The problems in textbooks tend to be organised according to the operation that is required to complete them and only occasionally are children expected to think about how to go about solving a problem. Little wonder then, that they cannot do such problems when asked to do them in a test situation.

You could respond to this dilemma by presenting a combination of challenging tasks and 'reassuring' or confidence-building tasks. A discussion with older children about the benefits of pushing themselves may also be of help. By being aware of the tension, you are best placed to reflect on how to respond to it with children in your class.

Revision and repetition

When a topic has been taught to children, it is useful to revisit it from time to time. Revising serves different purposes for different children. For some it will serve to consolidate material they already know; revising may help others to understand something they were unable to grasp the first time round. Whether revision is done weekly, fortnightly, monthly or just when necessary for teaching a new, related topic, it offers children a chance to look at material they have encountered before in a different way. It may be done using a quiz format, demonstrating for peers, creating a mind map, writing down what children know about a topic, listing questions children have about a topic, reading about the topic, creating a role play, viewing a video about it and so on.

Sometimes children can be resistant to repeating content. 'We did that poem with our teacher last year' is something they often say. However, the children are a year older now and will experience the poem – or other content – in a different way. Whereas children may be captivated by a poem's rhyme and sounds when they are younger, the content and the relationship between sound and theme may be something they learn to attend to when they are older.

In eastern cultures repetition in school seems to be valued more than in western cultures as a way to memorise content. Chinese students differentiate between memorisation through rote learning, and memorisation with understanding. Although rote learning has a bad name, memorisation with understanding is valuable. Repetition can 'create a deep impression', which helps memorisation. Repeated reading of a text may also deepen understanding of the text, just as any repetition that is 'concentrated and attentive' can promote understanding through helping children discover new meaning.[47]

Conclusion

In this chapter I have written about teaching approaches, strategies and methods and explained how educators mean many different things when they use these and related terms. I paid particular attention to discussions in teaching and learning, to the power of storytelling, to specific ways of making content explicit, to the idea of cognitive demand and to repetition and revision. But how are teaching methods related to the work of teaching? Frequently, teachers refer to *using* methodologies. However, by focusing solely on the *use* of 'methodologies', teaching can be reduced to a technical or formulaic activity. To think about how an activity or an artefact can be more than functional, I often think of one of my favourite buildings.

The Casino in Marino (Figure 3.4) is located near my workplace. Not a gambling casino, the neo-classical Georgian building was designed by Sir William Chambers and built between 1762 and 1775 as a summer house on what was then the country estate of James Caulfield, the First Earl of Charlemont. From the outside the building appears to be symmetrical and simple in design. But if you visit the Casino, you soon learn that much of it is different to how it first appears.

For example, the chimneys on the roof are disguised as Roman urns, and four of the Tuscan columns, which surround the building, are hollow and contain drainage pipes. What impresses me is the value placed on

Figure 3.4 The Casino at Marino in Dublin

the aesthetic appearance of the building. Although the project bankrupted Caulfield, he clearly wanted the building to be both pleasing and functional. In many areas of life today, it seems as if we are willing to sacrifice aesthetics in search of what is useful – think of mobile phone masts and electricity pylons that blot the landscape in many countries. We prioritise what the structures can do, and rather than savour their appearance, we tolerate them and hope that none will be erected near where we live.

A teaching strategy too can be used, purely as a means to an end. Viewed this way a teaching strategy can become a formula or a recipe that offers a means towards a predictable end, and the end takes precedence. But valuing teaching strategies in isolation from subject knowledge could be short-sighted.

Children may enjoy a demonstration of an erupting mini volcano, with baking soda and vinegar in its 'magma chamber' but they may learn little from it about volcanoes or about the chemical reaction of the two substances. Or children may role-play a family discussing the pros and cons of emigrating to flee war, famine or other disasters but may experience little empathy for the starkness of the choice to be made. Or a completed project may look good but most of the content may have been copied and pasted from internet and other sources.

Although we often hear that both process and product matter or that the journey is as important as the destination, a society that is focused on cost–benefit analyses and utilitarian values tends to prioritise product over process. In such a culture a journey often comes to be seen as something to be endured before arriving at a particular destination. St Augustine wrote that 'there are some things which are to be enjoyed, some which are to be used and some whose function is both to enjoy and use'.[48]

If teaching is a way to bring children closer to the disciplines embedded in the curriculum subjects, approaches, strategies and methods can be chosen which are integral to how knowledge is developed and tested in those subjects. There is no history without story, no mathematics without problem solving, no language without talk and discussion, no physical education without movement and skill practice, no science without experiments, no arts education without imagination and expression.

If a teaching strategy is looked on purely as something to be used, then it is considered to be inferior to the content that needs to be learned.[49] However, if an approach or strategy or method is an activity to be used *and* enjoyed, not only does it lead us towards the subject we are learning; it is an integral part of the subject. Teaching strategies need to be both used and enjoyed because they lead us to what we want children to learn *and* they are part of what we want them to learn.

Key points of Chapter 3

1 Labels that describe teaching 'methods' can be misleading in what they describe and in how a particular 'method' promotes learning.

2 Teaching and learning happen through deliberate, contemplative actions by students and teachers with objects and products using available resources.

3 Central to the teaching and learning that occur are the complex interactions among teachers, students and subject matter.

4 Practices or skills that are used to develop new knowledge in a subject can also be used when teaching and learning the subject.

5 Discussion, storytelling and making content explicit are useful teaching practices for beginning teachers to master.

6 Setting a task with a suitable challenge and maintaining that challenge while children complete the task is an important and difficult part of teaching.

7 Repetition and revision using various approaches are essential for consolidating learning.

Notes

1 A chef's tall white hat is called a toque.
2 The second half of this sentence is almost a direct quote from Leith (2011, p. 6).
3 See, for example, Leith (2011).
4 See, for example, McKee (1997).
5 Winch & Gingell (1999, 2008, p. 152). As evidence of the looseness with which the terms are used, in the very next sentence of the entry on pedagogy 'pedagogical techniques' have become 'methods.'
6 Shuell, Brown, Watson & Ewing (1988). Although the authors acknowledge that 'praise is not a teaching method in the strict sense of the term' they included it in their study of methods because 'there is a great deal of emphasis and discussion on the use of praise in the classroom' (pp. 341–342).
7 Ofsted (1996), cited in Sharpe (1997).
8 Irish National Teachers' Organisation (2007).
9 Anthony (1963); Richards & Rodgers (1986).
10 Stewart (1979).
11 Adamson (2004).
12 Richards & Rodgers (1986).
13 Lampert (2001).
14 For example, in Ireland, the Government launched *Literacy and Numeracy for Learning and Life: The National Strategy to Improve Literacy and Numeracy among Children and Young People 2011–2020*, in response to relatively disappointing results in the 2009 PISA tests (Department of Education and Skills, 2011).
15 This can be seen, for example, in how schools are funded, how new policies are justified, the status of teachers in a country, the role of religion in schools, the subjects taught, subjects on the curriculum.
16 This can be seen in what teachers, children, parents and society expect schools to achieve and what they expect teaching to be like.
17 Adamson (2004).
18 For example, when I was in college, patch studies were popular in history teaching, whereas they merit only a single mention in a more recent curriculum document (Government of Ireland, 1999a).
19 Collinge (1976).

20 Baroody (1989).

21 Rink (2001).

22 McGahern (1992).

23 http://www.theguardian.com/books/2004/jan/10/fiction

24 For more on this and on varying the dictation format see http://www.teaching english.org.uk/article/mutual-dictation, http://teflreflections.blogspot.ie/2013/ 11/dictations-are-fun.html, http://www.onlinetefltraining.com/10-dictation- activites-for-efl-classes/ and Davis & Rinvolucri (1989, 2002).

25 In a narrow sense, looking at things from the perspective of one's own pro- fession has been called '*Déformation professionnelle*' in French or 'Occupational psychosis' in English. See, for example, Langerock (1915). I am thinking about a teacher's inclination to seek teaching moments during the school day in a broader and positive sense, such as asking how many minutes to break time when teaching time in mathematics or using a second language informally for instructions or greetings during the school day.

26 See, for example, Darling-Hammond & Sykes (2009); Darling-Hammond, Wei, Andree, Richardson & Orphanos (2009).

27 Good starting points for such work are the 1970s TV series and book *The Ascent of Man* by Bronowski (1973), *The Story of Painting* by Beckett (1996), several books by Asimov such as *Asimov's Chronology of Science and Discovery* (1990), *The Way Things Work* by Macaulay (1988, 2005), various editions (book, audio-book and illustrated) of *A Little History of the World* by Gombrich (1985, 2011), and several books by David Attenborough, such as *Life on Earth* (1979).

28 See Singh (1997) and information about the BBC Horizon documentary can be found at http://www.bbc.co.uk/iplayer/episode/b0074rxx/horizon- 19951996-fermats-last-theorem.

29 Note that the term 'skills' can be used with different meanings. This can be seen, for example, across primary school curriculum documents in Ireland. In physical education the curriculum refers to ball-handling skills and movement skills. The English curriculum refers to skills in reading, listening and retrieval. In music skills refer to capacities such as keeping a steady beat and keeping a tune in pitch. In subjects such as science and mathematics, the term 'skills' is used with a different meaning. It refers to practices that are integral to how knowledge is developed in the subject. Included in this category are skills such as questioning, observing, predicting (science), reasoning, and problem solving (mathematics).

30 See Ball & Forzani (2009).

31 Government of Ireland (1999b, p. 32).

32 https://www.youtube.com/watch?v=8H_vJ33lrRo and 'The Joys of Storytelling' in *Birds of Heaven* by Ben Okri.

33 See Okri (1996, p. 32).

34 https://www.youtube.com/watch?v=8H_vJ33lrRo

35 McKee (2003).

36 Kieran Egan (1986, 1989) refers to the rhythm of a story involving an expectation, an elaboration or complication, and a resolution in which the expectation is satisfied.

37 'Making content explicit through explanation, modelling, representations and examples' is a high leverage practice identified by Deborah Ball and the team at Teaching Works. For more see http://www.teachingworks.com/work-of-teaching/high-leverage-practices.

38 As Leinhardt (1989) puts it: 'Experts, in general, tend to use something familiar to teach something new, whereas novices often use something new to teach something new' (p. 66).

39 See, for example, http://www.explainthatstuff.com/electricity.html.

40 Modelling has another specific meaning that is used in science and mathematics education. In mathematics education it refers to the use of representations or models such as graphs, equations or algorithms to study everyday phenomena from a mathematical perspective. Mathematical models might be used to make predictions about voting patterns, population change and the like (Abrams, 2001). However, the idea of modelling presented here is the more generic sense of the term.

41 Attributed to the late Seán Mac Réamoinn: http://radioeireann.blogspot.ie/2006/01/sean-mac-reamoinn.html.

42 See Appendix V for a sample of some such tasks.

43 See Doyle (1983).

44 Stein, Grover & Henningsen (1996).

45 Reasons taken from Stein et al. (1996).

46 In his book, *Horace's Compromise* (Sizer, 1984, 1992), Ted Sizer describes one compromise of teaching at post-primary school level as the unwritten rule between teachers and students where teachers agree not to challenge the students too much and in return, students agree not to make the teacher's life too hard (pp. 155–156).

47 See Dahlin & Watkins (2000) for more on this.

48 Green (1997, p. 9).

49 O'Donovan (1982, p. 381).

References

Abrams, J. P. (2001). Teaching mathematical modeling and the skills of representation. In A. A. Cuoco & F. R. Curcio (Eds), *The roles of representations in school mathematics*. Reston, VA: National Council of Teachers of Mathematics.

Adamson, B. (2004). Fashions in language teaching methodology. In A. Davies & C. Elder (Eds), *The handbook of applied linguistics* (pp. 604–622). Malden, MA: Blackwell.

Anthony, E. M. (1963). Approach, method, and technique. *ELT Journal, 17*(2), 63–67.

Asimov, I. (1990). *Asimov's chronology of science and discovery*. London: Grafton Books.

Attenborough, D. (1979). *Life on earth*. London: The Reader's Digest Association.

Ball, D. L. & Forzani, F. M. (2009). The work of teaching and the challenge for teacher education. *Journal of Teacher Education, 60*, 497–511.

Baroody, A. J. (1989). Manipulatives don't come with guarantees. *The Arithmetic Teacher, 37*(2), 4–5.

Beckett, W., Sr (1996). *The story of painting*. London: Dorling Kindersley.

Bronowski, J. (1973). *The ascent of man*. Boston: Black Bay Books, Little, Brown and Company.

Collinge, J. (1976). Teachers and teaching methods. *The Elementary School Journal, 76*(5), 259–265.

Dahlin, B. & Watkins, D. (2000). The role of repetition in the processes of memorising and understanding: A comparison of the views of German and Chinese secondary school students in Hong Kong. *British Journal of Educational Psychology, 70*, 65–84.

Darling-Hammond, L. & Sykes, G. (Eds). (2009). *Teaching as the learning profession: Handbook of policy and practice*. San Francisco, CA: Jossey-Bass.

Darling-Hammond, L., Wei, R. C., Andree, A., Richardson, N. & Orphanos, S. (2009). *Professional learning in the learning profession: A status report on teacher development in the United States and abroad*. Stanford, CA: Stanford University.

Davis, P. & Rinvolucri, M. (1989, 2002). *Dictation: New methods, new possibilities*. Cambridge: Cambridge University Press.

Department of Education and Skills. (2011). *Literacy and numeracy for learning and life: The national strategy to improve literacy and numeracy among children and young people 2011–2020*. Dublin, Ireland: Department of Education and Skills.

Doyle, W. (1983). Academic work. *Review of Educational Research, 53*(2), 159–199.

Egan, K. (1986, 1989). *Teaching as storytelling: An alternative approach to teaching and curriculum in the elementary school*. Chicago: The University of Chicago Press.

Gombrich, E. H. (1985, 2011). *A little history of the world*. New Haven, CT: Yale University Press.

Government of Ireland. (1999a). *History: Social, environmental and scientific education, teacher guidelines*. Dublin: The Stationery Office.

Government of Ireland. (1999b). *Visual arts, arts education: Teacher guidelines*. Dublin: The Stationery Office.

Green, R. P. H. (1997). *Saint Augustine: On Christian teaching*. Oxford: Oxford University Press.

Irish National Teachers' Organisation. (2007). Approaches to teaching and learning. Paper presented at the INTO Consultative Conference on Education, Sligo.

Lampert, M. (2001). *Teaching problems and the problems of teaching*. New Haven, CT: Yale University Press.

Langerock, H. (1915). Professionalism: A study in professional deformation. *American Journal of Sociology, 21*(1), 30–44.

Leinhardt, G. (1989). Math lessons: A contrast of novice and expert competence. *Journal for Research in Mathematics Education, 20*(1), 52–75.

Leith, S. (2011). *You talkin' to me? Rhetoric from Aristotle to Obama*. London: Profile Books.

Macaulay, D. (1988, 2005). *The way things work*. London: Dorling Kindersley.

McGahern, J. (1992). Sierra Leone. In J. McGahern (Ed.), *Collected stories*. London: Faber & Faber.

McKee, R. (1997). *Story: Substance, structure, style, and the principles of screenwriting*. New York: Regan Books.

McKee, R. (2003). Storytelling that moves people. *Harvard Business Review, 81*(6), 51–55.

O'Donovan, O. (1982). Usus and Fruito in Augustine De Doctrina Christiana, I. *Journal of Theological Studies, 33*, 361–397.

Okri, B. (1996). *Birds of heaven*. London: Phoenix.

Porter, A. C. (2002). Measuring the content of instruction: Uses in research and practice. *Educational Researcher, 31*(7), 3–14.

Richards, J. C. & Rodgers, T. S. (1986). *Approaches and methods in language teaching*. Cambridge: Cambridge University Press.

Rink, J. E. (2001). Investigating the assumptions of pedagogy. *Journal of Teaching in Physical Education, 20*, 112–128.

Sharpe, K. (1997). Mr Gradgrind and Miss Beale: Old dichotomies, inexorable choices and what shall we tell the students about primary teaching methods? *Journal of Education for Teaching, 23*(1), 69–83.

Shuell, T. J., Brown, S., Watson, D. G. & Ewing, J. A. (1988). Teachers' perceptions of the differential appropriateness of various teaching methods. *The Elementary School Journal, 88*(4), 338–356.

Singh, S. (1997). *Fermat's last theorem*. London: Fourth Estate.

Sizer, T. R. (1984, 1992). *Horace's compromise: The dilemma of the American high school*. Boston: Mariner Books (a Houghton Mifflin Company).

Stein, M. K., Grover, B. W. & Henningsen, M. A. (1996). Building student capacity for mathematical thinking and reasoning: An analysis of mathematical tasks used in reform classrooms. *American Educational Research Journal, 33 (2)*, 455–488.

Stewart, J. D. (1979). Teaching strategies: Is discovery one of them? *Canadian Journal of Education/ Review canadienne de l'education, 4*(2), 55–65.

Winch, C. & Gingell, J. (1999, 2008). *Philosophy of education: The key concepts*. Abingdon, UK: Routledge.

4

Teaching to reach all children

Differences among children

A casual observer in a classroom will see children who are similar in many ways – common interests, neighbourhood and age group, for example. A teacher too will recognise such similarities among children but will also appreciate differences that affect what they learn, when they learn and how they learn.

Differences in children's pace of learning, means of learning and capacity for learning can be expected in every classroom. Just because some children learn something later than their peers does not mean that they are unable or unwilling to learn. Before starting school most children reach key milestones in life such as walking, talking and dressing themselves at different times. Such variations are accepted and by the time most children start school they can manage such tasks competently.[1]

Children differ in how they learn and in the skills, interests, motivation, attitude, work rate and knowledge they bring to learning. Such differences quickly become apparent even when you are student teaching and you set a task for the class. Despite giving the same instructions to all, the task is undertaken in diverse ways with diverse results; or no sooner have some children begun working on the task when another raises their hand to say, 'I'm finished. What do I do now?'. Differentiation refers to how you teach in order to accommodate differences among children in a class.

Approaches to differentiating instruction

Two broad ways of thinking about differentiation in lessons have been identified. One is to assess the children and tailor the instruction for each individual child or small group of children depending on their current performance and perceived needs. We can call that approach the 'United States' approach or the 'individual' approach to differentiation, and applying it in a large class is particularly challenging.

Another approach is to view differences as an intrinsic feature of any group of children and to see those differences as a resource arising from different ideas and ways of approaching tasks that can lead to rich discussion among students. All the children benefit from sharing and comparing ideas and making connections among them. This is the 'Japanese' or 'whole class' model of differentiation.[2] Whereas the United States approach is to offer a custom-built torch to each student who needs one, the Japanese approach is to switch on the lights.

Each approach has different implications for how teachers plan. In the United States approach, different teaching strategies are used for different children. That means that the more similar the children are, the easier it is to teach them and the more diverse a class is, the more difficult teaching becomes. However, a classroom where all children are the same is as rare as it would be dull, so differentiating in this way makes particular demands of a teacher.

The Japanese approach requires a teacher to consider how different children will think about a new topic – what kinds of misconceptions they will have and how an idea can be explained and represented in different ways to take account of the differences. Children can share their insights with each other when they have grasped an idea and if they are confused, they can express their questions and seek a response from a peer who sees the idea more clearly.

An example of planning for differentiated instruction

Various ways teachers can differentiate have been identified: by task, outcome, choice, group, resource, support, pace and dialogue.[3] To see what might be involved in such differentiation, let's see how it could apply to the following task[4] a teacher might use as part of a second-language lesson for a senior class. Imagine the following task was presented in the targeted second language:

Box 4.1 Second-language task for differentiating

You are working as a chef in a hotel. Tell a colleague how to prepare a suitable drink or some food for breakfast. Afterwards, write the directions in the form of a recipe.

Table 4.1 shows how this task might be differentiated.

TABLE 4.1 Examples of different ways of differentiating a task

Differentiation by	Strategy
Task	The core task could be modified by asking some children, who find writing in a second language difficult, to draw pictures accompanied by key words instead of writing the full 'recipe'. The task could be extended for high achievers in the language by asking some children to make a breakfast recipe booklet that includes steps for making a range of breakfast foods and beverages such as tea, toast, cereals and various kinds of egg
Outcome/choice	The outcome of this task is open ended and allows room for student choice. Some children may choose to describe the steps for making orange juice, tea, toast, boiled egg, scrambled egg, cereal or something more elaborate; the teacher could restrict the choice for children who find it difficult to decide where to begin
Group	Most children will work on the oral activity in pairs, with each person taking a turn to describe the steps orally to a partner before each person writes the steps individually. Children who are less competent in speaking the language, however, could be paired with another child, and each pair of children could describe the recipe to another pair; subsequently the recipe could be written by a pair of children
Resource	Some children may not know the vocabulary in their first language for preparing the chosen food or drink. To support such learners, recipe cards illustrating steps for making one food or beverage could be prepared and made available to support those children; they could first put the pictures in order and then use a word or phrase from the language being learned to state what is to be done in each one

(Continued)

TABLE 4.1 (Continued)

Differentiation by	Strategy
Support	The support given to children by the teacher could vary according to what children need; support may include clarifying the requirements of the task, keeping some children on task, prompting children with needed vocabulary (squeeze, boil, toast) or directing children to where they would find the necessary vocabulary, and prompting children with recipe suggestions
Pace	If some children finish quickly, the teacher could suggest that they illustrate the steps or create a mini-book of breakfast recipes; the teacher can also alter the pace depending on the needs of the class, by saying, for example, 'you need to explain this very slowly and clearly because this is the person's first day working here' or 'you need to give the instructions quickly because guests in the hotel are waiting for their breakfast'
Dialogue	Questions directed to children may also vary so that children are challenged to respond with different levels of language sophistication: What do you use to make ___? What is this for? How do you make it? Did you ever make this at home? How? Which do you prefer to eat/drink? What would you serve with it?

Challenges and dilemmas in differentiating instruction

Although these steps for differentiation seem reasonable, devising and implementing them require plenty of thinking time and preparation for what is part of one lesson on one day. The basic task is open-ended and differs from the kind of task typically found in textbooks. Sometimes the scarcity of open-ended tasks in textbooks makes it difficult for a teacher to tailor tasks for children. Frequently, no suggestions for differentiation are integrated into textbook tasks or given to teachers in teacher manuals. The teacher must devise ways to extend or alter the task and outcome.

In one suggested alteration to the task above, a teacher needs to prepare pictures for use in the lesson (differentiation by resources). Even if suitable pictures can be downloaded from the internet, the teacher needs to print them and prepare them for class use. Although some steps for differentiation can be built into a teacher's work relatively easily – providing different kinds of support to children as they work on the task, asking different kinds of questions and varying the pace at which the task is completed – other steps make additional demands on a teacher's preparation time.

Differentiating by task, group, pace and so on creates dilemmas for a teacher. For example, how will the teacher decide who will be paired with a student who is finding the second language difficult? If a student is paired with another student who is also finding the language difficult, they may learn little from each other. If the struggling student is paired with a student who speaks the language well, the competent student may overwhelm the struggling student or the struggling student may diminish the competent student's opportunity to develop their language in the lesson. Perhaps the best solution is for the teacher to vary the pairs that are used from day to day or from week to week.

Keeping records of children's progress makes demands on the teacher because children are working on different aspects of the task. Although the teacher will have access to children's written work after the lesson, the oral language performance needs to be assessed while the children are present. The teacher needs to find a way to listen to the oral exchanges during the lesson, even though they are happening around the classroom simultaneously.

The teacher may try to listen to part of each pair's discussion during the lesson. This is difficult because as well as assessing progress of individual children, the teacher is providing support for children who need it, monitoring how well children generally are participating, and managing the overall work of the classroom.

An alternative way to assess individual progress would be to wait until after the pair work is complete and ask every child to repeat their recipe for the full class in order to make a record of each child's progress. That would be good because children would get to hear classmates other than their own partner speaking the language. But the teacher knows that asking every child to repeat the recipe may become repetitive and while it is happening, some children may become distracted. Although this need not be done every day, it needs to be done regularly enough for a teacher to monitor children's progress and to inform the teacher's future planning.

Making tasks accessible

Yet another approach to differentiation has been proposed by US researchers.[5] In the approach the teacher thinks about children in the class who have specific learning disabilities or difficulties and considers what strengths and weaknesses those children bring to learning mathematics. Strengths may be that the child has strong drawing skills and is able to create 2-D representations of 3-D shapes, is good at estimating and works well with a partner. Possible weaknesses are that the student's written work is disorganised and that the student has a poor memory for facts and is easily distracted.

The teacher then considers ways to build on the children's strengths and to ameliorate the difficulties in order to make lessons more accessible for all children. The teacher might model and teach strategies for organising work, provide calculators or multiplication and addition tables, or keep class discussions short and focused.

The researchers categorise several accessibility strategies under eight headings: helping children understand tasks, helping children access the subject in varied ways, building student independence, providing tools and handouts, promoting understanding through discourse, helping children manage tasks and organisation, adjusting tasks to children's needs and creating a supportive environment.[6] Although the strategies are applied specifically to mathematics, they can be extended to other curriculum subjects.

Many of the strategies identified make sense and can be implemented quite readily in a classroom. 'Post and reinforce classroom expectations', 'offer manipulatives', 'use charts or projected images', 'have students paraphrase directions and questions' and 'have children work in pairs or small groups' are relatively straightforward to implement. Some other strategies also make sense but they require even more discernment and preparation by a teacher. In relation to adjusting tasks to student needs, it is suggested to 'adjust level of difficulty' and 'use friendlier numbers'. Adjusting the level of difficulty of a mathematics problem is no trivial task. Take the following mathematics problem as an example.

Box 4.2 Fraction subtraction problem

If I eat $1\frac{1}{2}$ bars of the $3\frac{4}{5}$ bars of chocolate I bought earlier, how many bars of chocolate have I left?

This problem requires children to subtract one mixed fraction number from another where the denominators of the fractions are different. The difficulty of the problem could be reduced in several ways. The problem could be rewritten as 'I had $3\frac{4}{5}$ bars of chocolate and I ate $1\frac{1}{2}$ bars. How many bars of chocolate had I left?'. This would be easier because the numbers appear in the order in which a subtraction calculation is typically laid out.

A picture of $3\frac{4}{5}$ bars of chocolate could be placed alongside the text (Figure 4.1). This would be easier because children could try and visually subtract the $1\frac{1}{2}$ bars from the larger amount.

The problem could be written as a straightforward subtraction problem, i.e. as $3\frac{4}{5} - 1\frac{1}{2} = \_\_$, which would be easier because children would not have to figure out whether to add or subtract the fractions. Several changes could be made to the numbers to make them 'friendlier':

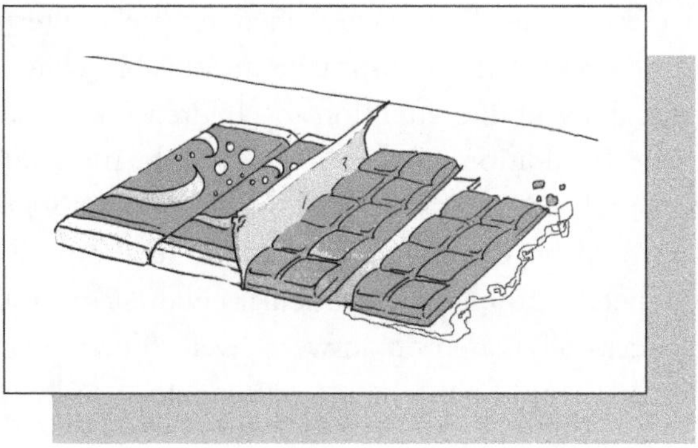

Figure 4.1 Visual aid for the chocolate problem

(Illustration by Emer O'Boyle)

- $3-1$ (remove the fractions);
- $3\frac{4}{5}-1$ (remove the fraction from the subtrahend);
- $3\frac{4}{5}-1\frac{1}{5}$ (change the fraction in the subtrahend so that it has the same denominator as the fraction in the minuend);
- $\frac{19}{5}-\frac{3}{2}$ (write both numbers as improper fractions);
- $\frac{4}{5}-\frac{1}{2}$ (remove both whole numbers so that only the fraction parts need to be subtracted);
- $\frac{4}{5}-\frac{1}{5}$ (remove both whole numbers and use the same denominator in both fractions).

Various combinations of these changes could also be made.

Which change should the teacher make to the problem to adjust the level of difficulty? Answering that question requires knowing a good deal about students, mathematics and the practical running of a classroom. Some changes would make the problem trivial and others may make it no easier for children; others still may be so far removed from the original problem that what a child learns from doing it bears little resemblance to what the child's classmates are learning by working on the original problem.

Would the teacher need to change the problem in different ways for different children? Children typically complete many such problems in a day and consequently a teacher would need to adapt several problems. That is something that could, perhaps, be done in a one-to-one or small group setting but it seems to be onerous for class teachers if it were required every day.

At a practical level a teacher needs to decide where to display alternative problems for children in a way that does not take up valuable whiteboard space and that does not draw undue attention to children for whom the adjustment is being made. In addition, some problems may be more difficult to adapt because they are related to illustrations in the textbook. No doubt this is something that could be helped with electronic textbooks, where teachers could allocate specific problems to particular children; or problems could be allocated automatically based on answers given to previous tasks. Regardless of whether that would be desirable or possible at scale, such a system is not currently available in most schools.

The teacher could vary the number of problems solved by children, reducing it for low achievers and increasing it for high achievers. This is relatively easy to do. But frequently it is the content of the problems rather than the number of them that needs to be varied to support all learners.

A teacher must also decide who in the class should be given a problem with an altered level of difficulty. Sometimes it is easy to decide who needs an alternative problem but there will often be children who are on the borderline; they may be able to make a good attempt at the original problem or it may be frustrating for them. Is it preferable for a child to experience likely success on the adjusted problem, or to experience the challenge, and possible satisfaction of solving the more difficult problem, keeping in mind that it may be too difficult?

Children know when they are receiving a different level of support to their peers,[7] and the teachers' expectations for them may in turn affect their expectations for themselves and ultimately their achievement.[8] Although the effects of teacher expectations on achievement appear generally to be less strong than previously believed, self-fulfilling prophecies may disproportionately affect members of some social classes and ethnicities.[9]

When a teacher considers how best to respond to differences in the classroom, several options for differentiation and greater accessibility are possible. Whichever approach is chosen, the teacher needs to consider whether the approach will be implemented like the United States model, where instruction is designed for several individual children and small groups of children, or the Japanese approach, where the teacher implicitly expects children to have different prior knowledge, solution methods, and ways of understanding and expressing ideas, and plans lessons taking such differences into account. The decision will be based on each teacher's judgement taking into account the students, the subject being taught, the teacher's beliefs about teaching and learning, and the context of the classroom.

I'm going to use three examples to illustrate how I have tried to follow the Japanese approach to differentiation by incorporating various strategies into my whole class teaching. The first example is based on a series of lessons taught to children on the topic of area and perimeter in mathematics.

Example 1. Targeting questions in class discussions

In order to accommodate individual differences within the class I tried to make the ideas accessible to all children in the class who are in a position to learn them. While doing so I was trying to identify prior ideas and procedures on the topic that have not yet been mastered by children, and which makes the new content difficult for them. I also wanted children to practise skills – mathematical practices such as reasoning and communicating – that would stretch their understanding.

1 *Provide plenty of wait time before asking a child to answer a question.* Some children know answers to questions but they may take time to consider their answer or how they will express it. Such children are discouraged from contributing where responses from the fast responders are valued. Slowing down the pace of the discussion gives all children more time to think about their contribution to the discussion.

2 *Match questions to the anticipated knowledge level of the children.* The questions I ask are generally directed towards children who I know have a good chance of being able to answer them. The topic may be area and perimeter, but if a child cannot yet independently multiply two single-digit numbers, that child will be encouraged to understand and recall those facts and will become our 'expert' on multiplying such numbers, initially by using a multiplication table or other support. When the child develops knowledge and confidence, the support can be removed.

3 *Direct a question to a student who will answer incorrectly.* Occasionally, however, when choosing someone to answer a question, I call on a student who is likely to answer incorrectly in order to illustrate a common difficulty. That is done not to humiliate a child but to use the error as a resource for everyone's learning so that it can be discussed in some detail. I thank the child for bringing up that potential source of confusion in learning the topic and discuss how as a class we can ensure that we won't be confused by it in future.

4 *Direct a question to quickly move along the discussion.* At other times I direct questions to children who will almost certainly answer the questions correctly so that the lesson can proceed.

5 *Allow a discussion to become more difficult.* Sometimes, I will permit a class discussion to continue even if the content is not on the curriculum or is difficult for several children. This has happened when the children venture into discussing a topic such as infinity, for example.

6 *Reduce the difficulty level of a discussion.* Other times, the discussion may be allowed to become very easy for most of the 10-year-old children, if we need to revise the value of the tens and units digits in a two-digit number, for example.

7 *Ask children to explain ideas for one another.* Sometimes, I'll ask a child who understands an idea to explain it to one who doesn't yet understand it. This is done either with the whole class listening or with the pair working quietly, depending on matters such as how familiar the rest of the class is with the idea, how relevant the idea is to what the class is currently working on, how competent I consider the explainer to be and how desirable it is for all children to hear related ideas and explanations. In such pair work – public or private – the relations vary from time to time. Sometimes, each of the two children has some information that needs to be shared. Other times, one child deliberately teaches another child. Occasionally, one child may question another about a mathematical idea.

8 *Ask a question to check how well children are following the discussion.* By directing a question at particular bellwether children, you get an idea of how well children generally are grasping an idea.

Example 2. Choosing tasks carefully to differentiate instruction

A key teaching decision is selecting problems to work on. I look for problems that can be approached at multiple levels. The following is an example of such a problem:[10]

Box 4.3 Zoo area problem

Your local zoo has just received two new sheep for the Family Farm section of the zoo. The zoo keeper wants to build an enclosure for the sheep. She decides that the enclosure must be square or rectangular with an area of 100 square metres.

1 Which different configurations could she build?
2 How many metres of fencing will she need for each possible design?
3 Use the graph paper below to draw and scan all the possible rectangular or square designs.
4 Include a key to tell how much each unit on the grid paper equals.
5 Which fence would you recommend that the zoo keeper builds? Why?

Some children may complete the entire problem in the allotted time and others will not. Take part 1 alone. Some children may come up with only one or two configurations, whereas other children may come up with some that involve numbers in fraction or decimal fraction form. No matter how much of the problem a child completes, everyone should have done enough to be able to make some contribution to the subsequent discussion of the problem.

One such problem may suffice for one or more lessons. I generally follow a number of steps with the full class: reading the problem together; discussing what the mathematical problem is; identifying what we know; establishing what we have to find out; relating it to other work we've done; and responding to questions or initial thoughts the children have. At this stage I refrain from discussing *how* to solve the problem.

In devising their solutions, children often need to apply knowledge and practices from more than one mathematical topic (e.g. length, multiplication, decimals, area). Children work on the problem alone, or in pairs or in a combination of individual and pair work. Afterwards, children share and discuss answers and approaches used. In subsequent classes, follow-up problems related to the main problem we're working on are often assigned.

I encourage children to pose their own mathematical problems; sometimes the questions they create are simple or derivative; other times their problems capture the interest of other children, like in one lesson about time where one child challenged classmates to figure out how many hours in a year.[11]

Sometimes, after we discuss a mathematics question in class where no consensus on a solution is emerging, I ask children to write in their copy books what *they* think the answer to a question is and why. I regularly request children to write down questions or confusions they have in their copy books at the end of the lesson so that I can incorporate them into subsequent lessons.

Problems like the one above differ from the problems often found in mathematics textbooks. Those problems are usually shorter, require a single answer and typically call on predictable operations to solve them (often because they are placed at the end of a chapter where that operation is introduced). Textbook problems rarely offer a manageable entry point for all children, where the challenge begins relatively low and is incrementally ramped-up for children who can handle more demanding mathematics.

Although rich, open-ended problems are currently rare in textbooks, you may be able to adapt some textbook problems to compensate for this shortcoming. In addition, you could begin to compile such problems from various sources for use in class, and over time you would develop a bank of problems you can choose from to differentiate instruction.[12]

Example 3. Revoicing and related ways of differentiating

The third teaching example illustrates the use of revoicing.[13] Revoicing typically happens in three steps. First, the teacher repeats or rephrases something said by a child. The repetition or rephrasing is done to enquire if the teacher understands what the child is saying rather than to evaluate what the child said. Then the teacher asks the child if the teacher has accurately interpreted what the child said. The child who made the original utterance either affirms the accuracy, corrects the interpretation or amends their original stance. Here is an example of a teacher using revoicing. It occurs in a class with eleven-year-old children.[14] The teacher has asked one child, Maria, to go to the top of the class and to build a cuboid[15] using eight individual cubes. Maria uses the cubes to construct a shape that is two cubes wide, two cubes high and two cubes deep. When Maria is finished, the following discussion takes place.

Teacher: Is that a cuboid that Maria has just made?

Damien: No, it's a cube.

Teacher: So, Maria, you're saying that you've made a cuboid. Damien says your shape is not a cuboid, it's a cube. What do you say to that Maria?

Maria: Well, a cuboid only has to have, emm, the cuboid only has to have six sides. It doesn't have, and it doesn't . . . with a cube they have to be the same. But it, as a rectangle, a rectangle can be in the shape of a square so a cuboid can be in the shape of a cube. But a cube can't be shape, in the shape of a rectangle. But it is a cuboid, if you get what I mean.

Teacher: And is it a cube?

Maria: It's a cube as well. But it's also a cuboid.

Although Maria's first response seems confused, it is because she is struggling to express her mathematical understanding and she had little time to prepare what she was going to say. The gist of what she is saying is that just as a square is a special type of rectangle, a cube is a special type of cuboid. In other words, just as a square is both a square and a rectangle, a cube is both a cube and a cuboid. That is her response to Damien's claim that the shape she made was a cube and not the cuboid that she had been asked to construct.

Maria's initial contribution is implicit in her action rather than expressed orally in that she publicly creates a shape to meet specifications set by the teacher. However, one student challenges her contribution by claiming that the shape does not meet the required specifications of being a cuboid. The teacher summarises what Maria did and the critique of what she did and asks Maria to respond. This is different from a frequent classroom exchange pattern where the teacher asks a question, the student responds and the teacher evaluates the response. In this example Maria is asked to reconsider her construction in light of Damien's comment. In justifying her initial contribution, Maria is required to elaborate on her understanding of a mathematical idea.[16]

One aspect of revoicing is that it puts the student and the teacher on an equal footing because the student is asked to evaluate if the teacher has expressed the student's views correctly.[17] I also see revoicing as a mechanism for differentiating in the classroom because an idea can be repeated, giving children an additional chance to hear it and to consider if it is correct; or it can be rephrased, allowing children to hear it in a different way. The idea can also be further elaborated or clarified. Thus, revoicing is a means to repeat, amplify and refine the expression of ideas, making it one form of differentiating content.

Furthermore, a teacher can use other strategies related to revoicing, as a way of differentiating lesson content for children. For example, you may ask one child to repeat what another child says. Or you may ask a child to paraphrase what another child says. Or you may ask one child to explain what another child has just done. Such forms of interaction allow children who may be struggling to contribute to the class by listening to, engaging with and responding to ideas of other children in the classroom. I believe that where one child repeats another child's statement, the child who repeats the idea is likely to be more invested in the discussion that follows, and having restated the idea, that child may begin to reflect on its content (even if they didn't fully understand it at first).

Summary of strategies for differentiation

These strategies for differentiation are built into the lesson planning. Many of them are based around class discussion. I have given examples from mathematics, but most of the ideas could be applied to differentiation in other subjects. They include:

- targeting questions to stretch all children;
- discussing topics that are advanced for a particular class level;
- discussing topics that involve revision of previous work;

- encouraging pairs of children to help each other;
- seeking a wrong answer to surface potential confusion;
- seeking a correct answer to move a lesson along;
- selecting tasks that can be accessed by children at different levels of achievement;
- discussing a task in great detail;
- having children pose tasks of their own;
- recording questions, ideas and confusions in their copy books;
- revoicing and related strategies.

These strategies for differentiation are consistent with the Japanese approach because rather than offering different experiences to different children, the approach to teaching assumes that children are different and the lesson is planned to take account of such differences.

I am not claiming that the Japanese approach to differentiation is superior to the United States approach. Sometimes, even when the lights are on, you need a torch to make some areas visible. However, it is helpful to be aware of both general approaches and to reflect on your specific teaching context in order to decide when it is preferable and practical to direct specific tutoring to individual children who require such intervention to advance their learning, and when it is preferable and practical to plan your teaching around the diversity and differences that occur naturally in any group of children.

Learning styles

Much has been written about learning styles. The general idea is that children learn something best when they encounter it in a specific format, such as visual, auditory or kinaesthetic. Consequently, many people claim a child will learn best if teaching is geared towards their preferred learning style. Let's take an example. If you are teaching children about the First World War and what it was like to be in the trenches at the time, a 'visual learner' would need to see lots of pictures or videos of soldiers in the trenches. An 'auditory learner' would need to hear a soldier talking about his experiences of the time or some sound effects of life in the trenches. A 'kinaesthetic learner' would need to build a trench (or a model of a trench) and act in role as a soldier in order to learn what it was like. A reading–writing learner would learn by reading newspaper articles from the time or by writing imaginatively about life in the trench.

My experience of children is that such divisions are fluid. Each of the learning experiences mentioned could enhance every child's understanding of what life was like in the trenches. So-called 'visual learners' will learn from listening to soldiers' accounts, 'auditory learners' will learn from reading newspaper reports, and 'kinaesthetic learners' will learn from writing.

Learning happens in lots of ways and it is good for all children to experience a variety of ways of learning. In other words, I would plan lessons where a variety of stimuli are included to bring topics to life for children, but I wouldn't necessarily be thinking that 'Mark is a visual learner and this part of the lesson is for him' and 'Maya is a kinaesthetic learner and that part of the lesson is for her'. The full lesson is for every child in the class.

Up to 71 different models of learning styles have been proposed, some of them commercial.[18] They are developed in university departments of business studies, education, law, medicine and psychology.

However, two Dutch researchers[19] have dubbed the idea of learning styles as an 'urban legend'; they are difficult to measure and most children do not fit neatly into one specific learning style. There is no doubt that providing a variety of ways for children to learn in the classroom is helpful; indeed the learning styles literature serves as a reminder for teachers that how we learn is complex and variable. You cannot assume that what helped you learn when you were in primary school will work for every child you teach. However, identifying an individual child's learning style across several domains of learning and matching it to a specific teaching or learning activity is as unreliable as it is impractical.

As an aside, apart from differences among children, different subjects may require different means of teaching, learning and assessment.[20] The means may be influenced by how knowledge is developed or validated in a subject. In history, for example, interrogating primary and secondary sources in depth is necessary to help older children learn how different perspectives and biases influence our understanding of historical events.[21] However, subject matter is often neglected in discussions about learning styles.

Universal design for learning

Another response to the different ways people learn was developed by Anne Meyer and David Rose and their colleagues at CAST.[22] Universal design for learning applies to education the architectural principle of universal design, where designing streets and buildings to meet the needs of specific groups of users makes the street or building better for all users. For example, dropped kerbs were originally installed to help wheelchair users but they also benefit people pushing buggies, riding bicycles or dragging trolley suitcases (Figure 4.2).

Universal design for learning centres on three broad principles where learners are provided with multiple means of engagement (to get them interested and keep them motivated), representation (to help them understand ideas) and action and expression.[23] It draws on research in neuroscience, instructional design, technology and education.

When these principles are applied, a digital textbook may enable children to listen to text being read, to have links to definitions, maps, relevant videos and other means of representing information. It will allow children to change the size of the text. Crucially, the supports are not just given to children with disabilities but they are built into the classroom materials and children can choose to use them or not to support their learning.

Figure 4.2 Dropped kerbs were developed to support the mobility of people in wheelchairs. However, their presence also benefits the mobility of parents wheeling buggies, young cyclists and travellers pulling luggage

Universal design for learning has potential to transform curriculums to make them more accessible to all learners and many teachers are already drawing on its ideas. However, for it to be widely adopted by schools, several practical and research questions need to be answered, such as whether teachers or product developers are best placed to design instructional materials for classrooms using these principles and how the application of universal design for learning is different from assistive technologies (generally offered to specific children with specific disabilities).[24]

Children who finish work early

Sometimes you assign a task to the class that is expected to take, say about fifteen minutes. While the children are working independently on the task, you may plan to work with an individual student or a small group, or you may want to provide individual support to several children in the class. However, after five minutes a couple of children say they've completed the main task. You glance at their work and it meets, at least, the minimum requirements that were specified for the task. It's difficult when you are working with another child or group of children to identify or seek work of superior quality from someone who finishes quickly. Perhaps the early finisher could be required to state how the completed work meets or exceeds the task requirements.[25]

The point remains that some children still have finished at a stage when most other children need another ten minutes and the teacher would like to continue targeting children who need specific support. What does a teacher say to the children who have finished early?

The easiest answer may be, to ask them to complete additional work. Some children will relish that but over time most will come to see it as punishment for finishing early. Such a realisation may prompt them to work more slowly or try to distract a classmate when they have finished, disrupting the work of several class members. On the other hand, if the prospect of finishing early leads to an attractive alternative, such as playing an educational game on a computer, children may take less care with the set task in order to finish early.

Frequently, children who complete tasks early are asked to create a picture or to take out a book and read it. Both may be reasonable tasks and most children enjoy doing one or the other. Yet, if the lesson is not a visual arts lesson or an English lesson, children are losing out on time in the subject being taught. Given that some children will always complete their work before others, thinking in advance about what early finishers will do can help such children use their time in an educative way and free up teacher time to work with individual children.

Many teachers display in the classroom a list of activities to be completed by children who finish early. Many lists of such activities are available online[26] and they include activities such as writing or drawing about the strangest dream you ever had or what you would do if you were in government. Children often keep a special copy in which to complete one hundred such tasks; completed tasks are recorded by crossing out the relevant number on a hundred square. Those activities tap into children's creativity and imagination and although they may not always be completed to the standard a teacher might like, they enable the teacher and some children to continue working with minimal interruptions. Such activities are relatively easy to set up in a class.

Over time a teacher may find that some of the tasks on such activity lists offer work that keeps children busy rather than work that is core to their learning. If the activities are worked on for a short time, they may be approached in a shallow way and may be fragmented from one to the other. It can be hard for a teacher to find time to follow up on such tasks to offer motivation or feedback. Furthermore, some of the activities may not be related to the subject being taught; a high-achieving child may end up spending less time on such a subject and not stretch themselves as much as they could. One way around that would be to classify the activity lists according to subjects on the curriculum. Alternatively, it may be worth rethinking how children who finish early can use discretionary time to benefit their education.

Activities for early finishers could be planned to help children acquire persistence and to learn to work independently. Children who are persistent in how they approach their work have been found to achieve better than those who are not. Persistence consists of children's ability to do a task (i.e. read it, understand it and answer it), their motivation to work hard at it (to follow instructions, to stay focused on what they have to do) and their willingness to guess an answer even if they are not sure of it.[27]

Children are unlikely to develop persistence if they engage in tasks which are designed to be completed in a relatively short amount of time, which they frequently may not get to complete and of which they have little ownership. Children may develop a disposition towards perseverance if they get to observe the kind of 'techniques, habits and skills [that are] used in persisting with a challenging problem'.[28]

Tasks they can work on over time would be better – tasks they choose themselves and for which they are accountable. Examples may be to write a book (story, biography, novel, poetry etc.), design a website, write a film script (documentary, musical, comedy etc.), choreograph a dance, solve a complex problem, plan a scientific investigation, design a building, plan an itinerary. Each project could tap into children's interests and into various curriculum subjects. Children could choose which activity they wished to work on and whether they wanted to work on it alone or with a partner. The project would be on a scale where it can be done in discretionary class time over several days or weeks. In younger classes the activities may require more teacher direction. Activities in younger classes may include some of the above as well as dramatic play; working on large jigsaws; collecting pictures, shapes, leaves and so on; counting as high as possible (in 1s, 2s, 3s etc.).[29]

Having children take individual responsibility for working on sustained projects over time may be new for children. Therefore it is worth taking time to discuss with the class the reasons behind it and how it works early in the year. You could initiate a list of possible activities and children are likely to expand the list. Time invested early in the school year explaining, clarifying and modelling the procedures for this is likely to pay dividends as the year unfolds.

If children are to develop persistence, they need to be able to work independently. Although this is a worthwhile aspiration for learning in the long term, it also yields benefits in the short term if a child can complete one task and transition to another without interrupting the teacher.

Children who work independently, either inside school or outside school, have been found to use specific strategies. These include: seeking information from sources such as libraries, the internet and dictionaries; keeping records of discussions, of things learned or things that the student got wrong; organising themselves by making a plan to do their work; seeking teacher assistance; thinking about positive or negative consequences of doing or not doing work; reviewing notes, textbooks or tests in preparation for class work or future tests; seeking peer assistance; seeking adult assistance; rehearsing and memorising; setting goals for themselves and matching them with timing and a sequence of actions to achieve the goals; setting up the physical environmental to make it conducive to doing work; and checking over their work.[30] Even as adults, many of us have not mastered all of these strategies. Yet, by knowing about them, a teacher can take time to discuss some of them with the children from time to time to make them aware of how they may be able to help children work independently.

Many examples have been documented of children at primary school level who show both motivation and willingness to take responsibility for their learning. The examples have shown that children can pursue projects of interest (such as creating comic strips) even when the teacher will not be evaluating their work;[31] they can revise their work in writing or in other subjects; they can learn from sharing and discussing work with their peers, and by having teachers model, enact and withdraw support in tasks such as computer programming with Logo or Scratch.[32]

Specific conditions

Recent decades have seen an increase in research and awareness about many conditions that affect learning. As understanding of conditions has increased, the language used to describe them has evolved.[33] Although the language and the perception of learning disabilities has evolved, teachers have long been aware that children differ in how they learn, what they learn and when they learn. Increased knowledge about conditions such as dyslexia, autism and attention deficit hyperactivity disorder (ADHD) helps teachers better understand the kind of challenges children with such conditions experience when learning. Creating awareness of such conditions is particularly important for teachers who have no personal experience of them. As you become aware of and sensitive to the kind of learning disabilities your children may have, you will find many resources to help you better understand how the conditions impact on learning. This helps you to provide the support necessary for all children to learn despite their difficulties.

However, if labels to describe learning disabilities are used to define a child, the label may adversely affect your relationship with the child. Although children may share a disability, each child is unique; children's learning and their achievement in school or in life cannot be predicted by or solely determined on the basis of a diagnosed intellectual disability. It would be as foolish to ignore a diagnosis of a learning disability as it would be to use it to predetermine experiences for and expectations of any child.

Diagnoses of learning disabilities have sometimes been controversial.[34] Such controversies often receive coverage in the media and the coverage is not always accurate and balanced. Research developments in relation to such conditions are typically published in a wide range of specialised journals.[35] For teachers, keeping up with the evolving understanding of psychological conditions, where contradictions and nuances abound, is difficult; access to information can be prohibitively expensive, time consuming or partial.

No doubt much remains to be learned about such conditions that will inform teachers. That is the case because each condition occurs in a person and it varies in degree and in manifestation. A condition exists alongside a combination of personality traits, knowledge and resources that is unique to each one of us. Developments in neuroscience, psychology and technology are likely to advance our knowledge of this area substantially in the coming years.

More is known about some conditions than others. Similarly, supports for teachers may be more accessible for some conditions than others. However, a range of societies exist to support children with various conditions and they may be able to direct you to reliable information on the internet about any condition that affects children in your class.[36]

Exceptionally able children

From time to time you will have in your classroom a child who is exceptionally able, sometimes referred to as 'gifted'. You may be in awe of such a child, who exhibits ability and talents that are superior to what is expected given the child's age. Although you may admire such a child, the child also presents challenges. You may worry less about such a child than about a child who cannot read or who has difficulties in communicating. Yet, such children need to be sufficiently challenged and motivated in school and have their talents developed. Simultaneously, exceptionally able children need to socialise well with peers and in time be well placed to use their talents for their own fulfilment and for the good of society.

Sometimes such a child is obviously able in one or more areas such as sports, mathematics, science, visual arts, music, writing and so on. More often children in a classroom will display a range of low and high achievement levels and you may wonder if a child who is achieving at a high average level is exceptionally able. It's like ageing; although most of us may use the adjective 'old' to describe a person, it is more difficult to identify a specific point when the transition is made from young to old and it can be relative to those who are around us. Identifying exceptionally able children is similar; many children are high achievers in various fields but will not necessarily meet the criteria to be considered exceptional.

Indeed, little consensus exists about what constitutes exceptional ability. Among the components associated with it are above average ability, motivation, creativity, analytic and practical intelligence, wisdom, self-concept and environmental supports.[37] Despite the many possible components of exceptional ability, many scholars rely on intelligence tests to identify children who are exceptionally able, where an IQ score of at least 120, and more often 130, is required. Others identify exceptionally able children using the results of achievement tests or based on general academic achievement. Sometimes a combination of features is looked at and they may extend to performance in extra-curricular activities, interviews, portfolios and recommendation by teachers or parents.[38]

Sometimes you need to stand back from day-to-day classroom interactions when considering signs of exceptional ability in a student. Someone who produces high-quality work and conforms to classroom expectations may not be exceptionally able, whereas a non-conformer who produces untidy work may exhibit a talent for thinking, creativity or performance that is exceptional.

Researchers have identified many recommendations to support the education of exceptionally able children: provide daily challenge in their specific area of talent, offer consistent challenge across all curriculum areas, provide opportunities and support for independent work and study, afford opportunities for accelerated learning, offer opportunities to socialise and learn with other exceptionally able children, give them differentiated materials or curriculum tasks, make classes fast paced with limited practice and revision, and teach from the big picture (concepts, principles, issues and generalisations) rather than from isolated or disconnected facts and terms.[39]

Few teachers would argue with the contents of such a list of recommendations but transferring the list from paper to practice is more than a matter of 'copy and paste'. Like many other priorities for teachers, catering for exceptionally able learners requires specific preparation, knowledge, flexibility, materials, cooperation from the school principal and colleagues, perseverance and even a degree of happenstance (because it is easier to provide for two or more exceptionally able children in a class than it is to support one). A teacher will try to implement such recommendations while also catering for children who are struggling with content, and the teacher may have to justify – to the children or their parents – why the support is provided only for specific children in the room. Let's consider what implementing these recommendations might involve.

Ideally, high-achieving children would have access in school to learning support from teachers with suitable expertise as is the case for low-achieving children.[40] Given policy priorities and constraints on resources this is unlikely to happen in many countries in the short term. Therefore classroom teachers need to try to do the best they can to support such children.

In order to provide daily challenge for a child who is proficient in an area, a teacher may be able to direct the child to a mentor outside of school; this would be like attending music lessons, sports coaching or an acting group as many children already do. Such mentoring may be harder to come by in more academic areas such as science, mathematics or writing.

A teacher may be able to set up a pair or small group in the class to work on more challenging work than their classmates. The children may be given challenging problems to solve in mathematics from a project such as NRICH.[41] Alternatively, they may be asked to engage in some computer-programming tasks using Logo or programs such as Scratch or Python. Before encouraging children to work on such tasks, a teacher needs to be satisfied that the children have mastered the regular curriculum. Children can be asked to demonstrate mastery of a topic, before moving on to working in groups or independently. As teacher, you need to find time to check on and to record children's progress on the task, and to know what a suitable challenge for a child is. Children themselves will often be able to help with identifying subsequent challenges.

In some classrooms, this will involve an individual child working independently on projects. Even where there is more than one exceptionally able child in a class, such children often enjoy working independently.

Nevertheless, most children rarely work well independently, either on their own or in groups, if a teacher just 'leaves them at it'. Teachers need to teach children to work independently, whether they are working alone or as part of a group. One way of doing that is the five-step 'Autonomous Learner Model', developed by George Betts.[42] The steps are:

1 orientation (children receive an overview of the model and learn about themselves as learners and about working as part of a group);
2 individual development (children develop the skills – social, emotional, cognitive and physical – concepts and attitudes, they need to become independent, lifelong learners);
3 enrichment (children explore ideas, investigate concepts, work on a project, participate in cultural and service activities);
4 seminars (in small groups children present research findings to the rest of the class);
5 in-depth study (learners create and implement a plan for their own study in an area of interest and the work is assessed).

Such skills can be of use to all learners as they grow older.

Providing opportunities for exceptionally able children to engage in accelerated learning can take various forms. It may involve a child entering school at a younger age than would otherwise be the case or permitting a child to 'skip a class' and proceed into the next higher grade. Alternatively, a child may work with children in an older class for a particular curriculum subject. This requires coordination of timetables between classes, though multi-grade classes have an inbuilt advantage here. Children may be encouraged to participate in programmes such as those offered by dedicated schools or centres[43] or children may be encouraged to participate in an online course in an area of interest to them.[44]

One controversial area of teaching relates to the benefits and drawbacks of putting children in ability or performance groups for instruction. Many claim that exceptionally able learners benefit academically from various kinds of grouping by ability or performance, with the exception of pairing such children with lower-achieving children.[45] Another view is that the academic benefits are more limited and that the main benefits are for within-class grouping for mathematics in senior primary classes or for grouping children across class levels for reading (where, for example, some children in third class read with second class and others read with fourth class).[46] Still others argue vehemently against grouping of any kind, claiming that it reproduces inequality and adversely affects children's lives in and beyond school.[47]

Intuitively it makes sense that high achievers should be extended and low achievers should be allowed to work at a slower pace, with more repetition: such an arrangement should make teachers' work more manageable because teachers work with children who are generally at the same level. However, the problems with ability grouping are that children are often put in groups based on performance on a single test, lower ability groups tend to receive instruction in lower order skills, movement between groups rarely happens, children can become demotivated to learn, group members tend to be stigmatised, and many poorer and minority children tend to be placed disproportionately in low-achieving groups.[48] When grouping does take place, it tends to be for reading and mathematics.

Research on grouping is contradictory because different people have different expectations of and priorities for schooling – academic achievement, achievement in other areas like music, sport or drama, or equality of opportunity, for instance. Furthermore, in research little attention is paid to what happens in the groups. The materials the teacher uses with different groups, the tasks the teacher assigns and how the teacher works with children in groups all make a big difference in determining the effectiveness of group work. Differences have also been identified across ability groups in terms of teacher interactions, reward systems, student motivation and self-esteem, student behaviour and peer influences.[49]

Working in groups

Regardless of a teacher's stance on grouping by ability, it is likely that some kind of group work will be used from time to time. This may involve working on a project in history or geography, creating a piece of art or collaborating on a role-play in drama. In the past I had some reservations about grouping children for instruction related partly to my own preference for working independently and also to a concern that if children are working in a group, they may be off task. Children may be discussing sports results or television programmes or what they are planning to do after school rather than focusing on the task are required to complete.

However, the more I participate in various work-related groups myself, the more I realise that almost every group spends some time off task. Indeed such time is probably necessary for the smooth functioning of the group. What matters is the balance between time spent on and off task. Indeed, at least one study found that the more autonomy a group is given to interpret a task and work on it, the more likely it is that group work will contribute to child achievement.[50]

Working constructively in a group with a shared sense of purpose is something that needs to be learned. It requires social skills of trust, mutual respect and tolerance, and sensitivity to others; it requires communication skills such as turn taking, active listening, questioning, suggesting, expressing and seeking opinions and ideas, helping, explaining, arguing and refuting, persuading, and summarising. It also involves more advanced skills such as coming to consensus, compromising, encouraging reluctant contributors, and planning.[51] These are skills that children develop when they engage frequently in group work and when they are helped to develop such skills.

For example, children may be helped to become active listeners by discussing what active listeners do – make eye contact, use various facial expressions, nod, not interrupt, ask a question for clarification. After discussing the necessary elements, children can be encouraged to engage in a class discussion where they practise using such skills. This can be repeated for the other skills of participating in groups.[52]

As with any human activity, children working in groups may encounter problems from time to time. Some children may fail to deliver what they promise, some may spend excessive time off task, some may dominate the work and be reluctant to allow all members to contribute, some may argue and some may be offended by words or actions of others. Such incidents are to be expected and need to be dealt with in an open and respectful way, either by the children themselves, or with some teacher leadership or intervention.

Multi-grade classrooms

Many teachers teach in multi-grade[53] classrooms.[54] Although some teachers see more positives to teaching in multi-grade classes than others, widespread agreement exists across countries that teaching in such classrooms demands more time for planning and allows less time for helping individual children.[55] Here's the problem. Teachers require materials such as textbooks to support their teaching. Textbooks are typically designed for one grade level in terms of the subject content, the reading level and the tasks.

If the teacher uses a different textbook for two or more class levels, the teacher may have to introduce similar ideas at different times, and children have to do a lot of independent work while the teacher directs and supports children in other class levels. If a teacher uses one textbook for two or more class levels, some children may either be over-challenged or under-challenged; it might be stimulating for a high-achieving seven-year-old child to be interacting with nine-year-old children and content, but by the time that former seven-year-old child becomes nine, the content may have turned stale. A low-achieving nine-year-old may benefit from easier content being explained to eight-year-old children but the gap to be bridged may become more apparent and frustrating the following year when the now ten-year-old child is in a classroom with other ten- and eleven-year-olds.

If the class-level splits in a school coincide with how the content of the curriculum is laid out (e.g. with the content laid out in two-year bands), the teacher's work becomes marginally easier. However, class level splits in schools do not always coincide with the class level splits in the curriculum. Consequently, most teachers who find themselves teaching multiple class levels find that they have to learn on the job. Pre-service teacher education programmes often pay insufficient attention to teaching in multi-class settings[56] and in-service courses are often designed with single-grade settings in mind.[57]

Later I'll address how teachers can teach the same content to children in different class levels. But first I want to consider two subject areas that pose particular challenges for teachers who work in multi-grade classrooms – first-language reading and mathematics.[58] Teachers sometimes need to teach specific content in reading and mathematics separately to children in each class level. If a teacher in a multi-grade setting decides to teach reading in groups, the first decision to be made is whether to work with class groups or to group in another way – by student ability or flexibly.

As already mentioned, research provides little guidance for teachers because little consensus exists about the merits of various ways to group. Some researchers point to examples of ability grouping working well within classrooms where: (i) teachers believed that in time all children could read independently; (ii) supportive, well-graded texts were available; and (iii) grouping was combined with having children work individually, in pairs, and as a whole class.[59]

In response to criticism of ability groups, flexible grouping has been proposed where children are grouped for different purposes at different times. Groups may be formed based on a skill some children need to develop, an interest they can share, knowledge they have, something they can do, the task to be completed, a way of working they have mastered, social reasons, random assignment or student choice. The groups may be individual, pairs, small group, large group, half class or whole class.[60] Continuous assessment of children and analysis of what they need to learn next guide teachers in deciding what kind of grouping is desirable.[61]

No matter which way a teacher in a multi-grade class decides to group children, a teacher needs to think about what the children who are not working directly with the teacher will do. In reading class, children who are not working with the teacher could be engaged in using digital books, reading alone, reading to a classmate or a small group of classmates, writing about a text they have read, writing in response to text or developing questions about a piece of text.[62]

In addition, from early in the year, children in a multi-grade class need to learn to work independently, either alone or with other children. Many children will need to be explicitly taught how to seek help from sources other than the teacher – peers, a dictionary, an answer key, for example – when they need assistance and about the importance of speaking quietly when the teacher is working with another group.

Sometimes teachers find teaching mathematics in multi-grade classes tricky. Therefore, I want to describe how one experienced teacher I observed taught one mathematics lesson. Fourteen children (ten-year-olds, eleven-year-olds and twelve-year-olds) were present in the class and the teacher – let's call her Ms Ryan – taught a lesson focusing on 2-D and 3-D shapes. The goal of the lesson was to complete a table on a wall-chart indicating the number of edges, vertices and faces on various 3-D shapes, to name the shapes and to decide if the shapes were polyhedrons or not.

Ms Ryan did not use a textbook in the first 36 minutes of the 56-minute lesson and all children worked together to complete the table on the chart. Next, Ms Ryan worked on a game with all the children, asking individuals to use the language they had just learned to describe 3-D shapes concealed in a 'feely' bag, while the rest of the children tried to guess the shape. In the third phase of the lesson (after 36 minutes) the three eleven-year-old children were asked to construct shapes using nets of shapes. The ten-year-old children were asked to do textbook work based on what they did when completing the table; they were advised to refer to the 3-D shapes they constructed previously when responding to the textbook questions.

At 37 minutes Ms Ryan called the six twelve-year-old children to the board and she worked with them intensively on some mathematics problems involving weight and money. The children were asked to calculate the cost of various weights of vegetables given the price of 100 g or 1 kg of the vegetables. Meanwhile the other children worked quietly on the work set for them. Mostly the ten- and eleven-year-old children worked quietly, encouraged by an occasional comment from Ms Ryan along the lines of 'I hope you're working there, not just chatting'. She closed the lesson by checking in with the ten-year-old children who had been completing the textbook activities.

How an individual teacher teaches mathematics to children in a multi-grade setting will vary depending on the class level, the topic, the number of children in the class and the routines the teacher has established with the children. The example above is provided as one example of one teacher teaching mathematics to three class levels in one setting.

For teaching other curriculum subjects in multi-grade settings, it is useful to have a continuum in mind when teaching a topic in any subject. For example, over the course of the primary physical education curriculum, children will need to develop their throwing skills progressively as they move through each class level. Even if a teacher is only teaching one class level, it is good to know what children are likely to have worked on in previous classes and to know what they will have to work on next. When teaching a lesson to a multi-grade class, the focus may be on throwing, but the instructions and expectations for children in specific classes can vary along the lines of Table 4.2.

Similar continua can be applied in other subjects. Take drawing from observation in the visual arts and children's developing awareness of line from grade to grade (Table 4.3).[63]

In history the same topics may be taught at different class levels but the details, concepts, methods of investigation and treatment become more

TABLE 4.2 Continuum for throwing skills in physical education

Junior classes	Lower middle classes	Upper middle classes	Senior classes
Throwing for height and distance Beanbag Under-arm	Experiment throwing various objects for height and distance Under-arm Over-arm	Over-arm throw of beanbag, ball, foam javelin from standing position Short run and release object Throw medium-sized ball from standing position	Develop over-arm throw Short, fast-paced approach run and throw Develop shot-put throw from standing position using primary shot

TABLE 4.3 Continuum for drawing from observation and developing awareness of line in the visual arts

Junior classes	Lower middle classes	Upper middle classes	Senior classes
Draw line and shape seen in natural and made objects	Draw a variety of natural and made objects Draw a classmate	Draw still life arrangements Draw aspects of the environment from different angles Draw the human figure	As for previous classes Draw details of human figure
Begin to represent familiar figures and objects with free lines and shapes	Develop personal symbols to represent familiar figures and objects visually	Interpret form, creating surface texture in line, pattern and rhythm	Interpret the human figure and progress beyond personal symbols

complex in older classes.[64] It is quite conceivable for a teacher, therefore, to work on one topic in a particular year but to adjust how it is treated according to the class level of the children.

In a subject such as Social, Personal and Health Education (SPHE), it may be necessary to separate the classes in a multi-grade setting when working with sensitive strands. This is something that is likely to have been already discussed and planned at school level.

As I close the chapter on differentiation an image comes to my mind from my own days as a child in primary school. It is of my teacher at the back of the room wielding a cane over three children who regularly experienced the cane – not because of misbehaviour but because they didn't learn as well or as quickly as the rest of the class. Clearly the teacher was frustrated with children who struggled to grasp concepts in various subjects. But did the teacher not realise that if the children could have learned, they would have? Fear of the cane alone would surely have made that happen. But for whatever reason – perhaps the content was too difficult; perhaps the teaching method was too abstract – they could not learn what the teacher wanted them to learn.

Dealing skilfully with differences among children is a key part of what teachers do. If all children learned in the same way, at a consistent rate and were motivated to learn independently, a teacher's job would be easy. Teaching would require less skill and the work of a teacher would be more easily replaced by technological solutions where learning is parcelled in digestible, logical, linear packages. Teaching remains for now an essentially human activity and that means understanding, respecting and supporting differences among children.

A more hopeful note on which to end this chapter on differentiation is Bruner's claim that 'any subject can be taught effectively in some intellectually honest form to any child at any stage of development'.[65] If what Bruner claims is true, it can only be done by a teacher who understands the material, who understands learning and who understands students with all the rich variations they bring to learning.

When we're older, if we attend classes in art, dance, guitar or languages, we expect that the levels of proficiency among our classmates will vary and we notice these differences relatively soon. Very often children in primary school classes know themselves when they are struggling compared to their classmates. As one gym instructor modified a task for various levels of proficiency, he commented that it was because 'maybe you're not there yet'. Such an expression is helpful and hopeful in that it recognises that children may be at different levels but that everyone can aim higher.

Key points of Chapter 4

1 Teachers can differentiate by task, outcome, group, resource, support, pace and dialogue.

2 Strategies can be used to make tasks more accessible to children by helping children understand tasks, providing multiple ways to access the subject, making children more independent, providing supports, interacting with

the children, helping children get organised, adjusting the task and creating a supportive environment.

3 Whole class teaching can be differentiated by choosing suitable tasks, by carefully directing questions in a discussion and by using the strategy of 'revoicing'.

4 Ideally early finishers will develop independent study skills and embark on substantial, multi-subject projects over a school year.

5 Reliable, up-to-date knowledge can be sought as needed about how children's specific conditions can impact on their teaching and learning.

6 When a child exhibits signs of being exceptionally able, supports – in school and out of school – need to be put in place to support the child's learning and development.

7 Multi-grade teaching makes particular demands on a teacher, including knowing how curriculum content develops across the class levels in a school.

Notes

1 Analogy from Tomlinson (2001, p. 41).
2 I use the country names to distinguish between the approaches and not to generalise or make presumptions about how teachers in either country approach differentiation. The patterns were observed by Stigler & Hiebert (1999, pp. 94–95) in videos of mathematics lessons in the United States and Japan.
3 See, for example, National Council for Curriculum and Assessment & Council for Curriculum Examination and Assessment (2007).
4 The task was inspired by a task for third/fourth class in Rialtas na hÉireann (1999, p. 159).
5 See Brodesky, Gross, McTigue & Tierney (2004) and http://www2.edc.org/accessmath/.
6 See http://www2.edc.org/accessmath/resources/StrategiestoConsider.pdf.
7 See Weinstein, Marshall, Brattesani & Middlestadt (1982) for one account of how this works.
8 See Brattesani, Weinstein & Marshall (1984).
9 See Jussim & Harber (2005) for a review of literature on teacher expectations.
10 Based on a problem on the NCTM website.
11 The children made this more challenging for themselves by attempting to incorporate into their calculation the fact that there are $365^{1}/_{4}$ days in a year.
12 One useful starting point in mathematics is the website http://nrich.maths.org/frontpage. An example of such a problem from Lampert (2001, p. 11) is

'Condition: A car is going 55 mph. Make a diagram to show where it will be A. after an hour B. after two hours C. after half an hour D. after 15 minutes'.

13 Revoicing is an idea from linguistics that was identified in classroom discussions by people such as C. O'Connor & Michaels (2007); M. C. O'Connor & Michaels (1993).

14 Example based on Mathematics Laboratory Class video, Time Code 08, from 25'40". Names have been changed.

15 A more widely used mathematical term for this is 'rectangular prism' but 'cuboid' is the term used in Government of Ireland (1999b).

16 C. O'Connor & Michaels (2007).

17 C. O'Connor & Michaels (2007).

18 Coffield, Moseley, Hall & Ecclestone (2004).

19 Kirschner & van Merriënboer (2013).

20 Coffield et al. (2004).

21 Tally & Goldenberg (2005).

22 Meyer & Rose (2000).

23 Meyer, Rose & Gordon (2014).

24 See Edyburn (2010) for a list of such questions in the form of propositions that need to be considered.

25 Idea from Tomlinson (2001, p. 37).

26 See for example thinking cards: http://www.nicurriculum.org.uk/curri culum_microsite/TSPC/the_think_pack/thinking_cards/index.asp or graded lists of activities that can be accessed from http://merrybeau.edublogs.org/ 2013/05/04/the-1000-question-challenge-the-first-100-prompts/.

27 For more see Boe, May & Boruch (2002).

28 Bass & Ball (2015, p. 21).

29 A report on the topic of perseverance that refers to many additional resources that are available is Shechtman, DeBarger, Dornsife, Rosier & Yarnall (2013).

30 Zimmerman & Pons (1986).

31 This example is taken from Jervis (1986) and recounted in Corno (1992).

32 For more details about such tasks see Corno (1992).

33 An illustration of this for the condition attention deficit hyperactivity disorder is contained here: http://www.cdc.gov/ncbddd/adhd/timeline.html.

34 See Elliott & Grigorenko (2014) for an example of this debate in relation to dyslexia.

35 Examples include *Journal of Learning Disabilities*; *Focus on Autism and Other Developmental Disabilities*; *Disability and Society*; *Learning Disability Quarterly*; *International Journal of Disability, Development and Education*; *Scandinavian Journal of Disability Research*.

36 For example, Down Syndrome Ireland has produced a handbook for teachers titled *Including Children with Down Syndrome in Your School* and it is available on http://downsyndrome.ie/wp-content/uploads/2012/08/primary-book.pdf.

37 Miller (2012).

38 Carman (2013).

39 The recommendations or 'lessons' are taken from Rogers (2007).

40 Archambault et al. (1993).

41 See http://nrich.maths.org/frontpage.

42 See for example: http://www.learningnetwork.ac.nz/shared/professional Reading/LIFELONG11.pdf and http://presentlygifted.weebly.com/autono mous-learner-model.html.

43 For more information about these programmes see: http://www.education scotland.gov.uk/parentzone/myschool/choosingaschool/centresofexcellence/ index.asp, http://www.dcu.ie/ctyi/index.shtml, or http://www.nace.co.uk/.

44 Examples of such courses that are offered in the United States are listed here: http:// www.ctd.northwestern.edu and here http://cty.jhu.edu/ctyonline/courses/ index.html.

45 Rogers (2007).

46 Slavin (1987) has a review of articles on this topic. Although it is almost thirty years old, and many of the reviewed articles are older, it is still widely cited.

47 See for example Boaler (2005).

48 Literature on this topic has been summarised by Poole (2008).

49 Taken from Hallinan (1990).

50 See Nystrand & Gamoran (1993) for an article about this in relation to English literature.

51 Taken from Baines et al. (2009).

52 Many activities to help children acquire such skills are listed in Baines et al. (2009).

53 In research articles many terms are used to describe classrooms where children from more than one class level are taught. Terms such as combination classes, multi-grade, multiple-grade and split grade are used to describe classes which necessarily consist of two or more adjacent grade levels in response to student enrolments (Mason & Burns, 1997). I have heard the terms multi-class or split class used to refer to similar classes that are grouped out of necessity. Mulryan-Kyne (2004) says that the term 'consecutive grade' class is used to describe a specific multi-grade class that consists of two class levels. A more infrequent scenario is one where grade distinctions are deliberately removed for educational or philosophical reasons and the terms used here are multi-aged classes, non-graded, mixed-age classes (Mason & Burns, 1997) or vertical grouping (Little, 2001). However, the terms used to differentiate between enforced and inten-tional grouping are not consistently used in research literature. I shall refer mostly to situations where such grouping is a necessity rather than a choice and shall use the terms multi-grade and multi-class interchangeably to refer to where two or more class levels are taught in the same room. Where I wish to refer specifically to such a class with two class levels only, I shall use the term consecutive grade.

54 In 2013, 54 per cent of primary schools (1,764 out of 3,293) in Ireland, for example, had seven teachers or fewer, which in most cases requires some multi-grade teaching. However, larger schools will often require some degree of multi-grade teaching where the numbers enrolled at a given class level necessitate it.

55 Mason & Burns (1995); Mulryan-Kyne (2004).

56 Little (2001); Mulryan-Kyne (2004).

57 Mulryan-Kyne (2004).

58 Mason & Burns (1995, 1997); Mulryan-Kyne (2004).

59 Wilkinson & Townsend (2000).

60 These points are taken from Flood, Lapp, Flood & Nagel (1992); in the article the approach is described in more detail and accompanied by an illustrative example.

61 Castle, Deniz & Tortora (2005).

62 Ideas from Wilkinson & Townsend (2000) and Flood et al. (1992).

63 Taken from Government of Ireland (1999c).

64 See, for example, Government of Ireland (1999a, p. 37).

65 Bruner (1960, p. 33).

References

Archambault, F. X., Westberg, K. L., Brown, S. W., Hallmark, B. W., Emmons, C. L. & Zhang, W. (1993). *Regular classroom practices with gifted students: Results of a national survey of classroom teachers.* Storrs, CT: The University of Connecticut.

Baines, E., Blatchford, P., Kutnick, P., with Chowne, A., Ota, C. & Berdondini, L. (2009). *Promoting effective group work in the primary classroom: A handbook for teachers and practitioners.* Abingdon, Oxon: Routledge.

Bass, H. & Ball, D. (2015). *Beyond 'You can do it!' – Developing mathematical perseverance in elementary school* (White paper). Chicago, IL: Spencer Foundation. Downloaded from http://www.spencer.org/sites/default/files/pdfs/bass_ball_mip_0415.pdf.

Boaler, J. (2005). The 'psychological prisons' from which they never escaped: The role of ability grouping in reproducing social class inequalities. *Forum, 47*(2 & 3), 135–143.

Boe, E. E., May, H. & Boruch, R. F. (2002). *Student task persistence in the Third International Mathematics and Science Study: A major source of achievement differences at the national, classroom, and student levels* (p. 34). Philadelphia: Pennsylvania University, Center for Research and Evaluation in Social Policy.

Brattesani, K. A., Weinstein, R. S. & Marshall, H. H. (1984). Student perceptions of differential teacher treatment as moderators of teacher expectation effects. *Journal of Educational Psychology, 76*(2), 236–247.

Brodesky, A. R., Gross, F. E., McTigue, A. S. & Tierney, C. C. (2004). Planning strategies for students with special needs: A professional development activity. *Teaching Children Mathematics, 11*(3), 146–154.

Bruner, J. (1960). *The process of education*. Cambridge, MA: Harvard University Press.

Carman, C. A. (2013). Comparing apples and oranges: Fifteen years of definitions of giftedness in research. *Journal of Advanced Academics, 24*(1), 52–70.

Castle, S., Deniz, C. B. & Tortora, M. (2005). Flexible grouping and student learning in a high-needs school. *Education and Urban Society, 37*(2), 139–150.

Coffield, F., Moseley, D., Hall, E. & Ecclestone, K. (2004). *Learning styles and pedagogy in post-16 learning: A systematic and critical review*. London: Learning and Skills Research Centre.

Corno, L. (1992). Encouraging students to take responsibility for learning and performance. *The Elementary School Journal, 93*(1), 69–83.

Edyburn, D. L. (2010). Would you recognize universal design for learning if you saw it? Ten propositions for new directions for the second decade of UDL. *Learning Disability Quarterly, 33*, 33–41.

Elliott, J. G. & Grigorenko, E. L. (2014). *The dyslexia debate*. New York: Cambridge University Press.

Flood, J., Lapp, D., Flood, S. & Nagel, G. (1992). Am I allowed to group? Using flexible patterns for effective instruction. *The Reading Teacher, 45*(8), 608–616.

Government of Ireland. (1999a). *History: Social, environmental and scientific education*. Dublin: The Stationery Office.

Government of Ireland. (1999b). *Primary school curriculum: Mathematics*. Dublin: The Stationery Office.

Government of Ireland. (1999c). *Visual arts: Arts education*. Dublin: The Stationery Office.

Hallinan, M. T. (1990). The effects of ability grouping in secondary schools: A response to Slavin's best-evidence synthesis. *Review of Educational Research, 60*(3), 501–504.

Jervis, K. (1986). A teacher's quest for a child's questions. *Harvard Educational Review, 56*(2), 132–150.

Jussim, L. & Harber, K. D. (2005). Teacher expectations and self-fulfilling prophecies: Knowns and unknowns, resolved and unresolved controversies. *Personality and Social Psychology Review, 9*(2), 131–155.

Kirschner, P. A. & van Merriënboer, J. J. G. (2013). Do learners really know best? Urban legends in education. *Educational Psychologist, 48*(3), 169–183.

Lampert, M. (2001). *Teaching problems and the problems of teaching*. New Haven, CT: Yale University Press.

Little, A. W. (2001). Multigrade teaching: Towards an international research and policy agenda. *International Journal of Educational Development, 21*, 481–497.

Mason, D. A. & Burns, R. B. (1995). Teachers' views of combination classes. *The Journal of Educational Research, 89*(1), 36–45.

Mason, D. A. & Burns, R. B. (1997). Reassessing the effects of combination classes. *Educational Research and Evaluation: An International Journal on Theory and Practice, 3*(1), 1–53.

Meyer, A. & Rose, D. H. (2000). Universal design for individual differences. *Educational Leadership, 58*(3), 39–43.

Meyer, A., Rose, D. H. & Gordon, D. (2014). *Universal design for learning: Theory and practice.* Wakefield, MA: CAST Professional Publishing.

Miller, A. L. (2012). Conceptualizations of creativity: Comparing theories and models of giftedness. *Roeper Review, 34*(2), 94–103.

Mulryan-Kyne, C. (2004). Teaching and learning in multigrade classrooms: What teachers say. *Irish Journal of Education, 35*, 5–19.

National Council for Curriculum and Assessment & Council for Curriculum Examination and Assessment. (2007). *Exceptionally able students: Draft guidelines for teachers.* Dublin: National Council for Curriculum and Assessment.

Nystrand, M. & Gamoran, A. (1993). Using small groups for response to and thinking about literature. *The English Journal, 82*(1), 14–22.

O'Connor, C. & Michaels, S. (2007). When is dialogue dialogic? *Human Development, 50*, 275–285.

O'Connor, M. C. & Michaels, S. (1993). Aligning academic task and participation status through revoicing: Analysis of a classroom discourse strategy. *Anthropology & Education Quarterly, 24*(4), 318–355.

Poole, D. (2008). Interactional differentiation in the mixed-ability group: A situated view of two struggling readers. *Reading Research Quarterly, 43*(3), 228–250.

Rialtas na hÉireann. (1999). *Gaeilge: Teanga, treoirlínte do mhúinteoirí.* Baile Átha Cliath: Oifig an tSoláthair.

Rogers, K. B. (2007). Lessons learned about educating the gifted and talented: A synthesis of the research on educational practice. *Gifted Child Quarterly, 51*(4), 382–396.

Shechtman, N., DeBarger, A. H., Dornsife, C., Rosier, S. & Yarnall, L. (2013). Promoting grit, tenacity and perseverance: Critical factors for success in the 21st century (draft). Washington, DC: U.S. Department of Education, Office of Educational Technology.

Slavin, R. E. (1987). Ability grouping and student achievement in elementary schools: A best-evidence synthesis. *Review of Educational Research, 57*(3), 293–336.

Stigler, J. W. & Hiebert, J. (1999). *The teaching gap: Best ideas from the world's teachers for improving education in the classroom.* New York: The Free Press.

Tally, B. & Goldenberg, L. B. (2005). Fostering historical thinking with digitized primary sources. *Journal of Research on Technology in Education, 38*(1), 1–21.

Tomlinson, C. A. (2001). *How to differentiate instruction in mixed-ability classrooms.* Alexandria, VA: Association for Supervision and Curriculum Development (ASCD).

Weinstein, R. S., Marshall, H. H., Brattesani, K. A. & Middlestadt, S. E. (1982). Student perceptions of differential teacher treatment in open and traditional classrooms. *Journal of Educational Psychology, 74*(5), 678–692.

Wilkinson, I. A. G. & Townsend, M. A. R. (2000). From Rata to Rimu: Grouping for instruction in best practice New Zealand classrooms. *The Reading Teacher, 53*(6), 460–471.

Zimmerman, B. J. & Pons, M. M. (1986). Development of a structured interview for assessing student use of self-regulated learning strategies. *American Educational Research Journal, 23*(4), 614–628.

5

Reinforcing teaching at home

Few fans and fewer benefits?

It's hard to find anyone who has a good word to say about homework. Many children see it as drudgery and they pore over it for hours every week. Other children see it as an inconvenience – something to be done quickly and quickly forgotten about. For parents and guardians homework is another source of family tensions, like arguments about bedtime or doing household chores.

Setting and checking homework in school eats into teaching time. And responding to half-hearted efforts and excuses when it's not done often starts the school day on a disagreeable note. Almost everyone views a night off homework as a relief. Yet despite the battles it causes, most schools require children to bring work home. With the inconvenience it causes for teachers, parents and children, it's difficult to see why homework is so widely accepted.

Despite its name, homework is often not done at home; a homework club, a childminder's house, in school or on the bus journey to school are other possibilities. In many homes parents check homework and sign a notebook to confirm they have done so. Teachers in turn check homework either first thing the following morning or during the day when the relevant subject is being taught. Children who have it done are commended and those who have not done it, with no explanatory note from a parent or guardian, may be reprimanded.

Most schools have homework policies[1] which articulate the purpose of homework, the kind of homework that is given, how long it should take, how teachers check the homework, and parent guidelines for monitoring homework. Homework policies are typically developed in consultation with parents. Nevertheless, for various reasons, only a minority of parents typically gets involved in the review or development of school policies.[2]

Differences among children affect how they view and do homework. Children understand the content of homework differently and they bring different study skills to completing tasks. In addition to this, children experience different levels of support for homework from the adults in their lives. Some children, whose parents don't speak the language of the school, are disadvantaged compared to children whose parents speak the language of the school.

Instructional reasons for giving homework include practising, revising or extending work already done in school, to prepare for future learning, or to do work on a project that applies or synthesises skills and ideas learned in school. It is also given to help children develop a work ethic and to learn independently. Non-instructional purposes are to demonstrate the complementary roles of parents and teachers in their children's education, to involve parents more in school work, to comply with school policy or to punish misbehaviour.[3] Although for post-primary students the benefits of a certain amount of homework are relatively clear, the benefits of homework for primary children's achievement are non-existent[4] or at best ambiguous.[5]

Giving homework is a practice around the world. But even when you search across several countries, it is difficult to find any concrete benefits of homework. One study looked at the relationship between mathematics homework and performance on the Third International Mathematics and Science Study (TIMSS) mathematics test. The study found a negative relationship between national average achievement scores in mathematics and the frequency or amount of homework given. In other words, less homework was associated with better results on the TIMSS test. The authors conclude that giving children more mathematics homework is unlikely to improve national achievement in mathematics.[6] That study found that the amount of mathematics homework given varies from just over fifty minutes per week in the Czech Republic to over three hours a week in Romania.

Despite the lack of research support for homework, many teachers believe that homework raises children's achievement, encourages good work habits and prepares children in older primary classes for secondary school. Other teachers give homework because it is part of the convention of schooling – like wearing a school uniform, taking a school bus or packing a school lunch. It is as predictable as a spelling test on a Friday morning or a day off for heavy snow. Requiring children to work a 'second shift'[7] is part of the familiar tradition and culture of schooling; criticising it seems unorthodox.

Besides, research that dismisses the value of homework could be problematic given the variety of activities and approaches covered by the term.

When I was teaching, I sometimes assigned homework just because I was expected to do so. I believed that parents' perception of my effectiveness was related to the homework I gave. Assigning homework gave me a way to show parents that I was interested in children's progress and committed enough to my work to spend time checking and following up on it the next day.

As much as they find it inconvenient, many parents expect their children to have homework. It is familiar; it reassures them that their child is going through the same ritual *they* went through at that age. When the current generation of parents were children, they probably didn't realise how much grief homework caused their parents many years earlier. Nevertheless, continuing it with their own children reassures them that a tradition continues.

But calling homework a tradition or a ritual tends to trivialise it. Surely it must have some benefit for children's learning? It seems counter-intuitive that children could spend so much time on homework and not have it improve their achievement. Perhaps the benefits of homework are about more than simply boosting children's academic success. For example, it may be to improve communications between home and school, to help children develop a work ethic of study from an early age, or to help train the children to work independently. Such factors have been investigated by few research studies.

Despite the limitations of homework, I doubt if it will cease to be a feature of schooling any time soon. Therefore I'm going to discuss aspects of giving and checking homework. Later I'll discuss some alternatives to homework that might be worth considering.

Assigning homework

In selecting tasks for homework, you could think about work that was done in class during the day that would benefit from additional consolidation or clarification at home. It might be something children found interesting or difficult. For example, a child might be asked to retell a story told in class to someone at home; or to write down two questions they have about improper fractions; or to find ways to organise a list of animals/objects.

Alternatively, it may be worth looking ahead to later in the week or beyond to consider how children could prepare for a future lesson topic or activity by gathering artefacts (such as objects from other countries, photographs, family memorabilia, or objects made from various materials) or investigating some phenomenon (such as a survey of trees or car types in an area, what life was like for their grandparents when the grandparents were the ages the children are now, or identifying a potential hazard in the home as a precursor to a lesson on safety). Homework tasks need to be sufficiently substantial that the children will engage with them but sufficiently easy that they can be done independently by most children in a reasonable amount of time.[8]

Setting and responding to homework can eat into class time, especially in senior classes where many teachers write the homework on the board and ask children to copy it into homework notebooks. Some children write down their homework quickly but others struggle with it because they are slow to write, or they are disorganised in getting started, or each time they look from the board to their notebook and back to the board, finding where they left off is a challenge.

It's useful for a teacher to check how children transcribe their homework in order to spot children who have not written down all the homework to be done or who have transcribed it incorrectly. Homework that is recorded inaccurately or incompletely begins a domino effect where the child does not know what homework to do,[9] a parent cannot help, and the child may get into trouble the next day for having done the wrong homework or none at all. Although homework can be communicated from school to home by e-mail, text message, social media or website, this could further disadvantage children who have no access to the relevant technology at home.

Doing homework

Given the range of circumstances in children's homes, it is difficult for teachers to set uniform homework that provides similar challenge for all children. Perhaps the best way to do that is to try and set open-ended tasks that can be approached at various levels and to be conscious of the diverse sets of circumstances and supports available to the children in your class.

Doing homework takes longer than teachers think. Most teachers expect homework for nine-year-olds to take less than an hour. Although children may be better than their parents at estimating how long they spend on homework,[10] a quarter of parents say their child spends more than an hour doing it.[11]

Despite how long it takes, most children do their homework most of the time. Only about one student in twenty does not complete homework regularly. Failure to do homework is typically explained by children having fewer supports and less motivation for doing homework than their peers. Children who might be susceptible to not doing homework regularly and who would benefit from some extra support or motivation from a teacher are children from single-parent families, from lower social class families, from less educated families, and boys.[12]

Checking and responding to homework

When children arrive at school, they know their homework from the night before is likely to be checked in class. The kind of checking may depend on whether the homework involved writing or memorising. When checking memorised work, it is helpful to discuss with children *how* they learned tables or spellings. Some children will talk about what they found difficult, and others may share strategies that helped them learn.

Because spellings are generally used in writing rather than orally, it makes sense to check them in writing. This could be done using a short dictation that includes the spellings learned, or the children could try and compose their own sentences using the spellings they learned. When checking spellings, it is the pattern of errors that matters more than the quantity. Children may omit letters, insert additional letters or spell in a bizarre way. A good alternative to a weekly spelling test is to look at how children spell in their free writing.[13]

Number facts may be checked using loop games ('I have 12, follow me if you have 7 + 2' etc.), asking children to count in 2s, 4s, 8s, 3s, 6s etc. with a partner (timed or untimed) or completing missing parts of a blank addition or multiplication table. The learning focus of such checking is to help children discover, understand and recall patterns and relations among number facts.[14]

A teacher may check written homework in different ways, depending on the kind of homework, the time available and other plans for the day. Checking may involve glancing at each child's work simply to see if it is done. Or it may involve quickly inspecting if answers given are correct or incorrect. Checking and correcting written homework can eat into teaching time, and teachers adopt various strategies to manage homework as efficiently as possible. Although homework checking may include some teaching and learning, it may also be diluted by time spent on administrative matters.

In junior classes, homework can usually be checked quickly each day. If children complete work on pages, storage may be problem. Some kind of folder for each student can be useful for keeping each child's completed work together during the year. It can be emptied and brought home to parents from time to time, and children may be asked to select their best work samples coming up to parent–teacher meeting time.

In senior classes, children may be able to check their own homework or check the homework of a classmate under the teacher's guidance. Some teachers require children to have two notebooks for doing homework. On a given night, children could bring notebook A home while the teacher checks the work in notebook B; the next night work done in notebook A is checked while that night's homework is done in notebook B.

When homework is incomplete or not done

Checking and recording homework done by the children in a class can be complicated. First, it may be done or not done. If written homework is done, you'll usually be able to check how well it's done but occasionally it may be left at home, in the car or on the bus. If it's not done, it may be excused by a parent or guardian, or it may not be excused. If it's not excused, a child may be upfront in admitting it's not done or you may have to discover that yourself. With so many possible options, much time and effort could be expended just policing homework.

An occasional case of missing homework is not a major problem, especially well into the year when your expectations have been communicated to children. But where a pattern of non-completion is developing, further action may be required. In order to observe a pattern, some record of homework done is needed. In fact, given that most children in most classrooms do their homework most of the time, it is probably easier to keep a record of occasions when homework is not done. Such details could be kept in a specific homework diary or on an individual child's record.

If homework is consistently not done, a teacher needs to investigate why. Some teachers may take the view that what happens at home is a matter for the parents alone. However, where homework is not done, and no consequences follow, some children may deduce that the teacher is indifferent to their completion of school work in general.

Many factors can explain why homework is not done on a regular basis. A child may try to get away with not doing homework because they think they can. In that case, discussing the problem may help. In other cases, persistent undone homework may indicate that the child is experiencing a lack of support at home. You may discuss this initially with the child but further discussion may be needed with the school principal, a home–school liaison teacher, or with a parent to see if the child can be given any additional support to complete the homework. In most classes only one or two children may be in need of such supports and consequently supports can be designed on a case-by-case basis. In consultation with the principal, parent and child, as necessary, you can decide whether a firm or a compassionate approach is merited for a particular child.

Teachers' knowledge of how homework is done

Although homework takes up a substantial amount of a teacher's time, the act of doing homework is largely invisible to teachers. They see the outcome or the absence of an outcome from homework but they do not see the homework being done. As a result, children's completion of homework is a mystery for teachers. When do children do homework? Where do they do it? Who is with them when they do it? What else is going on in the background? How do children do the different parts of their homework? In what order do they complete it? What aspects of the homework are challenging and what aspects are easy? How much help, if any, do they get? What takes most/least time? Although important, teachers miss out on this information.

If teachers allow children to do homework in class or if they supervise a homework club and observe children doing homework there, they may learn something about how children approach their homework. However, doing homework in school or a homework club is different to doing it at home. In class or in a homework club children are surrounded by their peers who may help or side-track them. Other temptations present at home, such as television or computer games, are not available to distract them. Unlike many homes, the time and the space in class and homework clubs are structured to encourage and facilitate school work. At best, teachers who supervise the clubs get a partial glimpse of how children do homework.

Teachers may recall their own experience of doing homework. Because teachers were generally high achievers in schools, their experience may resemble that of only a handful of the children they teach and their memories of doing homework may be selective. Personal experience therefore is unlikely to be a reliable guide for how homework is approached by most children.

Many teachers say that their view of homework changes when they have children of their own. Teachers with children begin to see from a parent's perspective the impact homework has on home life and how it shapes the post-school day. But even this view is partial because a teacher's children may not be typical. They may be well-organised and efficient at homework or they may reluctantly struggle to complete it over a couple of hours. And a teacher's knowledge is a resource that is not available in most homes for helping a son or daughter with homework. Although being a parent helps a teacher see the impact of homework on a family, the teacher does not see the diverse ways and contexts in which children in a class undertake the work.

Learning to study through homework

Not only is the process of how children do homework not seen by the teacher, it is not seen by other children. Some children may occasionally collaborate on homework, but they still do not get to see how someone works independently with their homework and how they organise themselves to do the work. As a result, children typically must develop their own strategies for doing different kinds of homework. Sometimes these strategies may be effective and other times not.

If homework is about developing better study habits, then perhaps teachers could explicitly teach children study habits that would help them when they do their homework. In Appendix IV some strategies are identified that may be useful for teaching children how to become better at studying independently. The idea is that you could regularly engage in discussions with children about the process of doing their homework. How long did it take you? What part did you enjoy most? Did anyone help you? How did you learn the spellings? How did you go about doing the writing? What did you find difficult? As the discussions develop, a child may say that they found it difficult to learn their tables, or they found it difficult to get organised.

Feedback from children about doing homework provides an opportunity for you to introduce study strategies like these described in Appendix IV. Children will develop and hone their study skills over several years, and it is better for them to find and practise using one or two strategies that work well for them rather than being told about several.

Variations in children's capacity to do homework

Homework competes for time, energy and attention with many structured and unstructured after-school activities. Competitors include all kinds of extra-curricular activities such as scouts, music lessons, horse-riding and football. However, not all children are involved in such after-school activities; participation in clubs and structured after-school activities increases with family income. Boys are more likely to be involved in sports clubs and girls are more likely to be involved in cultural activities.[15] Extra-curricular activities appear to benefit children, especially if they are related to the school in some way, because they contribute to children's social networks.[16]

Homework also competes with social activities such as attending birthday parties, spending time with friends and helping family members. Many children spend time watching television[17] and playing video games. When allocating homework, it is good to remember that it is just one of the demands on children's time after school.

Possible approaches to assigning homework

So given the differences among children, assigning homework which will satisfy the teacher, the child and the parents or guardians seems impossible. A teacher's challenge is to set homework for up to thirty or more different children in a class when each child has a different capacity for doing it. Moreover, children are going home to different home environments where their parents or guardians can offer varying levels of interest in and support for doing homework. In responding to such a challenge, you could weigh up the guidelines provided by the school policy with your knowledge of the lives of children and their families.

Given how difficult it is to be fair and reasonable in setting homework, a teacher could be tempted to believe that giving no homework would be the best option. At least that would remove the challenge of trying to find work that was suitable for every child at home.

If teachers stopped giving homework, parents would have to make a conscious effort to find out what their children are working on in school. Parents may be less likely to detect if a child is having difficulty with a topic; they might have to wait until they meet with the teacher or receive a child's school report. If a parent doesn't have homework to check, they are less likely to reinforce or supplement the teacher's work by helping a child understand at home something that wasn't fully grasped in school. Furthermore, giving some homework may stimulate children to think about what they did in school during the day.

Children 'teach' someone something for homework

An alternative approach would be to set homework but make it optional. The teacher could identify certain work to do and children could decide to do it if they have time or if their parents wished it. If the parents and child decided against doing the homework, that would also be acceptable. Indeed I have read at least one school policy that permits parents to write to the school if they wish to excuse their child from homework activities.[18]

However, making homework optional would not solve much for the teacher. As long as some children do it, the teacher needs to follow up on it in class. Setting and checking homework would be messy if only some children do it. And it makes record keeping even more difficult for the teacher. Such an arrangement may do little to address the inequality of the education system if it meant that some children receive feedback and support from the teacher and other children do not.

Other flexible approaches to homework are where children are given homework for the week on a Monday and they can complete it anytime during the week, or where schools require children to do homework on three out of five days. Such approaches would lead to setting and checking homework on a weekly rather than a daily basis. Although it gives flexibility to children, the assigned homework may be less directly connected to the work being done in class on a specific day, because that cannot be precisely predicted at the start of the week.

An alternative approach would be for teachers to set a different kind of homework – homework that takes into account the children's different achievement levels, and the different homes in which children live. Homework needs to connect to work that is current and alive in school. It is often said that the best way to learn something is to teach it. A possible task could be for the child to 'teach' something that was done in school that day to someone at home.

If the children are learning about the Normans, for example, they could teach a younger sibling something about the Normans, or they could revise the topic for a parent, guardian, grandparent or childminder. That would help address children's different levels of achievement because each child would do it at their own level, based on their understanding of the topic. This would be a kind of 'show and tell' in reverse where the child brings ideas from school and shares them with someone at home.

The following day the teacher could follow up on the 'lessons' the children taught. Who did you teach? How did you teach them? What did they already know about it? What questions did they ask you? How did you answer them? What questions do you have now? Did you have to prepare much to teach them? Did you show them any pictures? All children will learn from both the process and the subsequent class discussion that takes place based on such homework. Not every child will have something to contribute but enough of them will have something to add that will deepen the class's exploration of the topic.

The children's questions could be recorded for investigation in subsequent lessons. Perhaps the questions presented by the children could overwhelm the teacher. The teacher would no longer be taking on questions just from children in the class, but many of the parents or grandparents would be posing questions to the children who in turn would share them with the entire class. Some children will need to return to their 'pupil' – parent, grandparent, childminder – with answers.

The teacher may be able to answer some of the questions. Other questions may stump the teacher. Children may be prompted to research answers on the internet, verifying answers found for accuracy. The teacher may need to offer the children other sources of information. The teacher will certainly need to know the topic well. But such homework would make a genuine connection between school and home; children, families and teacher can learn together.

I suggested the Normans as a topic. That is a rich topic and many other topics likely to engage learners are possible – especially in Social, Environmental and Scientific Education: world wars, earthquakes, map reading, science experiments for instance. Children could teach these topics at home.

But what about subjects like a second language, or maths or English grammar? Children could teach new words or new rules in the second language at home, or they could teach how to subtract or multiply or divide. In preparation for such homework the teacher may need to discuss with the children during the lesson in school how the children would teach the content to someone at home. Thus children are encouraged to think about what they are learning with a view to teaching it as well as learning the content for its own sake. Some children may discover that the way they are learning something in school, like a topic in mathematics for example, is different to the way their parents learned it and this could lead to follow-up discussions in class.

But whereas some families may willingly participate and engage in the lesson and ask questions of their child, acting in the role of 'teacher', other children may struggle to find even one 'pupil' at home who has any interest in being taught. We know that among nine-year-olds, almost three-quarters of children can have regular support from an adult when doing their homework. The children who might find this kind of homework difficult are the minority of children who rarely or never receive homework support from an adult.[19]

Teachers might worry about whether or not children would take such homework seriously. Children are not required to write anything. Despite the importance of learning off spellings and reading, some children consider only the written work to be homework. Although most children are happy to learn spellings and tables and do some reading, it is the written homework that makes the most demands, takes the most time and is consequently treated most seriously. Would children really try and teach something to someone at home for homework? If the teacher is seen to take the homework seriously the following day, most probably would.

Asking children to teach someone at home won't solve every homework problem. First, children may tire of having the same homework every evening so some variety will be required. The 'pupil' at home may also become weary of being taught, especially if there are few options for different family members or neighbours to be involved from day to day. Without having to write something, some children may coast and rarely if ever do the teaching they are expected to do at home. Could the teacher sometimes ask the children to write 'notes for teaching' instead of doing the teaching? Given their recent memories of that task, beginning teachers might be reluctant to inflict such a task on primary school children but children might be happy to record a few sentences outlining what they would say about a topic if they were going to teach it. They need not write objectives or state how they will assess the lesson content!

Other forms of homework

Not all homework would have to be approached with the 'student as teacher' format. Written homework could still be given from time to time. For English grammar, the children may bring home some writing they did in school and edit it for grammar points. Does every sentence begin with a capital letter and end with a full stop? Are question marks included? Do all proper nouns have capital letters?

In mathematics, children could attempt one or two problems similar to those worked on in class. When problem solving in class, it is typically possible to give a challenging problem, because several children may eventually contribute to solving it; a problem assigned for homework will usually be more procedural. It is unfair to ask children to try out a new kind of problem for the first time at home given the amount of time it may take and when children's capacity in mathematics and the supports available to them at home vary so much.

Some teachers send school library books home on a regular basis and ask children to read them for homework. Teachers of some classes have been drawing on technology and getting children to create blogs that are visible to members of the classroom community.[20] Using dedicated software,[21] the children can create digital portfolios of their work and receive comments in response to their work from peers, moderated by the teacher. This extends the audience for the children's homework beyond the teacher.

A final word

From time to time in a class, children will do voluntary homework. They will write a story, complete a page of a workbook or share a poem they enjoyed with the teacher. When a student presents such work to a teacher, the student would like a response. It's difficult for children to appreciate how busy a teacher is and how hard it can be to reach even one additional demand. Yet, presenting independent work to a teacher is a way of paying a tribute to the teacher. It shows that the student has been inspired in some way by the teacher's teaching and that the student believes that the teacher cares about promoting every child's learning. If a teacher can take a moment to acknowledge the child's work, it may mean a lot to the child and inspire them to continue to try and excel.

Although research has identified few benefits of homework for primary school children, the practice is so embedded in our schools that it is unlikely to change soon. Conducting research into homework is by no means straightforward. If a study was designed to investigate the benefits of school work, few would take it seriously because it is too general. The *kind* of work that is done in school would influence the outcomes. For example, differences may be found according to how the teacher teaches, what the teacher teaches, how the children learn, the materials used in class and so on.

However, homework is frequently investigated as if it consists of much the same work; research typically measures homework on the basis of time spent on it rather than on what children do. Often homework is studied as if the only potential benefit of doing it is higher test scores.

Furthermore, many of the published studies available are from the United States. In those studies what counts as homework may be different to European countries and therefore may limit the application of such research findings to schools elsewhere in the world. Teaching can be informed by research; however, research cannot answer every question teachers have. Based on research findings and the circumstances of their class, teachers make decisions about homework and other matters in the best interest of their children's learning.

Key points of Chapter 5

1 Homework is widely given to children internationally but most published research has found few if any benefits of it for primary school children.

2 Homework can be assigned to follow-up on or prepare for work done in class and can be checked in a variety of ways.

3 Persistent lack of homework done needs to be responded to on an individual basis.

4 The process of doing homework is often hidden from teachers and from other children, and making the process more transparent may improve how homework is done.

5 Alternative forms of homework could be considered such as asking children to teach content to a family member or neighbour.

6 Homework can be used as a pretext to deliberately help children learn independent study skills.

Notes

1 See for example http://www.scoilmhuireabbey.ie/homework_policy.html, http://www.stpatsbray.ie/index.php/2011-06-13-22-43-43/homework-policy .html,orhttp://www.conventprimaryroscommon.ie/pageDetail.php?entid=115 &pageid=16

2 Notwithstanding that fact, one study found that the level of consultation with parents by schools can vary according to the policy area that is of interest at a particular time (O'Gara, 2005).

3 From Cooper, Robinson & Patall (2006).

4 See for example Kohn (2006a).

5 Cooper et al. (2006).

6 Baker, LeTendre & Akiba (2005).

7 Kohn (2006b).

8 Cooper (2001) describes a '10-minute rule' where it is recommended that the time allocated for homework be the child's grade level, multiplied by 10 minutes (p. 65).

9 Unless they remember it or phone a friend to check what it is.

10 Cooper et al. (2006).

11 From Growing Up in Ireland (2009); 96 per cent of teachers give homework four nights a week, 99 per cent expected it to take less than an hour and 26 per cent of parents said it took longer.

12 Williams et al. (2009).

13 Suggestions from Brendan Culligan on http://insideeducation.podbean.com/2010/02/21/programme-33-spellings-and-news-21-2-10/.

14 Baroody, Bajwa & Eiland (2009). See also https://numberstrings.com/

15 Williams et al. (2009).

16 Cosden, Morrison, Gutierrez & Brown (2004).

17 Watching television in moderation (1–2 hours per day) has been found to be positively associated with academic achievement but longer time spent in front of the box was associated with decreasing achievement. Of course the content of what is watched matters; educational programming is generally beneficial, whereas entertainment programmes, especially violent programmes, have been negatively associated with academic achievement. Fewer studies on video games have been conducted and the results have been mixed. One study did link video games with superior spatial skills. See Kirkorian, Wartella & Anderson (2008) for more information.

18 http://www.conventprimaryroscommon.ie/pageDetail.php?entid=115&pageid=16

19 Williams et al. (2009).

20 Read one teacher's account of using a blog with a class here: http://www.seomraranga.com/2012/09/blogging-with-kidblog/.

21 Examples of such software are http://kidblog.org/home/ and https://www.edmodo.com/.

References

Baker, D. P., LeTendre, G. K. & Akiba, M. (2005). Schoolwork at home? Low-quality schooling and homework. In D. P. Baker & G. K. LeTendre (Eds), *National differences, global similarities: World culture and the future of schooling* (pp. 117–133). Stanford, CA: Stanford University Press.

Baroody, A. J., Bajwa, N. P. & Eiland, M. (2009). Why can't Johnny remember the basic facts? *Developmental Disabilities Research Reviews, 15*, 69–79.

Cooper, H. (2001). *The battle over homework: Common ground for administrators, teachers, and parents* (2nd ed.). Thousand Oaks, CA: Corwin Press.

Cooper, H., Robinson, J. C. & Patall, E. A. (2006). Does homework improve academic achievement? A synthesis of research, 1987–2003. *Review of Educational Research, 76*(1), 1–61.

Cosden, M., Morrison, G., Gutierrez, L. & Brown, M. (2004). The effects of homework programs and after-school activities on school success. *Theory into Practice, 43*(3), 220–226.

Growing Up in Ireland. (2009). *Growing up in Ireland, Key findings: 9-year olds, No. 3, The education of 9-year olds.* Dublin: Economic and Social Research Institute, Trinity College Dublin, Office of the Minister for Children and Youth Affairs.

Kirkorian, H. L., Wartella, E. A. & Anderson, D. R. (2008). Media and young children's learning. *The Future of Children, 18*(1), 39–61.

Kohn, A. (2006a). Abusing research: The study of homework and other examples. *The Phi Delta Kappan, 88*(1), 8–22.

Kohn, A. (2006b, 6 September). The truth about homework: Needless assignments persist because of widespread misconceptions about learning, *Education Week*.

O'Gara, A. (2005). *Perspectives on consultation with parents in the development of the school plan.* (PhD), University of Dublin, Trinity College, Dublin.

Williams, J., Greene, S., Doyle, E., Harris, E., Layte, R., McCoy, S., . . . Thornton, M. (2009). The lives of 9-year-olds: Child cohort. *Growing up in Ireland: National longitudinal study of children.* Dublin: The Stationery Office.

6

Assessing learning and teaching

The link between testing and assessment

Many countries require owners of cars of a certain age to have an annual or biennial test of vehicle safety.[1] Before that test some motorists bring their cars for a service to check out the essentials and repair what's broken. By doing so they feel more confident when the car is checked by vehicle safety test staff. If the car needs a service, bringing it for a vehicle safety test wastes time and money. Teachers test children to check their mastery of what's taught. But just as doing the vehicle safety test won't ensure the smooth running of a car, testing children alone does little to enhance learning. Like a car needs regular servicing, teaching requires assessment approaches that go beyond testing.

But for many people assessment and testing are synonymous. Primary school children in senior classes typically take written tests in various curriculum subjects from time to time. Testing is even more prevalent in secondary schools. Tests are regularly set, done, marked and returned to students, partly to monitor and partly to motivate. Although other assessment occurs in schools, tests constitute the visible face of assessment.

Purposes of assessment

Because exams for national or state qualifications play such a prominent role in school life, it's easy to forget that assessment has purposes other than placing children in rank order, and ultimately sorting them for entry into college, work or various post-school training positions or programmes.

The origin of the word assess comes from an Old French word meaning to 'sit by' which has the suggestion of someone looking over your shoulder and maybe giving some guidance rather than the widely publicised and rigorous demands of state exams, such as the General Certificate of Education Advanced Level, the Leaving Certificate or the Scottish Higher. The term's original meaning is a reminder that assessment in teaching has many purposes, other than ranking children. And assessment is not always as obvious or as visible to children as a test.

One reason why teachers assess children is to find out what they already know so that what they know can inform subsequent teaching. No matter what topic you are going to teach, some children, at least, will know something about it beforehand or will have an opinion on it. They may even know more than you. I remember one Monday morning telling some children in second class about a bird I had seen the day before, running up the trunk of a tree 'like a mouse'. A girl in the class was able to inform me that it was a tree-creeper and that when creeping up the tree, it was looking for insects to eat.

Even if children's ideas on a topic are incorrect or inaccurate, their ideas can inform the direction a lesson takes. Eliciting children's ideas is not so much about assessing individual learners but about assessing the collective prior knowledge of the class to see how that knowledge can be used as a resource for learning. If you were teaching a lesson about India and some children in the class had seen a film such as *Gandhi*, had read a book such as *One Grain of Rice* by Demi, liked Indian food or were from India, this could influence where to begin learning about the country. Information that children have gained from such prior learning experiences can enrich your teaching of a topic.

Another reason for assessing children's knowledge is to inform yourself about how effective your teaching is. Suppose you are teaching the class about weather and you have done some work on clouds, rainfall, temperature and wind direction. Then you bring the children outside and the majority of children in the class can correctly identify the clouds in the sky that day as being cumulonimbus, they can tell the direction of the wind, and they forecast that rain is likely to be associated with the cloud. That provides feedback to you that your teaching was effective and that most children could apply what they learned to analyse a fairly straightforward weather situation. If the children were unable to accurately analyse the weather, you may need to revisit the topic, taking a different approach so that the class understands it. This is about the collective knowledge of the class rather than what individual children know.

Such collective assessment of learning informs what is taught and how it is taught. Often it is referred to as 'assessment for learning' or formative assessment. It shows children that you care about what they already know about a topic and it helps you link what you plan to teach to their collective knowledge. Teaching is difficult without being able to assess the individual and collective knowledge of a class before and during lessons.

Feedback

Sometimes assessment is so informal and seemingly casual that you might not think of it as assessment. Yet, whenever you glance at work done by children in order to provide feedback, you may be assessing – identifying a strength, an error, or a misunderstanding of the task. Such assessment could become the basis of learning for one or many children. When I was teaching fulltime, my feedback to children was often of the form 'Well done' or 'That's clever', 'Good girl, that's right' or 'Excellent work'. Most children like to be praised – privately, at least.

However, such feedback about the student as a person – rather than about what they are doing or how they are doing it – is less helpful than other kinds of feedback. Better is feedback about the task, feedback about how well children are working towards achieving the learning goal of a lesson, and feedback about how aware children are of how they're approaching the task.[2]

Let's consider what each kind of feedback might sound like in practice. Suppose you know that children in your class are interested in wildlife. You set a task requiring each child to prepare a one-page overview of a chosen plant, tree or animal. The overview will be in the format of an encyclopaedia entry to be read by children of their own age. The task integrates the subjects of social, environmental and scientific education (plants and animals) and English (writing).

Feedback on the task

Feedback on the task may refer to matters such as how accurately or neatly the student has completed the task or part of the task. An example of such feedback may be that 'You have written that penguins live mostly in polar regions, but perhaps you could be more precise about the pole to which they are native' or 'It is clear that you define trees native to Ireland as the trees that reached the country after the last Ice Age, before the country was separated from the rest of Europe'.[3]

Feedback on the process

Feedback could also be about how well a child or a group of children attempts a task. This feedback is a way to help children learn about how they approach a school task and organise their work. It might take forms such as 'You have a lot of facts there about oak trees and you sourced a lot of it on Wikipedia. It would be a good idea to compare that information with information in this library book to check it for accuracy' or 'I see that you made out a plan for your entry before you began writing it out. That helped you be sure that you included all the information you had gathered'.

Feedback to promote self-regulation

Along with feedback from their teacher, children may receive feedback from peers, parents or themselves. Teachers sometimes display checklists on the wall to prompt children to monitor their own work in various curriculum areas. 'Did I begin every sentence with a capital letter?' or 'Did I do a warm-up activity before performing gymnastics moves?' are the kind of questions that children might be encouraged to ask so that they can provide feedback to themselves on their progress.

Successful children are those who learn to provide feedback to themselves about how well they are doing what they set out to do. Although feedback from a teacher may still be sought, it helps if children themselves can monitor how well they are performing a task.[4] To give themselves feedback, children need to almost detach themselves from the task they are working on so they can analyse how they are doing it, assess how well they are doing it and identify supports they need to complete it.

You may encourage children to engage in feedback to self with comments such as 'Did you include a map to indicate the place in which this plant/animal is native?' or 'Last week we talked about how to acknowledge sources in our writing. Make sure that you have acknowledged all the sources you used in this entry' or 'Have you used a dictionary to check any spellings you are unsure of?' or simply 'How well are you doing what you wanted to do?'.

No matter what kind of feedback you give your students or prompt them to give themselves, you first need to make some kind of judgement about students' work. Therefore, giving constructive feedback is one reason you need to know about assessment. Other reasons to know about assessment are to inform what and how you teach, to know about different ways of assessing, to report to parents about children's progress, to design and select tests and to interpret test results. Such knowledge about assessment may promote:

1 your understanding of assessment and accountability;

2 your adopting a positive attitude toward external assessment of student learning;

3 your ability to prepare tests;

4 your having a good moral compass about preparing children for tests;

5 your willingness to participate in developing assessments.[5]

Possessing such knowledge and dispositions about assessment means having to develop and clarify your own attitude to assessment and to acquire historical, political and professional knowledge of the topic. Assessment usually features heavily when education matters are discussed in the media – typically in relation to international comparative tests. It is useful to be able to view such matters against a broader backdrop.[6]

Four broad types of assessment can be identified: formative, summative, diagnostic and standardised. Although there may be overlap among them – standardised assessment may be summative, for instance – I discuss one type at a time.

Formative assessment[7]

Formative assessment is done to find out what children know while a topic is being taught, when feedback can be given or the teaching can be modified. If you are teaching drama, for example, and groups of children are planning drama presentations for their peers, you might assess each child's contribution to the group discussions. If you notice a child who is not cooperating or communicating with peers, you can discuss the situation either with the child or with the group to see if the student can participate more fully in the drama being prepared by the group. Such assessment is quite specific because you are both identifying particular strengths that children are demonstrating in a curriculum subject as well as spotting areas for potential improvement or a change of teaching approach.

Formative assessment is like the assessment a football manager makes during a game that leads to an adjustment in tactics or a substitution, as distinct from the post-match analysis that occurs when the game is over. Formative assessment happens at a time when the child or teacher can still take steps to improve the child's learning experience.

Formative assessment may be done through various activities such as posing oral questions to individuals or the class, giving all children an informal 'check-up' quiz on a topic, setting a task that requires children to apply what they have learned, or seeking children's written responses to a prompt. Prompts I have used include 'What do you know about . . . ?', What questions do you still have about . . . ?', and 'What else would you like to learn about . . . ?'. Because formative assessment occurs prior to or during the teaching of a topic, you can adjust the content or the teaching method as necessary.

Summative assessment

Summative assessment, on the other hand, is assessment that happens after a topic has been taught or when a term's work in a subject has been completed. Although it will vary from subject to subject, this kind of assessment often takes the form of a written test or a performance. Children may be asked to write a story in the first language of the school or in a second language, or to read a passage and respond to some questions based on the passage to test their comprehension. In more practical subjects, like physical education, children may have to create a gymnastics sequence or demonstrate some throwing and catching skills. These assessment results are usually communicated directly to the children themselves and sometimes to their parents through the school report.

An important element of summative assessment is the written record of the assessment. When children complete a written assessment – write an essay, complete a test, solve a problem and so on – written, tangible evidence of the work can be used as a record of the assessment. In assessments that are not written, you may decide to create some record of children's performances. This may take the form of a photograph or video (with student, parental and school consent if children's faces are recorded) or a checklist.

Checklists

You may use a checklist to record the assessment of children's performances in an area such as creating a gymnastics sequence. The checklist may contain a list of children's names on one side of a page and some criteria along the top, which the children are told about in advance. As each child or each group of children performs their sequence, you could assess the sequence for balance, weight transfer, travelling and fluency. The teacher may assess each aspect of the performance along a suitable scale, such as 'fair' to 'excellent'.

Rubrics

A rubric is usually a table or a grid that communicates to children what a teacher is looking for when checking an assessment and what constitutes excellent, very good, good and fair in assessed work. When a teacher uses a rubric, giving feedback to children is easier. A rubric also makes it possible for children to assess themselves.[8] Imagine you set a task in music for groups of three or four children in a senior primary school class to arrange and perform for their classmates a song with which they are familiar. You might assess the performance of the song using a rubric such as the one in Table 6.1.

TABLE 6.1 Sample rubric for group task of arranging a familiar song and performing it for classmates

	Excellent	*Very good*	*Good*	*Fair*
Awareness and control of pulse (beat) and tempo (speed or pace)	Tempo chosen was aligned with the mood of the music throughout the piece and maintained constantly — may include deliberate variation for expressive effect	Selected tempo was aligned with the mood of the music and maintained throughout the piece	Made an effort to align the tempo with the mood of the music, but was not consistent throughout the piece (e.g. speeding up)	Tempo not obviously matched to the mood of the music and/ or tended to vary throughout the piece
Awareness and control of pitch (high and low sounds)	Melody is produced accurately and in tune without accompaniment	Melody is produced accurately and in tune with accompaniment	Melody is accurate but may exhibit some hesitation, even with support	Song is not pitched accurately *or* Song melody contains several inaccuracies
Awareness and control of dynamics (loud/soft), phrasing and expression suited to the words and mood of the song	Aesthetically pleasing performance of the song as a result of attending to dynamics, phrasing and expression relative to the words and mood of the song	Obvious implementing of decisions around dynamics, phrasing and expression related to the words and mood of the song	Some evidence of attending to dynamics, phrasing and expression to suit the words and mood of the song	Little evidence of use of varying dynamics, phrasing or expression to suit the words and mood of the song

Source: Terms and explanations adapted from Government of Ireland (1999).

A rubric can be adapted in different ways. It may have more or fewer columns for classifying levels of performance, or it may have more or fewer rows for identifying dimensions of performance, and each cell may have more or less detail. The columns may have different headings such as expert, skilled, capable, novice.

But regardless of the level of detail included, it takes time to develop and apply such rubrics. Therefore rubrics may have limited application in your teaching, at least in your first couple of years or when you are teaching a full class. They may be more practical in a learning support or resource teaching situation where fewer children are present at one time. However, even with a whole class you may occasionally find it a useful tool for assessment. Many rubrics are available online and some may be adaptable for use in your setting for a particular assessment.

A rubric can provide rich detail about performance, but summative assessment is often associated with a simple percentage mark or a mark out of ten. Although awarding a numerical mark to children for work done is widespread today, the practice only dates from the late eighteenth century.[9] Providing written feedback to children on their work is more beneficial for children than giving a mark.[10] Nevertheless, awarding percentages and grades to children for work done is so widespread at all levels of education today that it is difficult to imagine an education system that did not test children using numbers.

Interpreting test results

Despite the ubiquity of marks, it can be difficult to interpret a particular mark on a class test. In one classroom or in one subject 65 per cent may be the highest mark and in another classroom or another subject it may be the lowest. The percentage mark may be more meaningful for a parent if they are told what the highest and lowest marks in the class are.

Alternatively, they could be given the mean (sum of all the marks in the subject divided by the number of children who took the test) or the median (the middle mark when the marks are listed from lowest to highest) or both. The advantage of the median over the mean is that some exceptionally high or exceptionally low marks can distort the mean.

Norm-referenced tests and criterion-referenced tests

However, many educators object in principle to using tests because so many of them are norm-referenced. That means that they only make sense when a given mark is compared to the marks of other test-takers. The idea of ranking children by performance on the test is inherent in such tests. Critics dislike them because they believe that tests encourage schools to shift their focus from educating children for life to being test preparation centres.[11]

Criterion-referenced tests differ from norm-referenced tests in that they are based on certain criteria, usually related to the curriculum, and they set out to check if children can or cannot show that they have mastery of a particular skill or concept. An example of a criterion-referenced test is the driving test. In order to pass it, a candidate must demonstrate competence in specific aspects of driving and knowledge of rules of the road. A learner's task is to meet specific criteria and not to achieve the same score as someone else of the same age; the learner's performance is considered in its own right and is not ranked or compared to others.

Observation as assessment

Observation is a potentially less formal kind of assessment. But consistently recording casual observations of children is no trivial matter. A format for doing so and a focus for observation are necessary; specific time needs to be set aside for the activity. Now and again, a teacher may set some independent work for the children and take time to observe how they go about completing it. Who seeks further clarification about what is required? Who has the materials they need when they need them? Who begins working immediately? Who takes a long time to get started? Who applies themselves well throughout the lesson? Who is easily distracted by, or distracts, others? Who independently consults reference sources such as dictionaries and atlases? Who works well in a group? Who prefers working alone?

Some of what is observed can be recorded in writing for future reference. The focus here is more on how children work rather than on what they do. You might formally observe children just for a short time once every three weeks. A teacher will notice other actions and interactions from time to time. It might be a child asking an intelligent question, or a child who is constantly spending time away from their desk, or a child who complains about another child, or a child who shows passion or knowledge for an area of schoolwork. Making a note of such observations when they happen or at the end of the day can help you build up a rounded picture of a child during the year.

Records of assessment

Things happen so quickly in school from a teacher's point of view that from one day to the next it is very easy to forget things. Written records can counteract the risk of forgetting pertinent observations and incidents relating to individual children (Box 6.1). Furthermore, so much happens in a class that many things remain unseen by the teacher. It is incredibly easy for you to miss things that are going on in the classroom in front of you.[12] Knowing that you will take some time, even just five minutes, at the end of the school day to record such observations, helps to heighten your awareness of what is happening.

When I teach maths lessons, I make notes at the end of class about what I observe. This is something I cannot do immediately when the children leave the classroom. I either need to note it on the spot when something happens – which is often impractical – or I need to take a short break immediately after class has ended before doing so. Only after such a break can I gather my thoughts about things that happened during the day. It always amazes me that this break is needed but I think it is because of the busy, concentrated nature of teaching.

Assessing children by observing them and recording the observations is just one extra teaching task alongside many others. And because it is an extra task, one that doesn't have to be done in the moment, it is easy for a teacher to overlook it. That is understandable but if it can be done, many anecdotes and incidents can be garnered that will provide a parent with a concrete sense of how their child is getting on. Along with other assessment information, it helps the teacher create a rounded picture of each child.

Box 6.1 A note on storing notes

Notes may be kept on a card and stored on a card file; a notebook may be kept with a page for each student; notes may be kept electronically using a word-processing document or a package such as Evernote. Such notes need to be stored carefully, especially when they contain information that is sensitive. When creating the notes, sensitive information may be entered using a code, using children's initials or using a language other than the language of the school. A notebook may be stored in a locked press and a laptop or electronic file can be protected using a password. Because they are so portable, USB keys can easily go missing and information stored on them may be vulnerable.

Communicating test results to parents

Looking at a child's performance allows you to identify strengths a child has and areas the child can work on. Whether a child is struggling, excelling or somewhere in between, a variety of assessment information provides you with broad knowledge about the child so that you can convey to parents a vivid, detailed description of how their child is doing in each subject and how the child can make further progress.

Although communicating with parents encompasses more than reporting to them about their child's performance on tests, interpreting children's test results for parents is an important part of what a teacher does for parents and guardians at parent–teacher meetings. Such interpretation is important because a percentage mark on its own provides little useful information. Parents need to know what a given mark means relative to what the curriculum expects children to be able to do, relative to peers in the class and relative to children of the same age nationally.

If the mark is representative of the child's competence, parents can be told that. However, a child's performance on a summative assessment on a particular day might not be representative for several reasons. Perhaps the test was too long and some children didn't have time to attempt every question. Responses that were written may not do justice to what some children know, especially children who have dyslexia or other specific learning difficulties or who have minority language status. Some ethnic minority children may lack cultural knowledge that is required to answer questions in summative tests.

Diagnostic assessment

Another kind of assessment is diagnostic. I experienced the potential of diagnostic assessment recently when I took some swimming lessons. I was taught by two different swimming teachers. For many weeks one teacher asked me to repeatedly practise my freestyle stroke and each time her comment was the same: 'Your ankle is too rigid. You need to point your toes towards the wall, not towards the floor'. This was her response every time I swam even though I was trying but obviously failing to do what she advised.

Then one week a substitute teacher, with a very different approach, took the class. The new teacher took a broader view of my swimming and showed me how I was wasting effort with my arms by not following through with the stroke, she showed me that I was holding my breath until just before inhaling which was unnatural and slowing me down, she noticed that not only were my toes not pointing at the wall, but that I was bending my knees too much and not kicking from my hips as I should be.

Both of these teachers could swim and both of them could give instructions. But what made the second teacher helpful to me was the way in which she could look at my performance on a task, break it into steps and identify where the problems were. Like other acts of teaching, assessing diagnostically highlights the difference between being competent at a task yourself and being able to break down that task to analyse the competence of another. Although a primary teacher is working with many more students than my swimming teacher was, the principle is similar.

A diagnostic test is one you give a child to find out what is blocking the child's optimal performance. Suppose, for example, you notice that a child has answered several subtraction word problems incorrectly, many reasons could account for the errors. Maybe the child cannot read the subtraction word problem. Perhaps the child can read the problem but does not know that subtraction is required. It could be that the child is unable to lay out the numbers symbolically on the page. The child might be unable to subtract any numbers or the problem may be specific to numbers that require renaming. The child may be unaware of equivalent representations of a number – that 53 can be written as five tens and three units or as four tens and thirteen units (i.e. $53 = 4\,T + 13\,U$), for example.

In order to identify the source of the child's errors you could give the child a test that would help surface each of the possible difficulties and see which ones apply to the specific student at a specific time (see Figure 6.1). The test you give might have calculations written out both as number problems and as word problems. You could give some problems that require renaming and some that do not. Some problems could require the child to provide equivalent representations for various numbers. You could set some problems that are laid out horizontally and some that are laid out vertically. You could even give part of the test orally. This would help you identify where any misunderstandings lie and ascertain the extent to which other children share the difficulties. You can then plan a programme of work to help the relevant children avoid such errors.

Sometimes diagnostic information can be gleaned by studying a child's performance on regular work given to the class. You can look closely at the child's answers and see what patterns of errors exist. Which questions does the child get right and which are wrong? On other occasions you could give a child a specific diagnostic test, say if you had concerns about how a child is getting on and wanted to find out what the child knows and what the child does not know.

A learning support or resource teacher will often carry out a diagnostic test using commercially available diagnostic tests, especially if a child has performed poorly on a standardised test. Learning support teachers have

Laura has 135 books. Sarah has 19 books fewer than Laura. How many books has Sarah?

Mark had £758 in savings. He spent £125. How much savings had he left?

```
  1 3 5
-   1 9
```

```
  £ 7 5 8
- £ 1 2 5
```

135 = 1 hundred, 3 tens and 5 units = 1 hundred □ tens and 15 units = 13 tens and □ units = 10 tens and □ units

$4 3 5 - 1 2 3 = $ ___

```
  4 3 5
- 1 2 3
```

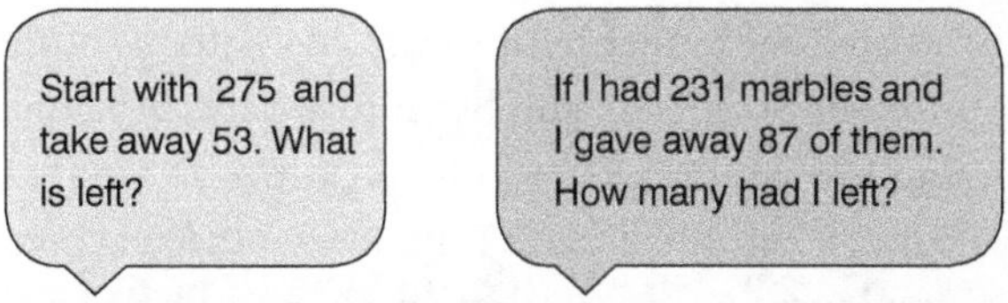

Start with 275 and take away 53. What is left?

If I had 231 marbles and I gave away 87 of them. How many had I left?

Figure 6.1 Diagnosing difficulties in understanding subtraction

access to tests that classroom teachers don't use. An educational psychologist can recommend diagnostic tests that can be used, such as the Basic Number Diagnostic Test and the Neale Analysis of Reading Ability.[13] In exceptional cases, an educational psychologist may be asked to administer a diagnostic test where a child seems to have a specific learning disability.

Referring a student to an educational psychologist

Referring a child to an external specialist such as an educational psychologist or a speech and language therapist – either privately or through a public educational psychological service – is an important decision for a teacher to make. On one hand, they are scarce and expensive resources and some parents may be concerned if their son or daughter is recommended for such a consultation. On the other hand, in many cases children derive greatest benefit the earlier such an intervention is made.

Your school may have protocols for such a referral which involve the headteacher or the Special Education Needs and Disabilities Coordinator or a similar post-holder depending on the supports available to you where you are teaching. In general, a number of steps need to be followed before recommending that a psychologist or speech and language therapist be asked to assess a child. You need to have some evidence that a child has learning difficulties across several topics in one or more subject areas. If that is the case, you could first check if the difficulties can be explained by factors such as unsatisfied physical health needs, safety needs, belonging needs or esteem needs.[14] A child who is hungry, tired or caught up in a troubled relationship at home is unlikely to perform well in school.

You could then inform the principal of your concern to find out if the principal or a colleague knows anything about the child's circumstances of which you are unaware, including the existence of a report from either a psychologist or a speech and language therapist. If no prior knowledge or report exists, you could meet with the child's parents, outline the concern, provide any relevant evidence and listen to what the parents have to say.

Conducting a meeting where you recommend a referral of a child to an external agency can be difficult for a beginning teacher, especially if the parents are previously unaware of any problems. The first time I had to do this I worried beforehand that the parents might blame me for the child's problems. They did not, of course, and most parents appreciate receiving concrete information about their child; they realise that the teacher too wants what is best for their child.

It is only natural, however, that a parent may be anxious, upset or apprehensive on receiving a recommendation to seek specialist advice for their son or daughter. Most principal teachers are happy to sit in on such meetings if asked. They can provide further information for the parents or answer any questions you may be unable to answer.

A practical concern for parents may be how to go about getting a psychological or a speech and language assessment. Waiting lists may be long and costs may be high, creating a barrier for some parents. Nevertheless, when received, expert reports should be able to diagnose the specific difficulties a child has and identify steps that can be taken to remediate the difficulties. A psychologist or a speech and language therapist will typically request a report from the teacher about how the child behaves and performs in class and in the school playground. Information from various kinds of continuous assessment is helpful when preparing such a report.

Standardised tests

Standardised tests are administered in many schools. They are designed so that children's performances on the test in one school can be compared to the general performance on the test of children of the same age or in the same class level around the country. When a standardised test is being developed, the questions are given to a large representative sample of children of the same age or class level. Test developers can then estimate where an individual child's performance stands compared to the performance of other children of the same age on the test. The test developers can then estimate standard scores and percentiles for children.

Standard score

A standard score is the score a child of average ability in the subject being tested is expected to achieve and it is typically set at 100. Most children's standard scores will be between 85 and 115. In order to find out a student's standard score, the teacher takes the raw score – the number of questions the student answered correctly – and uses a table to convert the raw score to a standard score.

STEN score

A second score often talked about is the STEN score. STEN (coined from the words standard and ten) scores are related to the standard scores and are presented on a scale from 1 to 10. One way of calculating them is to take the full range of standard scores (e.g. 60 to 140) and divide the range of possible scores into ten equal segments[15] and order them from 1 (lowest) to 10 (highest), and identifying the segment in which an individual standard score falls.

The score offers an impartial and comparative estimate of a child's performance on a test on a particular day. As an estimate of a child's achievement, the STEN score may be the most helpful and understandable score for parents. However, a STEN score makes most sense when it's complemented by other evidence of a child's achievement in that subject and across the curriculum.

Percentile

The other score calculated for each child based on their performance on the test is the percentile score. If a child's estimated percentile score is 25, that means that the child scored as well as or better than 25 per cent of the population of children at the child's age or class level in the test; or if the percentile score is 80, the child scored as well as or better than 80 per cent of their class or age population on the test.

The percentile is calculated based on a large sample of children who took the test when it was being developed. However, percentile scores don't consistently reflect similar gaps in children's performance across the spectrum of achievement. In other words, some children with the same percentile score may have different standard scores.[16]

Limitations of standardised tests

Although there is some benefit in knowing how children in your class performed on the test compared to other children of a similar age or class level, it is important to know the limitations of standardised tests. Some people – including teachers, parents and policymakers – treat them as if they are an end in themselves. They're not. Standardised tests are simply one indicator of how a student is getting on. They are typically only available for some subjects – language and mathematics usually, and occasionally science. That limits their usefulness because if teachers believe that only what is assessed on a standardised test matters, every other subject on the curriculum is devalued somewhat.[17]

The second limitation is that even in the subjects that are tested, only a few questions from each topic can be selected for the test. These questions are expected to represent a range of competences but the questions asked by no means assess all the content or skills children are expected to learn in a topic. If a test purports to test mathematics, only one or two questions are taken from each topic and the child's performance on the topic is estimated based on the answers to those sample questions. Subsequently the child's performance in a whole subject area – reading or mathematics, say – is extrapolated from the student's performance on the chosen sample questions.

Third, the test is limited by the kind of questions that can be asked. An essential skill to master when learning English reading comprehension is to summarise a passage of text. A standardised test is unlikely to test such an activity because it would be difficult to score the answer in a standardised way. Instead, the test will ask a proxy question, a question that tries to measure how well a student would have summarised the text if it could have been done in the test. The proxy question may or may not be a good way to estimate the child's ability to summarise.

Tests may also be timed. Even if no specific time is set, children become tired after a while or the exigencies of the school day (break times etc.) impose an effective time limit on the test. Such time limits place an additional constraint on children's performance. The bottom line is that a result on a standardised test is not an end in itself; it is only an indicator of how a child is getting on in limited sections of a limited range of school subjects.

Despite the limitations of standardised tests, sometimes schools are required to submit test results to a central department or agency. The motivation for doing this can vary. Its effect is to make the tests more 'high stakes'. This means that there are perceived potential consequences to having children in your school perform poorly on the tests. Unlike state exams, which are high stakes for an individual child, compiled standardised test results may have high stakes for the school. School principals may worry that if children in the school perform poorly on the tests, the school will be considered to be 'poorly performing' or ineffective. If a school's results were ever to be published, some parents could decide to move their children to a school where children achieved better results.

However, many legitimate reasons might explain a school's poor overall performance – such as having a high proportion of children whose first language is not the language of the school, or serving children in an area traditionally associated with disadvantage. Regardless of such legitimate reasons, no school wants to look bad when their results are compared to the results of other schools. This leads to the risk that teachers may begin to view standardised test results as an end in themselves. In response, teachers could be tempted to narrow the curriculum they teach. They could allocate additional teaching time to subjects that will be tested and reduce the time given to subjects that are not tested.

Within the subjects that will be tested, teachers may be tempted to prepare children to answer the kind of questions that appear on the test rather than focusing on wider learning objectives for the subject. So, to take my earlier example, children might not be asked to summarise passages of text in class but may instead be given practice answering questions to indicate how they might summarise texts so that they are prepared to answer the type of question that can be asked in the test. That is how a standardised test can narrow the curriculum. Given the importance for children of a broad, balanced education, narrowing the curriculum is best avoided.

Ethics of preparing children for tests

Where high-stakes tests exist, teachers are faced with ethical dilemmas. To what extent should children be prepared for a test? Clearly it is unacceptable to tell children questions that will be asked or to prepare children to answer specific questions that will be on the test. Telling children answers to questions when they are doing the test is similarly wrong.

The appropriateness of other ways of preparing children for a test may be more ambiguous. If the teacher knows that questions on a standardised test are in a cloze format, is it acceptable to prepare children for questions using that format? Or if the teacher knows that a passage on the test is on the topic of air travel, is it ethical to have children read books or articles about planes and airports before children do the test? One way to answer this question is to differentiate between 'teaching to the test' and 'teaching for the test.'

Teaching to a specific test is teaching children to answer items from a test or items similar to those on a test[18] and is unacceptable. Teaching for the test is 'teaching that prepares children to demonstrate their acquired knowledge of a broadly defined subject domain on multiple types of external assessments conducted by others beyond the individual classroom teacher'.[19] In other words, a subject should be taught in a broad way so that children could do well on any kind of assessment, irrespective of who sets or administers the test. That is acceptable because children are being prepared for taking various types of tests and not just ones that have been seen by or created by the teacher.

In other countries where high-stakes testing is in place, some responses to high-stakes test results have been more damaging than narrowing the curriculum. Some teachers have been tempted to prepare children explicitly for tests by providing study guides to children based on the test content.[20] In other situations instruction has been targeted towards children who are most likely to boost a school's overall results at the expense of children who are sure to pass and those who are most likely to fail.[21] Other teachers were found to have changed children's responses to test questions.[22] In other cases extra time was given, visual aids such as multiplication tables were displayed on walls during tests, and children were given help while doing tests.[23]

Such cheating and unethical practices have no place in education. It narrows what children learn, it deprives individual children of accurate information on their attainment, and it distorts the overall picture of results within a school. In every occupation there are opportunities to cheat; sport has drug using and match fixing; business has 'creative' accounting and insider trading.

In a profession such as teaching, which generally enjoys a high level of trust among the population,[24] ethical standards must be upheld. Even where standardised test results are valued by the system, the best response you can have is to work hard to provide education that is broad, well-rounded and of the best possible quality for the children you teach.

In summary, standardised tests can be used to track the effects of policy but they are not an end in themselves. For example, if policymakers wanted to be satisfied that a policy initiative to boost literacy was working, most people would have 'no problem looking at some assessments and seeing how well do kids do'. But it is important too to look at 'broader indicators' of change such as 'are people reading more …? That would tell … a lot about a society where books are valued more and where it's important to read'.[25]

International tests

International tests such as Trends in Measurement in Maths and Science (TIMMS) and the Programme for International Student Assessment (PISA) receive media coverage when the results are announced. Their design is similar to national standardised tests except that the goal is to compare the performance of students across countries.

Unless your school is chosen as a test school in a given year, they won't have too much of an impact on you personally. However, they can have implications at the system level. Politically, the results may be used to insti- gate policy change[26] and therefore it is at a policy level that the international test results tend to be noticed rather than directly in your own class.

Disappointing test results

It can easily happen that you may be disappointed with the test results achieved by a class – either on a class test or a standardised test. Many reasons can account for why children perform poorly on a test: they may have little experience of doing tests and may not plan their time well or they may not perform well under test conditions; perhaps their knowledge at the start of the year was below where it should be for their class level; the school may serve an area traditionally associated with disadvantage, which could impact on children's test results; several children in the class may not be native speak- ers of the language of instruction in the school; perhaps the teaching approach used or previous teaching approaches didn't help children learn; possibly the children didn't see the test as important; maybe the test was administered at a time of the day when the children were tired. Performance on a test is worth discussing with the children as well; their insights may be useful.

Analysing test results

Analysing a set of results after a test is neither a pressing task for a teacher nor one for which teachers have substantial preparation. Yet, taking some time to write a few sentences – with descriptions, hypotheses and questions – about results in a test may be worthwhile. A sample analysis of a set of results is produced in Tables 6.2–6.4 and Box 6.2.

TABLE 6.2 STEN scores received by students in a hypothetical primary school class in a standardised test

Student	Sten score
Anna	1
Barry	4
Claire	10
David	3
Ethna	10
Fiona	7
Grace	7
Hilda	6
Ivan	5
Jack	6
Kai	8
Laura	6
Mark	8
Nora	8
Oliver	6
Patrick	7
Quentin	6
Rebecca	7
Sarah	5
Teresa	7
Una	4
Vicky	6
William	8
Adam	2
Maya	7
Conor	4
Delia	2

TABLE 6.3 STEN scores organised according to the number of students in each category

STEN score	Number of students	STEN score	Number of students
10	2	5	2
9	0	4	3
8	4	3	1
7	6	2	2
6	6	1	1

TABLE 6.4 One way to interpret STEN scores

STEN score range	Descriptor	Fraction of students
8–10	Well above average	Top one-sixth
7	High average	One-sixth
5–6	Average	Middle one-third
4	Low average	One-sixth
1–3	Well below average	Bottom one-sixth

Source: Adapted from National Council for Curriculum and Assessment (2007, p. 63).

Box 6.2 Sample analysis of class scores on a standardised test

In this set of results the STEN scores range from 1 to 10, with most students (16) concentrated in the range of scores from 6 to 8. The number of students who received STEN scores of 4 or less was below the number that would be predicted (7 students in the class in contrast to the 9 students predicted) whereas the number of students who received a STEN score of 7 or higher was higher than predicted (12 students in the class in contrast to the 9 students predicted). This generally above-average score is consistent with what might be expected in a class where most parents value good achievement in school and convey to their children a desire for the children to do well in school.

STEN scores from the previous testing period are not available but it would be interesting to check whether students' scores were generally similar or higher or lower than when tested on previous occasions.

(Continued)

(Continued)

Only the results of Jack and Vicky caused some surprise to me. Based on their performance on other assessments and my monitoring of their work, I would have expected Jack to have received a higher score, and Vicky received a score that was higher than I expected. Jack missed some time during the year and this may have adversely affected his performance on the test.

Table 6.2 does not provide data on students' performance across domains of the subject. This would be helpful in indicating aspects of the subject on which students performed well or poorly during the year and would help inform how topics might be approached next year.

Anna, who received a STEN score of 1, has not been diagnosed with having a learning difficulty that would affect her performance in the subject, though this performance is consistent with what I have observed in my time teaching her to date. Raising this matter with her parents will be a priority and one that will be done in person rather than in the end-of-year school report. Some kind of additional support for her would be helpful to enhance her future performance in the subject.

Adam receives a lot of support from home, but has been diagnosed with a specific learning difficulty and this condition may be affecting his performance in this subject area as in others.

Delia's mother indicated that she herself found school difficult and that she didn't perform well in school. As a result, she is unable to help the student at home. This information needs to be conveyed to next year's teacher so that in-school support can be given to help her break out from what may be a family cycle of learning difficulty.

Although some factors affecting poor test performance are beyond the teacher's control, steps may be taken to improve performance in subsequent tests – steps that will be helpful to the children generally in life as well as on the tests. Children can be taught strategies to help them perform better in tests. For example, in a reading test children can be encouraged to preview and survey text and they can be encouraged to formulate a question about text before reading it. Other strategies include picturing what they read, reading more slowly than usual, re-reading text they do not understand, and taking notes as they read.[27] The priority for teachers is to maintain focus on educating children for life rather than for a specific test.

Spelling tests

Teachers in many classrooms administer a weekly spelling test to children. However, weekly spelling tests are of little value. Teachers will have frequently observed children getting full marks in their weekly spelling test only to misspell the same words in their independent writing shortly afterwards. One review of research in this area[28] concluded that the Friday spelling test contributes little and that it may even hinder children from learning words because it encourages them to commit words to their short-term memory rather than to their long-term memory where they are needed. In short, the *kind* of spelling errors a student makes matters more than the number of errors made in a test.

Self-assessment

Self-assessment by children is another aspect of assessment. As stated earlier, a rubric shared with children offers them a chance to self-assess. Most children can tell what they know and can do and what they do not know and cannot do. If they are given an opportunity to express that, they will do so.

I taught in one school where children were asked to self-assess as part of their school reports. Children were asked to self-assess by making affective judgements – about their behaviour, their effort and their interest in their work. In most cases the children were harsher in their assessment of themselves than I would have been.

Self-assessment should work well for more cognitive judgements too, but the statements need to be specific. Possible questions that could be used are to ask if it is true or false that 'I can name three geographical features formed by erosion' or 'I can retell a story about weather that was told to me by a parent, grandparent or neighbour'. This kind of assessment is good in itself and it complements other forms of assessment.

Sourcing and creating tests

Sourcing tests is another task to be faced by a beginning teacher. Some commercial textbook series include tests with the series and these are worth evaluating for their suitability for your class. Teacher-designed tests are also possible. They can be geared specifically towards the children in your class and towards the work you have done in a subject.

In any test it is important to assess the children's development of skills as well as their knowledge of content. For example, in mathematics, you don't just want the children to know how to multiply; you want to know if they can estimate the answer to a multiplication problem, if they can solve a multiplication word problem and if they can explain to others why their answer is correct.

Matching a test to your intention

Sometimes you will have to create a test for children and before doing so you need to be clear about what you want to find out. If it's an end-of-term test, you might want to ask questions from the full term's work but if it's a test after you've completed a particular topic, the questions may be more specific. You need to think about whether you are testing children's thinking processes – such as reasoning, communicating, problem solving, questioning and predicting – or their recollection of procedures and specific content. Typically there will be a combination of both, and the test questions need to reflect that.

For example, if you want to find out if children know which mathematical operation to select in order to solve a problem, there is no point in giving them questions in the form '36 × 42 = ___' because the format of the question tells them that multiplication is required. On the other hand, if you want to know if children have mastered the procedure of multiplying two two-digit numbers, such questions would be fine.

Having decided which aspect of children's knowledge you want to assess, you need to design questions that will help you do that. If you want to find out about children's mathematical knowledge, the questions need to test their mathematical knowledge and not something else. For example, if you give a multiple choice question and ask the following question, you might expect the children to multiply 4,236 by 3:

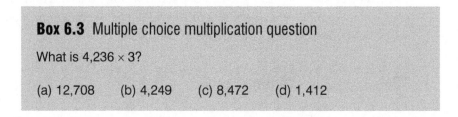

Box 6.3 Multiple choice multiplication question

What is 4,236 × 3?

(a) 12,708   (b) 4,249   (c) 8,472   (d) 1,412

However, at least some children will figure out that the answer is (a) by seeing that none of the other answers could possibly make sense because they are too small or because none of them has the digit 8 in the units place. This would be an example of a child using 'test-taking strategies' to answer a question, rather than using the mathematical knowledge the child was expected to use. Similarly, a question to test mathematics should not be couched in complicated language which could affect the mathematical performance of someone who finds reading difficult.

Question formats and types

It is good to vary the format of questions used in a written test so that children gain experience of responding to questions in various formats outside a test before they encounter the format in a test. Thus children may experience completion questions, multiple-choice questions, cloze-procedure questions, true–false questions, matching questions, short-answer questions and essay questions.

Possible types of question include: asking children to explain how they got an answer to a mathematics question; presenting an answer to a question and asking the children what the question might be; punctuating a paragraph that has no punctuation; looking at some completed answers to questions – correct and incorrect – and either confirming that the answer is correct or alternatively providing a/the correct answer.

Children could summarise a paragraph, or compare alternative summaries and say which one is better and why. A question could be asked orally by the teacher and the answer could be given orally or in writing. Children could order objects or events by size, by date or by some other criterion. Ask children to write all they know about a particular topic.

Each type of question will test different aspects of the children's knowledge, and a variety of question types may keep the children's attention. More importantly, a well-designed test will give children of different attainment levels a chance to succeed because it will have some questions that every student can attempt with some success.

The quality of test questions

Questions on a test are usually selected from a wide range of questions that could have been asked. Although teachers hope that the questions are representative of the full extent of what children should know, the particular selection of questions may have boosted some children's scores and lowered the scores of others.

The wording of a question on a written paper may be inaccurate or open to misinterpretation. For example, a teacher I know gave her class a test

Draw a line under the second word:

Ellen jumped over the puddle.

Figure 6.2 Misinterpreting the question

that included the instruction to 'Draw a line under the second word'. The teacher showed me a response by one six-year-old who had drawn a picture of a lion under the second word (Figure 6.2); the child got the sense of the question right by selecting the second word, but got it wrong by not knowing the difference between the spelling of line and lion. If similar instances occurred of getting answers wrong for the wrong reason, it could distort a child's result and this should be explained to parents.

On the other hand, a child's performance on a summative assessment may be better than expected based on the child's general competence in the subject. This may be because the assessment proved motivational for the child; or the set of questions chosen for the assessment favoured the child; or the child may have copied answers from another child. When it comes to providing a context in which children's summative assessment results can be understood, it is helpful to view them alongside a range of assessments conducted during the year.

Test-marking criteria

No matter what kind of questions you choose to ask, children need to know the marking criteria. This is not the same as telling them the answer. It is about communicating why a particular question is asked. You could say, for example:

If on the test you are given an answer and asked to provide the question, I want to know if you understand the material well enough to ask a question. There might be more than one possible solution, but if your one makes sense, you will get the marks.

By being explicit about marking criteria, the children learn to see the relationship between what they learn and how it is assessed. It helps them to learn about learning and about communicating what they have learned.

Wording questions

Some technical aspects of creating a test also need to be considered. The wording of questions in a test needs to be clear and unambiguous. For example, the question 'When did the D-Day landings take place?' could be answered correctly as '1944' on '6 June' or 'during World War II'. A more precise question would be 'In what year did the D-Day landings take place?'. That question is closed and invites a short, specific answer. It provides little information of value about what the child learned, but the question is easily corrected by the teacher or by another child.

In contrast, an open question might ask, 'What events followed the D-Day landings in World War II?'. This question permits a range of possible answers, some that may not even have been discussed in class. Marking such a question makes demands on a teacher's knowledge of history, if a child is aware of facts the teacher has not yet encountered. That provides an opportunity for a child to be asked to substantiate their knowledge or to justify a claim.

As a teacher you will learn a lot about test design from giving a test. Children will respond with answers you never thought possible. Given how difficult it is to come up with good questions and the time it takes to create a marking scheme for it, it might be useful to begin developing a bank of test questions that you build up over time and draw on when necessary. Perhaps such questions and possible answers could be exchanged with other teachers so that you learn from each other. Having a bank of questions and possible answers will make it easier to create subsequent tests.

Test papers

The layout of questions should be clear and easy for children to follow. A sans-serif font is easier for children with reading difficulties to read. You need to decide if children will answer questions on the test paper itself or on a separate page. Easier questions can be asked early in the paper to provide confidence to children before they attempt more challenging questions.

The more I've been involved with testing and assessment at various levels in education, the more I have come to appreciate the importance of reading a test paper several times before copying it for distribution to the children. I have frequently found spelling errors and grammatical errors in questions. It is helpful to ask a colleague to read over a test paper because someone who is new to it may spot problems you have overlooked.

Test administration

When you administer a test in class – whether it is a test you design yourself or a standardised test – some children will take the test very seriously and may even get anxious about it. Although it is no harm for children in senior primary classes to do a test in a relatively formal environment, you do not want children to worry about their performance in a test at such a young age.

Children will often take their cue from the teacher about how anxious they should feel. The main message to give children is that they should try their best when they are doing the test and not think too much more about it after that. They can be told that the test might indicate some things that they still have to learn and that they have plenty of time to do that.

Children often make great efforts to ensure that other children cannot copy their answers. Preventing copying of answers matters more if answers are relatively short and specific than if the questions are open-ended or personal. Usually guidelines for standardised tests recommend taking steps to prevent children copying each other's work.

Some children will inevitably finish a test before others; it is good to have a quiet activity for them to do when they finish, so that other children can complete the test in silence. When all children have finished, it is good to give the children something active to do and it is good if it coincides with a break time so that they can let off steam.

Tests are given in some subjects more than others. Children quickly learn in school that what is tested is what matters, even if they enjoy more the subjects that are rarely tested. Assessing children in a subject is a way to show that you value a subject. The kind of assessment will vary from subject to subject. In some subjects, such as the arts, assessment by portfolio or by performance is best. Again, it is good to know and communicate what criteria matter for such assessments.

Group assessments

In some subjects, groups rather than individuals may be assessed. Children could be asked to collaborate with others to complete a task.

Collaborating with other people on solving a problem or creating something is a much valued skill in the workplace. Lots of projects can only be accomplished if participants work as a team. Because of the competitive nature of state exams, schools may undervalue the importance of teamwork. However, children's achievement is raised when both group goals and individual accountability are built into group work.[29] Although children can be passive in a group for many reasons, they tend to be more participative in small group than in whole-class interactions.[30] Assessing and reporting on how well a child performs as part of a team contributes to a rounded assessment of the children.

Summary

A teacher could spend lots of time in the classroom assessing and not teaching. One union representative parodied this by comparing it to a farmer he knew who continually counted his cattle in the hope that the number in the herd would increase. However, in many cases assessment is integrated with teaching and happens at the same time: portfolios and performance for instance. Nevertheless, it is occasionally worthwhile to step back from the class and observe what is happening, making notes about individual children, either during such observations or at the end of the school day. Formal tests will usually take place at the end of a unit of work, at the end of the term or the end of the year, and they will mostly be in senior classes.

Assessment informs teaching. It can provide good information about how a child has performed in various areas of work. However, sometimes we expect too much of assessment and believe it can predict how a child will perform in the future. That is not the case and in many areas of life from selecting footballers to selecting teachers, no test can definitively predict future success.[31]

Although tests are only one part of assessment, they receive more attention than other assessment types. Yet, the expression that is often used in relation to the stock market applies too to test scores: 'values may fall as well as rise'. Such a warning should prevent us from reading too much into test results and prevent us from being concerned or complacent about children's performance on any one test. Above all, the limitations of tests remind us of the benefits of taking a broad view of assessment.

Key points of Chapter 6

1 Knowledge of assessment allows you to make judgements about children's work so that you can provide them with useful feedback and ways to assess their own work.

2 Formative assessment can take several forms and can be used to adjust teaching to promote better learning.

3 Summative assessment may take the form of tests or performances and outcomes may be recorded using checklists, rubrics and observation records.

4 A core teaching skill is to diagnose where a learner is having difficulty in learning what is being taught.

5 When used with other forms of assessment, standardised tests provide useful information but they have important limitations.

6 Self-assessment by children constitutes an important component of the suite of assessments used with a class.

7 Designing teacher-made tests requires thought and effort to ensure questions are clear, formats are varied and the test assesses what you want to assess.

Notes

1 See for example https://www.gov.uk/getting-an-mot or http://www.nct.ie/.

2 See Hattie & Timperley (2007) where the four levels of feedback are referred to as feedback about the task, feedback about the processing of the task, feedback about self-regulation and feedback about the self as a person.

3 Fact confirmed at http://treecouncil.ie/tree-advice/native-species/

4 This kind of feedback is known as self-regulation. See Butler & Winne (1995) for more.

5 Crocker (2003) identified these traits as being desirable in teachers.

6 *The Mismeasure of Man* (Gould, 1981, 1996) is a good introduction to the history of assessment. Newspaper articles and other media provide a perspective on political aspects of assessment and accountability.

7 This is sometimes known as 'Assessment for Learning'. See for example http://www.ncca.ie/en/Curriculum_and_Assessment/Post-Primary_Education/Junior_Cycle/Assessment_for_Learning_AfL_/.

8 Jonsson & Svingby (2007).

9 The initiative has been credited to a Cambridge examination moderator William Farish in 1792 (Hoskin, 1979), even though Stray questions the veracity of Hoskin's account (Stray, 2005).

10 Hattie & Timperley (2007).

11 See Kohn (2000) as an example.

12 This video by Daniel J. Simons illustrates this point very well: http://www.youtube.com/watch?v=IGQmdoK_ZfY.

13 See, for example, http://www.gmsen.co.uk/fileuploads/targets/assessment/general/AssessmenttoolsLONDONWANDSWORTH.doc, Department of Education and Science (2007).

14 Department of Education and Science (2007).

15 However, the first and tenth segment may be slightly wider than the other segments because of small numbers of extreme low and high scores.

16 This applies especially to children who have very high or very low scores.

17 For one fuller discussion of this in the Irish context, see Ó Breacháin & O'Toole (2013).

18 Popham (2001).

19 Crocker (2003, p. 9).

20 Although this may happen in many countries, examples from the United States receive substantial media coverage in English and thus are relatively easy to find. See, for example, http://www.washingtonpost.com/local/dc-elementary-school-teacher-reportedly-gave-students-illicit-help-on-standardized-test/2014/05/14/d5b66724-dbae-11e3-bda1-9b46b2066796_story.html.

21 For more on this see Booher-Jennings (2006).

22 See, for example, http://edition.cnn.com/2014/05/09/justice/philadelphia-school-cheating/.

23 From Wright (2009).

24 One survey conducted in the Republic of Ireland found that 68 per cent of 1,000 respondents considered teachers to be trusted or very trusted and only 11 per cent said they were not trusted or not at all trusted: http://www.teachingcouncil.ie/en/Publications/Research/Documents/Evaluation-of-Public-Attitudes-to-the-Teaching-Profession-Summary-of-Findings.pdf.

25 Listen to the full interview with Professor Jim Spillane from Northwestern University at http://insideeducation.podbean.com/2012/04/30/programme-137-jim-spillane-on-leadership-policy-and-change-in-education-29-4-12/.

26 For example, in Ireland the PISA results in 2011 were the catalyst for introducing a national strategy to improve literacy and numeracy (Department of Education and Skills, 2011) and analyses of the TIMMS results have led to

recommendations for minor changes to the Irish mathematics curriculum (http://www.erc.ie/documents/pt2011_context_report.pdf (p. 174)).

27 Wright (2009).

28 See Culligan (2009) for this review. Culligan's earlier book is another helpful resource for teaching spelling (Culligan, 1997).

29 Slavin (1991).

30 Mulryan (1992).

31 Gladwell (2008).

References

Booher-Jennings, J. (2006). Rationing education in an era of accountability. *The Phi Delta Kappan, 87*(10), 756–761.

Butler, D. L. & Winne, P. H. (1995). Feedback and self-regulated learning: A theoretical synthesis. *Review of Educational Research, 65*(3), 245–281.

Crocker, L. (2003). Teaching for the test: Validity, fairness, and moral action. *Educational Measurement: Issues and Practice, 22*(3), 5–11.

Culligan, B. (1997) *Improving children's spelling: A guide for teachers and parents.* Published by the author.

Culligan, B. (2009) *Spelling and handwriting.* Published by the author.

Department of Education and Science. (2007). *Special educational needs: A continuum of support.* Dublin: The Stationery Office.

Department of Education and Skills. (2011). *Literacy and numeracy for learning and life: The national strategy to improve literacy and numeracy among children and young people 2011–2020.* Dublin: Department of Education and Skills.

Gladwell, M. (2008). Most likely to succeed: How do we hire when we can't tell who's right for the job? *The New Yorker, 84,* 36–42.

Gould, S. J. (1981, 1996). *The mismeasure of man.* New York: W. W. Norton & Company.

Government of Ireland. (1999). *Music: Arts education (teacher guidelines).* Dublin: The Stationery Office.

Hattie, J. & Timperley, H. (2007). The power of feedback. *Review of Educational Research, 77*(1), 81–112.

Hoskin, K. (1979). The examination, disciplinary power and rational schooling. *History of Education, 8*(2), 135–146.

Jonsson, A. & Svingby, G. (2007). The use of scoring rubrics: Reliability, validity, and educational consequences. *Educational Research Review, 2,* 130–144.

Kohn, A. (2000). Burnt at the high stakes. *Journal of Teacher Education, 51,* 315–327.

Mulryan, C. (1992). Student passivity during cooperative small groups in mathematics. *The Journal of Educational Research, 85*(5), 261–273.

National Council for Curriculum and Assessment. (2007). *Assessment in the primary school curriculum: Guidelines for schools.* Dublin: Author.

Ó Breacháin, A. & O'Toole, L. (2013). Pedagogy or politics?: Cyclical trends in literacy and numeracy in Ireland and beyond. *Irish Educational Studies, 32*(4), 401–419.

Popham, W. J. (2001). Teaching to the test? *Educational Leadership, 58*(6), 16-20.

Slavin, R. E. (1991). Synthesis of research on cooperative learning. *Educational Leadership, 48*(5), 71–81.

Stray, C. (2005). From oral to written examinations: Cambridge, Oxford and Dublin 1700–1914. *History of Universities, 20*(2), 76–130.

Wright, R. J. (2009). Methods for improving test scores: The good, the bad, and the ugly. *Kappa Delta Pi Record, 45*(3), 116–121.

7
Communicating with parents and guardians about teaching[1]

Why teachers feel vulnerable

Parents and teachers contribute in different ways to children's education; therefore, communications between parents and teachers form an important part of a teacher's work. Indeed, parental involvement in children's education more generally appears to be related positively to children's academic achievement.[2] This chapter is about successfully communicating with parents at individual parent-teacher meetings, at group meetings of parents, and through school reports. But first I explain why beginning teachers often feel vulnerable when they meet with parents.

A teacher's job is never done. Rarely does a teacher enjoy the satisfaction of a finished product, a deadline met, or a project completed ahead of schedule. You can always do more to advance the children's education. As a teacher, your best work is always ahead of you. You have never enough time to do all you want to do for the children in your class. The unfinished nature of teaching can lead to professional vulnerability or insecurity; it goes with the job.

That may surprise a casual observer because at work the teacher has the demeanour of a queen bee. Often the teacher is the only adult in a room of 30 children who appear to follow the teacher's every request; sometimes they even seek permission to go to the toilet. If another adult – a teaching assistant or a special needs assistant – is present, the teacher still has a leading role. It seems that the teacher decides what happens, how it happens and when it happens. Although teachers have considerable professional autonomy, ambiguity or self-doubt can accompany the choices they make.

Should you spend discretionary time before and after class checking children's work, preparing a chart for an upcoming lesson, or trying to locate a poem that would relate well to the topic you're teaching? Would it be better to prepare an activity sheet for the children, to research a topic to be taught in geography, or to use time to source equipment for a science experiment? You are constantly making trade-offs. Teachers don't talk about it much but that realisation is always present.

Entrants to teaching tend to set high standards for themselves. Teachers are often high achievers and they want their students to achieve highly. They hope they can succeed in helping every child do well in school. Then they encounter factors they hadn't anticipated. Time is limited. The work is exhausting. Not all children apply themselves like the teacher did as a student. Not everybody is motivated to learn. Many children are not suited to being cooped up in a confined space for several hours a day. Not all children have the support of a loving family.

So what sustains teachers? The connection with children; teachers work with young children at a wonderful time in the children's lives. The children have a sense of wonder. They are mostly optimistic about the future. They are curious about the world and they want to learn more about it. From day to day, teachers put aside their insecurities and their doubts and they devote their energies to doing their best for the children. Teaching gives little time for teachers to dwell on their doubts and motives. The work is full-on. From the start of the year, from the start of the week, from the start of the day, teachers are propelled by the energy of the children, the impetus of the curriculum and the demands of the work; little time exists to dwell on omissions or shortcomings.

When teachers meet with parents or other adults, the pace and focus of the work change. In meetings about children, parents remind teachers of their insecurities. Parents don't intentionally do this. In fact, parents are teachers' allies. They have common goals: to do their best to help the children to be happy and successful in life. Teachers learn much by engaging with parents.

Parents share knowledge about their children that informs your work. You may hear about conditions a child has that affects their progress in school. Parents may inform you about family circumstances that impact on a child's attention in class. Many parents will let you know if a child is finding it difficult to grasp a concept or taking a long time to do homework.

They will inform you if they believe their child is being excluded or being treated unfairly in the playground. Such information may be shared through notes, phone calls or informal meetings. You always feel you know a child better after you communicate with their parent or guardian.

But as part of their communications with teachers, parents ask questions. Parents complain. Provided it is done in a respectful manner, parents are entitled to question and complain. But when complaints or questions coincide with the teacher's insecurities, they lead to anxiety, especially among beginning teachers. Teachers are taken out of the forward momentum of teaching to think about things they may not have done, not noticed or not thought about.

Teachers need to face their own doubts and insecurities about their work while reassuring parents that they are doing their best to ensure that every child is safe and flourishing in the classroom. On the inside, teachers worry. Am I doing a good enough job? Is this particular child responding well to my approaches? If this parent is unhappy, will the parent talk about me to other parents? Will that affect my reputation in the school? In the locality?

No matter how positive a parent is, the teacher will always focus on the question or the note of criticism. No matter how well several encounters with parents go, if one goes badly, we think about it for longer. That is a common phenomenon[3] that happens in college evaluations and other human interactions. So although teachers value meetings with parents, they approach the meetings with some apprehension.

Remember too that some parents may be nervous about meeting teachers. They worry that if they question or complain to the teacher, the teacher may give their child a more difficult time. Although such a fear is unfounded, it delays some parents asking a question or making a complaint until they believe they have no other option.

Parents may have had a negative experience of school themselves and they may feel uncomfortable asking to meet a teacher informally before or after school. 'The teacher is too busy', or 'My concern is too minor', they may think. Or if they contemplate writing a note, they may be concerned that a teacher will be critical of their poor handwriting or their incorrect spellings.

Communications between parents and teachers are laden with emotions on both sides. That is on top of the usual emotions that arise in any interaction between people where how we communicate is coloured by financial difficulties, relationship matters, joys and successes, illness and bereavement, and worry about or delight for family members. The presence of emotional barriers does not constitute reasons for parents and teachers not to communicate. Indeed they are reasons why communications between parents and teachers are 'the essential conversation'.[4]

Trust in parent-teacher relationships

The basis of relations between teachers and parents needs to be one of trust. Both parties are significant people for the child – the parent is present constantly and the teacher is present as a significant adult for a substantial period at a formative time in the child's life. It is good if the child gets consistent messages from both. Most of the time, this is easy.

Parents make it easy for teachers to trust them by communicating promptly when matters arise, by being courteous and by supporting the child doing homework. Teachers in turn make it easy for parents to trust them by showing interest in and knowledge of each child, by responding thoughtfully to children's work and by listening carefully to what parents say and taking seriously their concerns.

Trust breaks down when one party is concerned about what the other party does or does not do. A parent may worry that a child is learning little with a teacher. They may worry that a teacher is doing nothing to minimise bullying of their child. They may worry that a teacher is treating their child unfairly. They may worry that a teacher is inexperienced, incompetent, or has lost interest in their job.

A teacher may worry that a parent dislikes them or their approach. A teacher may worry that a parent will damage their reputation in a community by complaining about the teacher. At an extreme, a teacher might worry that parents will move their children to another school because they are unhappy with the teaching.

A parent can build trust by offering to help a teacher and by not making additional demands on the teacher; a teacher can build trust by listening to parents' concerns and by taking an extra step to support a child's learning. Trust is enhanced when parents and teachers cooperate.

Some parents may become involved in the school if they have time or skills they can share with the class to support your work. The skills may be in sports, knitting, sewing, art or sign language. They may have time to help out with listening to children reading, transporting children to activities or accompanying children on walks or trails. When parents and teachers spend time together, trust grows between them. The comfortable, trusting rapport between parents and teachers happens more easily in the junior classes when parents often accompany children to and from the school door; as children get older they often desire a clearer boundary between their home and school relationships.[5] As a result, older children may prefer their parents to spend less time in the school.

Informal parent-teacher communication

As a teacher you need to convey to parents that you are approachable and willing to engage formally or informally with them should the need arise. Sometimes we may think we're friendly and approachable but parents may have a different perception. Spending an extra minute at the school door at the end of the day when parents collect their children or making eye contact with parents at home time can make a big difference. Even a smile to parents can convey the message that you are available to talk should it be necessary.

A parent needs to decide which form of communication is most appropriate in a particular situation. A note, e-mail or text message may suffice if the purpose is to inform the teacher that a child will be collected by a grandparent after school or if a child found homework difficult one night. An informal word, face-to-face might work best for a minor matter, like the time a mother of a senior infant student asked me not to say that 'your homework tonight is . . .' because her child was insisting that the homework not be done until it was dark outside, on the grounds that the teacher said it was to be done that *night*.

If the concern is around ongoing difficulties about school work or concerns about relations with classmates a formal meeting or phone call could be scheduled. Teachers vary about when they prefer to meet with parents, before or after school. During the school day is generally not good. When a parent requests a meeting, it's good to reply promptly. Receiving the request in advance gives you time to prepare for the meeting by gathering information about the child before meeting the parents.

From time to time, a child, especially a young child, may bring strange stories home from school. A parent may be puzzled by a report from the classroom that seems strange. Or the child may bring strange stories from home to school. Parents would occasionally blush or bristle if they heard some of the tales teachers hear from home. Sometimes the stories have a grain of truth in them and other times messages are confused.

A parent should be encouraged to contact the teacher to clarify any story that is troubling. In most cases such matters can be resolved with a quick clarification. You should treat most information from home with discretion, unless the information gives reasonable grounds for concern that a child is at risk of abuse or neglect.[6]

Formal parent-teacher meetings

Many schools organise formal parent-teacher meetings once a year. On these occasions teachers meet several parents over a relatively short amount of time and need to convey vivid, individual information about each child to the parents during that time. Attending the meetings can be challenging for some parents because of work commitments or difficulties organising childcare. As mentioned earlier, some parents may be apprehensive about attending the meeting because of unhappy memories of their own school days or out of fear that a teacher will make a judgement about their child or a judgement about them. They may be happy or unhappy with how their child is getting on in your class. One way or another, the formal parent teacher meeting is often loaded with emotions for both teacher and parents.

Those background emotions form the backdrop for you talking to one or two parents or guardians about their child. Your field of vision zooms in from the general vista of a whole class to a specific, individual focus on one child. Detailed and clear knowledge about each child is required. Communications with parents go well when you know the child well and are honest in sharing that knowledge with the parent.

Knowing a child well means both knowing the child as a student, and knowing the child in a rounded, rather than in a narrow, way. Getting to know a child in this way takes time and acuity. A teacher knows a child differently to a parent. A teacher has a different, narrower view of a child than a parent. The teacher's view relates to how the child is learning only in the school setting, whereas the parent has a fuller picture of how the child is learning in many settings.[7]

However, as a teacher you see the child interacting in a social setting to which most parents are not privy. Because you work with many children, you can benchmark the child's achievement, behaviour and personality with the achievement, behaviour and personality of others, both in the child's own class and over time with other children you've taught.

Although incomplete, your perspective on the child as a student and on how the child behaves in the social setting of the classroom provides helpful insights to parents on their child's overall development. You draw on this information to answer a common question from parents, 'How is my child getting on?'. When parents ask this question, they mean different things. Some are really asking if their child is happy in school; others want to know how well the child is doing in some or all subject areas; others want to know how the child is doing relative to other children in the class.

In general I would avoid comparing how a child is doing in relation to other children in the class because the measure has limitations. The group of children in the class may be particularly high-achieving or low-achieving compared to other children of that age so a child who is a relative high achiever in one class may be a relative low achiever in another class. Therefore comparing a child to others in the class has little meaning. It's a bit like how a runner's position in a race is influenced by who else turns up to run the same race.

Furthermore, most of us are average, and describing ourselves as average, above average or below average doesn't tell us very much.[8] And most of us don't like to think of ourselves as average or below average. Parents certainly don't like to think of their children as average and some, at least, may be disappointed if you tell them that their child's performance is average or below average.[9]

Comparing a child to peers may have the effect of either putting undue pressure on a child or of providing a licence for a child to glide. It makes more sense to discuss the progress the child is making relative to the child's own capacity and what can be done to support further progress.

Parents really want to know, 'If you were in my shoes, would you have any concerns about my child?'. Early in their careers many teachers are not parents and may find it difficult to put themselves in the parent's shoes. And yet that question might be a useful one to ask as a way of preparing for a parent–teacher meeting. If you know the child well and succeed in answering that question, the meeting should go well.

Every parent harbours dreams for their child. Parents may be wondering subconsciously if their child is still on track to achieve those dreams. The dreams might be that the child will be some combination of a happy, successful, moral, literate, numerate, accomplished, enterprising, independent citizen who is ready for lifelong learning. Such dreams are compatible with many paths in life. The child must find their own path while parents and teachers do their best to help.

Teachers too have their views on what constitutes success in life. Parents' dreams and teachers' perceptions of success may have an unspoken presence at meetings between parents and teachers. Parents may seek assurance that their child can achieve the goals they have in mind. But teachers are not fortune tellers. The child is still developing in many ways. Many additional factors, luck included, will determine what happens in the future. All the teacher can do now is give an honest appraisal of how the child is in school and what can help the child develop in as rounded a way as possible.

To guide the discussion it is helpful to have tangible information to share with the parent like work samples, test results, feedback from assessments in all subject areas, a description of how the child interacts with peers, and suggestions for what parents or guardians can do to help the child at home. Every parent should receive some sincere, positive comments about their child. Even if a child is disruptive in class, parents need to realise that you know the child well enough to see some of the positive attributes the parents see in their child.

Yet, what you say needs to be more than platitudes. Parents recognise and are not impressed by platitudes; they suggest that you don't know the child very well. One teacher hopes that by the end of the parent–teacher meeting, the parents 'will have learned something about their child that they never knew'. She also hopes parents respond to the teacher's suggestions at the meeting in a way that shows the teacher their confidence in the teacher.[10]

Parents particularly appreciate hearing anecdotes about their child. They may be comments made or questions asked by the child publicly or privately in class, conversations overheard with peers, or other incidents that can enrich the parents' knowledge of their child. Although parents want data about their child, they also want to hear the teacher's overall impression of the child. As Lawrence-Lightfoot puts it,

> When parents hear the teacher capture the child that they know, they feel reassured that their child is visible in her classroom – that the teacher actually sees and knows him or her – and they get the message that she really cares.[11]

Conducting a formal parent-teacher meeting

You have choices to make about the conduct of parent–teacher meetings. Will children attend the meeting with their parent? I have usually given parents the option of doing this and in some cases parents took the option. It was helpful because the child could be included in the conversation from time to time. The child is the only person who has a view of both settings – home and school. Most parents, however, opted not to bring their child with them to the meetings.

When I began teaching, I was advised to begin every meeting by asking the parents, 'Is there anything in particular on your mind that you wanted to bring up at the meeting?'. Most parents would just say, 'No, not really. I was just wondering, how she/he is getting on'. The idea of that opening question was to find out immediately if there was any issue or concern worrying a parent that needed to be addressed and that might influence what would be said subsequently. Some parents dislike such an opening to the meeting; they want to hear first the teacher's assessment of the child's progress. Although I am less inclined now to stick to such an opening for every meeting, as a beginning teacher I found it to be a useful support.

In any parent–teacher meeting, you will draw on your competence in communicating. One aspect of communication is using clear language. Be wary of using terms that are familiar to teachers but may not be familiar to all parents. If such terms need to be used, they should be explained. They include assessment, phonics, learning style, print-rich environment, constructivist, concrete materials and many more. It is also good to avoid or explain abbreviations, many of which are unique to a given education system.[12]

Listening is a major part of communicating. If a parent has a question or something to tell you, it may take them some time to express it clearly. Remember that what the parents are discussing is of great concern to them; it may even be keeping them awake at night. And they believe you can help.

At first the parent should be allowed to outline their concern or question. You need to listen carefully to the parent. Make eye contact and allow the parent or parents to tell their story fully and completely. Help the parent by asking questions to elicit missing facts or to seek clarification as they share their concern.

Having listened to the parent's story, identify the parent's key concerns. Empathise with the concerns. Does the story concur with your perception of the child and the child's progress or the child's social interactions? Perhaps you can add information to what the parents have said. It may be possible to resolve the matter between you. Or perhaps someone else needs to be involved – the child or the principal, for example.

There may be silences during a meeting. One teacher compares this to the 'wait time' that teachers are encouraged to give before calling on a child to answer a question in class.[13] In class it allows children who are slower thinkers to gather their thoughts rather than having the teacher always call on the fast thinkers. Similarly in a parent–teacher meeting, parents may need time to gather their thoughts to reflect on what the teacher is saying. Perceiving the silences as thinking time may help you become more comfortable with those moments.

Some parents will raise matters that you did not expect at the meeting. A parent may question why you teach a topic in a particular way. Explain your thinking to the parent as honestly as you can and try to find out what prompted the question. The parent may have an interest in the area or the child may have reported liking or disliking an approach.

A child may be having a difficult time at home. A child may be having a difficult time in school. A parent may have a query about a school policy that is unfamiliar to you. Such questions provide an opportunity for you to learn about the child or about the school. If necessary, you can tell the parent that you'll get back to them with an answer.

A parent may compare you positively or negatively to a previous teacher. They may say that the child is happier in your class or that the child was happier in a previous class. In both circumstances, this needs to be taken lightly. The questions can be responded to by asking respectively 'What is it that she likes about my approach?' or 'What is it that he liked about the previous teacher's approach?'. Apart from asking such a question, there is little else you can say.

When you have time to reflect on it, you can decide if there is anything you can do differently. Or you may want to follow up with the child, one-to-one, by discussing your approach with them. It is not possible to bring back a previous teacher, so the questions might take the form of 'What did you like about how Ms M_____ taught this last year?' and 'What would help you learn it better this year?'. Sometimes a child may be able to articulate this and sometimes not. It may take some children time to establish a rapport with a new teacher but doing so is a part of learning.

A common question from parents is what they can do to help the child at home. This may be a general question or it may be in response to something you say about the child's behaviour or the child's progress in a particular subject. The question is so common that it is probably worth preparing a sheet to give to parents at the meeting.[14] The sheet could give suggestions of work to be done at home that could complement the work done in school and the sheet could recommend websites the parents could consult. The sheet could give specific advice for supporting the children's learning in every curriculum subject and for support in relation to behaviour or other matters that come up for children such as bullying or homework. It is the kind of sheet that could be developed from year to year.

Many parents will not request such information and will not have time to work on supplementary exercises with their child. Other parents may prefer to spend the limited time they have with their children on activities other than school-related ones.

At a meeting, parents may spill out various worries about their child that are on their mind. Their son has no friends. Their daughter never gets picked for the school team despite being really committed to training. A parent may ask for their child to be moved, to sit elsewhere in the class. A parent may complain about the amount of homework – too little or, more likely, too much. They may say that the previous year's teacher found that the child struggled with some aspect of work and they may request specific information on that aspect of the child's performance this year. In some cases you will need to take time to think about what the parent says and if that is the case, tell the parent so, note it and get back to them at another time.

Difficult parent-teacher meetings

Sometimes, you will need to make a suggestion that a parent will find difficult to accept. For example, you might want to recommend a psychological assessment for a child or suggest that the child would benefit from attending a learning support class. This can be a difficult situation for a teacher early in their career. Your goal is to outline clearly the basis for your recommendation while keeping in mind that a parent may be initially upset on receiving the advice. It is good if the advice is accompanied by a description of some genuine strengths the child displays in school. If possible, such a conversation might be better outside the regular schedule of parent-teacher meetings, where you can take more than the allotted time to talk and listen.

Although often short in duration, parent-teacher meetings are ritual events within our culture. Parents talk to other parents about them; teachers talk to other teachers. Parents and teachers have expectations of what will happen at the meetings based on discussions and based on memories of their own parents' meetings with teachers. In such an atmosphere, conflict between the parent and teacher can occasionally arise.

A parent may ask an apparently routine question but the teacher feels criticised by the question. In most situations, the questions are genuine and not intended to be personal or critical and it is good to give as honest an answer as possible. Or a teacher may make a comment that unintentionally offends the parent. If that happens, it is good to apologise quickly so that a constructive working relationship is maintained between you.

However, like teachers and everyone else, parents can be unreasonable at times. A parent may make a request to which you cannot accede, or a parent may accept a child's account of a classroom event that differs to yours, or a parent may be critical of you in a personal way. In such circumstances, you have to stand your ground. This can be done politely but firmly. It may result in two parties 'agreeing to disagree' or it may need to be referred to the principal. This should happen rarely but if necessary, you may need to be assertive, without being aggressive.

Because each meeting may be assigned a specific time slot, it is easy for meetings to run late and for subsequent meeting times to be delayed. For parents who have to take time off work to attend meetings, it can be inconvenient if they are waiting for long. It is good to think about a way of keeping meetings on time and to schedule for another time any meetings that are anticipated to run for longer than the allocated time. Few schools will have the luxury of a secretary to knock on the door when ten minutes are up. However, a list of names and times on the door, with a welcome note and a request for a parent to knock when their assigned time arrives may help.[15] A clock in the classroom visible to you and the parent might help ensure that you try and keep meetings on time.

Diversity among parents and guardians

Although the setting and preparation for meetings are consistent, every parent is different and their circumstances differ. Some parents have lots of interest, time and capacity to help their children at home, to supplement and complement the work done by the school. Other parents may lack the interest, or time or capacity to do so.

Among the people you will meet are mothers alone, fathers alone, couples together and guardians. Typically the parents live together; sometimes they do not. Some are unemployed, some are employed at a range of jobs, some work fulltime in the home. Some are older than you, others are younger. For some parents the child you are teaching is their first or only child, for other parents, the child you are teaching may have one or several older or younger siblings. Some parents you may know very well outside of school, some you may meet frequently in school and some you may never have met before.

Some may be colleagues. Some come in with a list of questions written down, others are happy for you to do all the talking. Some may be articulate, others faltering; some may be deferential and others demanding. Some may have plenty in common with you, others may have little in common with you. From culture, to language, to beliefs, parents, like children, come from all sections of society.

Given the diversity of people you will meet at your parent-teacher meetings, every meeting will be different. The common thread is that through life's circumstances all the parents have children who are currently taught by you. In the short time available to you, you need to help each parent to receive an honest appraisal of their child with regard to their progress in all aspects of school life. Parents know most aspects of their child better than you and that fact should be acknowledged.[16] The sharing of perspectives on the child should contribute to a constructive relationship between teacher and parents.

Where parents are separated, the meeting can be awkward for you if communication is difficult between the parents. You may not know that the parents are separated. In most cases both parents will be involved in the child's education. However, one parent may be receiving information about the child for the first time at the meeting, possibly information that was already known to the other parent. Only in exceptional circumstances, approved by the school, would separate meetings be offered to each parent.

A particular dynamic applies when a child's parent is also a colleague. In this situation you and the parent have ongoing access to one another at school. Minor questions or misunderstandings can be addressed informally and easily at mutually convenient times. Because a parent-teacher meeting is more formal than the usual chit-chat about a child, you may find the encounter more difficult than the usual exchanges.

Sometimes the colleague-parent will opt to have a spouse or partner attend a meeting instead of attending themselves. The preparation for such a meeting will be similar to those of other parent-teacher meetings. It becomes difficult if the child is struggling in some way. However, because you work alongside one parent, a word with the parent earlier in the year should avoid a situation where what you say surprises the parent. Similarly, you would hope that the colleague will not present you with an unexpected concern or question at the meeting.

When talking about parent-teacher meetings, teachers often say, 'The parents I most want to meet are the ones who don't show up'. That may be the case. However, teachers need to be patient with such parents. Teachers need to recognise that they may have had privileges in their upbringing that are not present for many of the children they are teaching or their parents.

You will encounter many parents who hold different value systems about schooling. If at all possible, it is great if you can reach out with goodwill and flexibility to all parents, even if the approaches are sometimes rejected.

One of the strengths of primary schools is that children come to them from vastly different home environments.

In some homes legal and illegal drugs are abused with consequent impact on the children. Some children describe to their teachers the different partners that their parents have in the home on a regular basis. Some children come from homes where extreme poverty is endemic, possibly because of unemployment, illiteracy or other factors that may have endured for a generation or two. Some parents have criminal records and have been absent from the children's lives due to time spent in prison. Some parents just don't value education – it didn't help them and they do not see how it will be of much help to their child.

For many children school is a refuge from a chaotic and tumultuous home life. Your role is not to judge the parents or their value systems, just to discuss your common concern, the child's education. Knowing about the diverse home environments from which children come to school can enhance how you help children to meet the expectations of the school, especially if school expectations differ from expectations in the home. The more all children can adapt to school the more likely are the children to stay in school for longer, which might just help a child break out of a difficult cycle.

A parent might not want to attend a meeting to hear about the difficulties a child is having with various school subjects or to be told about a chronicle of misbehaviour since the year began. The parent may already be at their wit's end not knowing what to do with the child. By not attending the meeting, a parent avoids such reminders of the child's troubles. A phone call to the parent may be an option. Although the parent needs to hear about all aspects of the child's progress, it would be good if there can be some encouragement for the parent as well.

Another parent may be totally intimidated by the school setting. I remember meeting with one mother who had memories of being in school and everything going over her head. Even though today the woman works hard and holds down a demanding job, which pays a reasonable wage, the mother is barely literate and cannot support her daughter with school work.

More than anything else the mother hoped that her daughter would do well enough at school to go further in the education system than her mother went. But for that mother, stepping into a classroom for a meeting brought back to her memories of the mornings many years before when tables and spellings were unknown, when workbook tasks were unfinished, and maths problems were unsolved. It brought back memories of a teacher's questions and the embarrassment of being unable to answer them. Perhaps a parent like that would welcome a phone call if the parent finds it difficult to visit the school.

Some parents place little value on schooling. They take for granted the education that is provided. Those parents see school as a convenient way to get one child or a few children minded for several hours every day. What the child does there doesn't really concern the parent very much and the parent sees no role for themselves in the children's education. That is the school's job. The parent sees no reason to ever attend a parent–teacher meeting.

However, the parents who cannot or will not attend parent–teacher meetings are in a minority in most schools. For many more parents the barriers for attending may be practical ones of being able to get time off work or having other children minded and such difficulties can usually be resolved with some flexibility on both sides.

School reports

The written analogue of the parent-teacher meeting is the school report. It is less spontaneous and more permanent than the meeting – I still have most of mine from post-primary school. Thanks to online primary school report templates,[17] guidance is available for the kind of feedback you might give parents. For example, you may comment or tick a box under aspects of children's progress such as the following:

■ the child as a learner;
■ the child's social and personal development;
■ the child's learning during the year (organised by curriculum subject);
■ how parents can further support their child's learning;
■ standardised test results (where relevant);
■ comments;
■ attendance;
■ punctuality.

A section for a child's self-assessment can also be included. Some forms refer to the language spoken at home and whether the child has special education needs.

Ticking boxes about a child can be difficult for you and interpreting ticks can be difficult for parents. Take, for example, 'interested in learning', a subheading of the 'child as a learner', (though the same could apply to any subheadings on a report). If you have to choose between options such as 'rarely', 'sometimes', 'most of the time', 'always', what counts as 'interested in learning'? It may indicate a child's application to completing class tasks; it may convey a child's curiosity and a willingness to ask lots of questions in class; it may capture a pattern of sourcing material at home related to topics discussed in class; or it may reflect a desire to help others learn in the class.

Even if there was unanimity among teachers about what constituted 'interested in learning', other factors may influence which box is ticked. Should the teacher consider the child's exhibiting of a trait relative to other children in the class, even if the class in general is high achieving or low achieving? Or should a teacher assess it specifically to each child and consider how well the child is doing now compared to earlier in the year or in a previous year? Should the teacher take into account supports a child receives at home in deciding which box to tick?

The teacher may even think about the effect ticking a given box will have on a child. Ticking 'most of the time' rather than 'sometimes' might encourage a child to show more interest in the future or perhaps a child will be more motivated by receiving a 'sometimes' – a challenge to improve.

If teachers differ in how they understand headings or how they decide to tick a given box, parents too may wonder how to interpret a judgement of 'rarely' or 'always' on a particular row of the report. Furthermore, parents may interpret such judgements differently depending on their background or expectations.

Report cards generally include a section for summative written comments. This is a space for you to place other comments, marks and tick-boxes contained in the report into perspective for the parent. These comments can be difficult to write and they are likely to get most attention from parents. If any information in the rest of the report is not typical of the child's general performance (say a score on a standardised test or a child's behaviour), this is where you can note the disparity or refer to potential mitigating circumstances that applied.

The general comments section invites you to capture your knowledge of a child in a concise, accurate and meaningful way that is encouraging and helpful. It usually includes one or two positive statements about the child's work or effort to date and it may prioritise one or two aspects of work or attitude that needs to be improved or that could benefit from support from home.

I remember how I used to agonise over these comments, trying to phrase them so that they were personal to each child. Many school report phrase banks now exist on the World Wide Web that teachers can use to help them write reports. They may be helpful for teachers in overcoming the writer's block that occurs when writing reports. But if there is a writing block, it may be because you are struggling with various interpretations that can be taken from different comments as noted above. Or it may be that you don't know the child as well as necessary. Or it may be that you need to collect different or additional data about some children in order to sum up their achievements in a meaningful way.

A school report should contain no major negative surprises for a parent. If a child has difficulties in a subject area, or if a child's behaviour has deteriorated, the teacher needs to invite the parent to a meeting before the parent reads about it in a report.

Because a report is a permanent record, it is worth re-reading all completed reports to check for grammatical, spelling or punctuation errors. The report also needs to be written in language that is accessible to the parents reading it. I remember a colleague describing a child as 'perspicacious' in the child's school report. Although any parent would be pleased to know their child exhibited the trait, they shouldn't have to consult the dictionary to know that.

Group meetings with parents and guardians

In addition to one-to-one communications with parents, many teachers invite all parents of the children in their class to a group meeting at the start of each school year. I found these whole-group meetings to be a useful way of introducing myself to the parents and explaining my approaches to teaching various subjects and classroom policies around matters such as classroom management, assessment, marking children's work, homework or technology use. It also allowed me to tell parents that my door was open if they wanted to see me about anything during the year and how to go about setting up a meeting.

My own parents still recall how one of my teachers used to flatter the parents who attended similar meetings she organised many years ago: 'The very fact that you walked out your door this evening to attend this meeting about your child's education conveys a strong message to your child about how much you value their education', she used to say to them. What she said is true because children notice when parents attend meetings in school. The comment also affirmed parents who made the necessary effort to attend the meeting.

In addition to discussing how you approach the teaching of various topics, meeting all parents gives you a chance to inform parents of ways they can complement at home the work that you are doing in class. Here are some examples that you could use. Suggest that parents try and have dinner together with their child at least two or three times a week. Such conversations contribute to children's language and literacy skills because these conversations often involve narrative and explanatory discussions and sophisticated words are often used.[18] Parents can be encouraged to keep track of how their son or daughter is getting on in school work. Suggest that parents ensure that the child has a place to study at home. Parents can also be advised to encourage their child to read.[19]

The meeting also gives parents an opportunity to ask you questions about any aspect of your approach. A note of caution about this: these meetings are different to the individual meetings that are held with one or two parents and questions can only be answered in a general sense, even if a parent asks a question that relates to a particular child. So the question, 'Why do you give so much homework? It took Mary more than two hours to do it this evening', needs to be answered without reference to Mary.

Key points of Chapter 7

1 Convey your approachability to parents and guardians and welcome interactions with them as a way to enhance your teaching.
2 Make parent-teacher meetings constructive by knowing each child well as a student, by listening carefully to what parents/guardians say, by sharing positive information about each child, and by suggesting ways for parents/guardians to support the child's further progress.
3 Be flexible and understanding about parents who cannot or do not attend parent-teacher meetings.
4 Avoid ambiguity or confusion in school reports by collecting a range of data about every child and writing clearly about each child.
5 In group meetings with parents and guardians, avoid making comments about the performance or progress of individual children.

Notes

1 Although this chapter is about communication with parents and guardians, for convenience I usually refer to parents but the term is intended to include both parents and guardians.

2 Fan & Chen (2001).

3 Peeters & Czapinski (1990).

4 Lawrence-Lightfoot (2003).

5 Lawrence-Lightfoot (2003, p. 51).

6 For more information on this topic see http://www.education.ie/en/Schools-Colleges/Information/Child-Protection/cp_procedures_primary_post_primary_2011.pdf.

7 Lawrence-Lightfoot (2003, pp. 193–194).

8 In a comedy film from the 1980s, Arnold Schwarzenegger and Danny DeVito played the roles of 'twins'. Their average height was 1.70 metres, but that tells you little about the height of either – Schwarzenegger is 1.88 m tall and DeVito is 1.52 m tall.

9 In Growing Up in Ireland (2009) it was reported that 60 per cent of parents believed that their child was 'above average' at reading, whereas teachers believed that 39 per cent of children were above average. In mathematics, 52 per cent of parents believed their child was above average, in contrast to 33 per cent of teachers who regarded children as above average.

10 Lawrence-Lightfoot (2003, p. 67).

11 Lawrence-Lightfoot (2003, p. 104).

12 Examples include Ofsted (Office for Standards in Education, Children's Services and Skills), DfE (Department for Education), DENI (Department of Education, Northern Ireland), DES (Department of Education and Skills), NEPS (National Educational Psychological Service), STEM (Science, Technology, Engineering & Mathematics).

13 Lawrence-Lightfoot (2003, p. 28).

14 Some suggestions are given on these webpages: http://merrybeau.edublogs.org/category/re-homework/ and http://seandelaney.com/2011/11/15/how-parents-can-help-their-child-learn-maths/.

15 Based on a suggestion on http://forum.educationposts.ie.

16 An idea expressed in Lawrence-Lightfoot (2003, pp. 89–90).

17 See for example http://www.ncca.ie/primaryreporting or http://det.wa.edu.au/curriculumsupport/reportingtoparents/detcms/navigation/sample-reports/.

18 Snow & Beals (2006).

19 Support for the final three points is contained in Yap & Enoki (1995).

References

Fan, X. & Chen, M. (2001). Parental involvement and students' academic achievement: A meta-analysis. *Educational Psychology Review, 13*(1), 1–22.

Growing Up in Ireland. (2009). *Growing up in Ireland, Key findings: 9-year olds, No. 3, The education of 9-year olds.* Dublin: Economic and Social Research Institute, Trinity College Dublin, Office of the Minister for Children and Youth Affairs.

Lawrence-Lightfoot, S. (2003). *The essential conversation: What parents and teachers can learn from each other.* New York: Random House.

Peeters, G. & Czapinski, J. (1990). Positive-negative asymmetry in evaluations: The distinction between affective and informational negativity effects. *European Review of Social Psychology, 1*(1), 33–60.

Snow, C. E. & Beals, D. E. (2006). Mealtime talk that supports literacy development. *New Directions for Child and Adolescent Development, 2006*(111), 51–66. doi: 10.1002/cd.155

Yap, K. O. & Enoki, D. Y. (1995). In search of the elusive magic bullet: Parental involvement and student outcomes. *The School Community Journal, 5*(2), 97–106.

8

Relating with colleagues when teaching

The people with whom you work influence your learning as a teacher. Navigating these relationships successfully will have a big impact on your workplace experience.

Relating with the principal

Your relationship with the principal colours your experience of working in a school. Whatever kind of school you're teaching in, the principal is the interface for everyone connected with the school – students, parents, teachers, teaching assistants, cleaning and caretaking staff, secretary, the board of management, the Department of Education and others. The school principal has a unique perspective on the educational needs, expectations and interests of these parties and where tensions and disagreements arise, it is usually the principal who tries to resolve the conflict and balance the various interests.

Just like teachers, principals differ in many ways. The principal sets a tone for a school. Often that tone reflects the principal's personality. It may be a frantic, active tone, where the underlying message is to keep busy and where the school moves from one demanding, whole-school event to another. Or the tone may be professional and focused on teachers maximising time in the classroom working with the children in their own class.

The tone may be laid back and good humoured, where the work gets done and no-one takes themselves too seriously. Or the tone may be lax where no-one seems to care much about what happens in the classrooms or in the school building more generally. Although the tone in your school may have some or no elements of those described here, it is one that is usually noticed rather quickly by visitors. But I really only appreciated how tones differ and the difference a tone makes when I moved school, experienced a change of principal or visited different schools.

Some principals are hands-on and want to know what is happening everywhere in the school all the time; others adopt a more laissez-faire approach and want only to know if some matter out of the ordinary arises. Whereas one principal might be direct in conveying wishes and stating clearly and firmly what you as a teacher should do in a given situation, another may take a more indirect approach and make a suggestion in the form of a question, like 'Did you ever consider doing . . .?'. Although the latter approach suggests a greater openness to other ideas, unless a better alternative is available, the best approach is probably to follow the implied suggestion.

Principals, like teachers, differ in other ways, including personality, approachability, competence, interest, helpfulness and motivation. It is good to learn about a principal's working style in order to engage productively with the principal. As with most people, your principal will have some traits you like and some you dislike; it is likely that those traits that irk or charm you have as much to do with you as with the principal.

It is important to learn to work well with your principal but it can be difficult to get to really know a principal. That is because in addition to the principal's actual traits, the principal gains a reputation among other teachers for having a certain style. Although a principal's reputation among colleagues may help you understand the principal, it is good to keep an open mind about the principal. Some of the reputation – positive or negative – may be deserved and true and more of it may be way off the mark. A principal's traits will be revealed over time in the decisions that are made, how they are made, in how matters are handled at staff meetings, and through your own individual encounters with the principal.

You may seek to meet with the principal for many reasons. You may have a question about a child, about teaching or about school expectations in relation to a given matter. A matter may have arisen in your classroom or you may have received information you don't know how to handle. Sometimes a colleague or a mentor may be willing and able to answer such questions and if they are, that's great. Other times, only the principal will do and if the matter is one that will take time to discuss, it can be good to ask the principal to suggest a convenient time to meet.

At other times, the principal will take the initiative to approach you. When you begin teaching, this may just be to check how you're settling in or to provide any necessary support. Over time the principal will want to make you aware of the myriad of policies in the school. The school will likely have written policies to deal with matters such as child protection, bullying, behaviour, health and safety, and assessment. Most principals will remember how overwhelming the first year can be and will try and disseminate school policies on a phased basis.

Other matters may not have written policies but expectations may have built up through custom and practice over many years. Such unwritten conventions may cover matters such as putting on a Christmas play, organising a school tour, responding to children's birthdays, distributing invitations to parties, children staying in the classroom at break times, or having a class party at particular times of the year. Many of these matters arise on a need-to-know basis over the first year in a job.

A principal may ask to see your written preparation at any time. This can be done in a supportive manner, in a routine way, or as a way of checking up on you. Your perception of the motive may be influenced by what you have learned about the principal's reputation. However, a principal is entitled to see such notes and it is probably best to assume that the motive is supportive.

A constructive relationship with the principal is well worth cultivating. At some stage a principal may need to approach you with feedback on your work from a parent. If that feedback is positive, it's easy to receive. But if the feedback is negative, it is good for the principal to know something about you and your approach to teaching in order to be able to share this knowledge of you with the parent. A principal can diffuse criticism directed towards a teacher when the principal has confidence in the teacher and believes in the teacher's general goodwill towards the job. Most principals will support a teacher who acts in good faith.

Nevertheless, sometimes principals receive complaints or queries about something that happened in class. When that happens, the principal needs to listen dispassionately to all sides and gather quality information about the situation. It is essential to be honest with the principal and to provide full, clear and honest information about a given incident as accurately as possible. With such information, even if you are at fault, the principal can put an error in context for a parent. Even when all parties are honest in their accounts, a principal may sometimes have to resolve two conflicting versions of a classroom incident. However, there is no excuse for a teacher to lie to the principal. It erodes trust between you and can create bad feeling that takes a long time to dissipate.

Of course, trust in a working relationship must be created mutually by both teachers and principal acting in a trustworthy way. Open and accurate communication, sharing of information and involving teachers in decision making all contribute to the creation of a trusting environment in which to work.[1] Although many of these actions must originate with the principal, it is good to recognise them when they occur because they cannot be taken for granted in a school or in any workplace.

Relating with teaching colleagues

Although most teaching occurs in classrooms with just one teacher, you will have opportunities to interact with colleagues at various times. You and your teaching colleagues are the most valuable resource available to children in the school and you will learn from them and with them. Your colleagues and you may have diverse perspectives on work and on life. Colleagues can offer support, when needed, personally and professionally. Indeed, with the support of colleagues, other potentially difficult aspects of teaching such as children's misbehaviour or conflict with parents can be mitigated.

Notwithstanding the support that teachers give one another, teachers tend to be parsimonious with praise of one another's work. This may be because we know little about what happens in each other's classrooms or it may be because of a sense of rivalry among colleagues. Whatever the reason, Andy Hargreaves concluded that 'if you want to be appreciated by your colleagues, it's best to get sick, have a baby, retire or die'.[2] Although the Hargreaves comment is made tongue-in-cheek, it has a sense of truth about it for teachers who desire affirmation in their work but who rarely give it to colleagues or receive it from them.

The paucity of feedback may be difficult for you as a beginning teacher. You may wonder if you're doing a good job. Occasional feedback from children, their parents or even from your colleagues may help but it's good to remember that people's perception of good teaching, like beauty, is in the eye of the beholder. I often received positive feedback from parents who were happy that their child was being taught by a *young* teacher. Although I accepted the 'compliment', it had little to do with the quality of my teaching. Try not to be seduced by flattery or stung by criticism; rather evaluate both praise and criticism through your knowledge of your own teaching.

Your teaching colleagues will likely include people who are quiet, out-spoken, energetic, lethargic, focused, distracted, confrontational, appeasing, scientific, artistic, good-humoured, earnest, steadfast, wavering, generous, mean, funny or serious and who can be considered to be initiators or followers. Sometimes the same people will meet several of these descriptors – even the contradictory ones – over a period of time. You can decide which of the boxes can be ticked for you on a given day.

Your colleagues will have varied interests. In larger staffrooms, staff members often group themselves into informal cliques according to such interests or their stage in life or career. Such subgroups could include those interested in sport, young singles, recent and prospective parents, teachers of certain class levels, newspaper readers or current affairs junkies.

How teachers relate to one another has been characterised in four categories: parallel play, adversarial, congenial or collegial. In parallel play everyone does their own thing with minimal interaction among one another. In adversarial relationships teachers may be overtly critical of each other or they may withhold insights about teaching that others could use. Congenial relationships are friendly and helpful but generally refrain from discussing teaching, and participants will certainly not question colleagues' practices. Collegial relationships happen where teachers talk about their work and share successes.[3] Collegial relationships are relatively rare among teachers.

Mostly relationships among teachers are congenial, but sometimes a relationship with one or more colleagues can deteriorate. A problem exists on a staff when you end up talking *about* someone on a topic of importance rather than talking to the person.[4] The principal and senior teachers can try to influence and shape the relationships within a school; a beginning teacher may often do little more than observe it and recognise that other kinds of relationship within a school are possible.

As you become established in a school you will find yourself exhibiting particular characteristics, adopting certain roles, and being drawn to specific groups in the staffroom. Regardless of your identity in school or informal membership of a group, it is desirable to keep on good terms with all colleagues as far as possible. General politeness is one way to maintain healthy relationships on a staff. Despite working closely together, it is good to remember that most people on the staff are acquaintances rather than friends. In other words, relations with most colleagues are more often characterised by friendliness rather than by friendship.[5] You have been chosen as part of a team and you need to do your best to play your part on the team and cooperate with one another as necessary.

But wherever people gather regularly, tensions can arise. In this way, a school workplace is similar to any other workplace. Tensions can arise over petty matters such as someone not paying their contribution for biscuits in the staffroom or around more substantial matters such as disagreements over who was appointed to a position in the school. If such conflict arises between you and a colleague, it is generally healthy to attempt to resolve it soon after it is noticed. Most conflicts can be resolved by approaching the person with whom the conflict exists, naming what you see as the conflict and discussing it. A useful principle to apply in such exchanges is to 'forgive yourself and forgive others'.

More rarely, however, conflicts can endure and even time won't heal them. If that happens, the best you can do is work around them as necessary in the interests of the children and your own sanity. This may include exchanging polite greetings when you meet. If the other person refuses to engage, you can show strength by not allowing someone else to dictate how you act. Sometimes it is necessary metaphorically to bite your tongue and avoid being drawn deeper into the conflict. Instead raise the work matter that needs to be addressed and attempt to deal with that as well as possible.

When tensions arise – petty or substantive, short-term or more enduring – it can be useful to imagine yourself on a balcony looking down, in a detached manner, on the petty behaviour below and to see it from a different perspective. Or you can simply ask yourself, who will give a toss about this matter in a month, a year, a decade, a century from now?

A different perspective on conflict is that it is natural, and neither positive nor negative. Conflict occurs widely in nature where oceans create cliffs, beaches, valleys and caves. When conflict occurs among people, it can be about learning, growing and cooperating rather than about producing a winner and a loser; it can lead to the acknowledgement and appreciation of differences.[6] Granted such an approach may seem difficult to accept when you have been offended, criticised, excluded or undermined. Yet the approach is consistent with the martial art of Aikido, where an attack can be made harmless without injuring the attacker. Thomas Crum has identified six principles that can help one apply such an approach: choose to be centred, accept your connectedness, learn the power of discovery, be willing to understand, be willing to change, and choose to co-create.[7]

Although I mention tensions and conflict, more often than not the atmosphere among staff members in schools tends to be characterised by cordiality and politeness, at least on the surface. This is good insofar as it leads to an atmosphere where teachers can approach one another for support or to discuss various aspects of the job. The flipside of such an environment is that teachers are rarely inclined to question or challenge colleagues[8] about an action or a teaching approach, even where they disapprove of an action or disagree with an approach. If one objects to an action or challenges a colleague, upsetting a staff consensus, one can be seen by others as difficult or contrarian. Shying away from conflict can make it more difficult to bring about change in school. This is not something you can do much about in your early years of teaching, but it is good to be aware of it and to recognise it.

Relating with special needs and classroom assistant colleagues

Although you may rarely work in the same room as a teaching colleague for any substantial length of time, you may work alongside a special needs assistant on an ongoing basis. Such colleagues can be invaluable in assisting with the smooth running of the class. They may know some or most of the children better than you do, at least initially and they may be familiar with the routines of the school. Despite the value of special needs assistants, their work in classrooms varies in terms of what they do and in terms of the responsibilities assigned to them. Your school may have guidelines[9] for such assistants and being familiar with such guidelines is a good starting point for identifying the kind of assistance that will help your class.

The relationship between a teacher and a classroom assistant resembles the relationship between a concert pianist and a page-turner. The page-turner needs to understand and follow the pianist's work, to remain alert and attend to what the pianist is doing, to anticipate what is coming next and to be alert to subtle communications from the pianist. Substitute 'classroom assistant' for 'page-turner' and 'teacher' for 'pianist' and the relationship is similar. Although the page-turner and the classroom assistant both play a vital role, it is the pianist or the teacher who takes overall responsibility for the success of the performance.

As the person with the overall responsibility for the education of all children in the class, you need to plan how the assistant in your class can best support the relevant children. Guidelines for how to work can be discussed with the special needs assistant. Both teacher and assistant can become upset if roles are not clearly defined. The earlier in the school year this can be done, the better.

Guidelines for special needs and classroom assistants may identify the kind of jobs the assistant will do and the jobs that will be done by the teacher, how much help and what kind of help can be given to children working on a given task, who provides feedback to children and how the special needs assistant can support children with special needs while caus-ing minimal disruption to other children in the classroom. Remember that some of the guidelines you prepare for a special needs assistant may differ to those adopted by a previous teacher, and it is important to listen to how the teaching assistant has worked in the past, to reflect on that and to explain why your approach is different if it is different.

Relating with school colleagues who mostly work outside the classroom

Other colleagues outside the classroom will play a prominent role in your working life and it is worth cultivating respectful working relationships with them. Although the role of school secretary can vary, school secretaries play a vital role in the smooth running of school communications. Most secretaries do great work cheerfully and have intimate knowledge of the school. Their job is a difficult one and they must endure constant interrup-tions to their work from phone-calls and personal callers, who may require or demand an immediate response.

The principal, teachers, parents and children frequently shape the workload of the secretary. In any interactions with the secretary, it is good to be mindful of the demands of the position and to be aware that only in exceptional circumstances is it reasonable to ask a secretary to drop a current task in order to do the task you perceive as urgent.

The caretaking/cleaning position in any school is very important. Schools that are not regularly and thoroughly cleaned quickly become unpleasant places to work in. Litter builds. Dust clings. Food rots. Grime spreads. Smells linger. Visitors notice. And effort is needed to restore a safe and pleasant workplace.

The work of cleaning staff is made easier when papers are removed from the floor and chairs are stacked as agreed. Asking children to tidy the class-room before they leave at the end of the day cultivates good working habits in the children and helps them see that rooms don't just tidy themselves.

One principal I know said that on taking on the position of head in a school serving an area of social and economic disadvantage, she wanted to ensure that the school was always bright, warm and clean. In cooperation with the entire school community, the cleaning and caretaking staff in a school help create such a welcoming environment that provides an attrac-tive backdrop for learning and teaching.

Key points of Chapter 8

1 Recognise the key role a principal has in setting the tone or atmosphere of a school and work to create a constructive, trusting relationship with the principal.

2 Although conflicts with teaching colleagues can arise, most such relationships are characterised by congeniality, which falls short of collegiality.

3 You may work closely with a special needs assistant and guidelines for how you work together should be established early in the school year.

4 Know about the work demands of secretarial and cleaning staff and see how your respective roles intersect.

Notes

1 Moye, Henkin & Egley (2005).

2 Hargreaves (2001, p. 523).

3 Barth (2006).

4 This comment was made by Rob Evans in a discussion with me. The discussion in which the comment was made can be listened to or downloaded here: http://insideeducation.podbean.com/e/programme-220-rob-evans-on-teacher-congeniality-collegiality-3-6-15/.

5 See for example Hargreaves (2001).

6 Crum (1987, 1988, p. 49).

7 Crum (1987, 1988).

8 Hargreaves (2001).

9 Guidelines for duties related to the role of special needs assistants are contained in the appendix of DES Circular 30/2014 (http://www.education.ie/en/Circulars-and-Forms/Active-Circulars/cl0030_2014.pdf).

References

Barth, R. S. (2006). Improving relationships within the schoolhouse. *Educational Leadership, 63*(6), 8–13.

Crum, T. (1987, 1988). *The magic of conflict: Turning a life of work into a work of art.* New York: Touchstone (Simon & Schuster).

Hargreaves, A. (2001). The emotional geographies of teachers' relations with colleagues. *International Journal of Educational Research, 35*, 503–527.

Moye, M. J., Henkin, A. B. & Egley, R. J. (2005). Teacher–principal relationships: Exploring linkages between empowerment and interpersonal trust. *Journal of Educational Administration, 43*(3), 260–277.

9

Integrating life, teaching and learning

Teaching takes time

Teaching and learning happen in time and over time. The blocks of teaching in a school day are punctuated by breaks. A topic that begins as a trickle on a Monday can have matured by Friday. The seasons and school holidays provide stepping stones around which teaching flows. Material is organised in timetable slots and units of work. A class of children work and grow with one another and with the teacher over the course of a year. Anything worth learning takes time. But how long? The time needed may vary from teacher to teacher and from child to child.

I always wanted to spend long enough on a topic for most children to get a good grasp of it but not so long that they were getting bored working on the same topic. A weekly time allocation is recommended for each subject but the feeling of curriculum overload – trying to teach an adequate range of topics in the full range of subjects in the limited time available – is real. As a beginning teacher, it takes time to get used to the ebbs and flows of the day, the term, the year and of the children and their learning.

Children can learn a lot in a single lesson or a single day. Many can memorise facts and poems, for example, quite quickly. Other forms of learning, like problem solving, subject/discipline-specific thinking, subject appreciation, working autonomously, and reasoning, happen more slowly, at each student's pace. Such capacities develop over time, and as a teacher you need to keep an eye on what children are learning in the short term and in the longer term. One day's teaching blends into the next, and it is over a year that a teacher's impact on children's learning is experienced. Sometimes a teacher's job satisfaction can come from the attainment of a short-term goal, but many of the achievements of teaching – for example, developing 'an appreciation and enjoyment of aesthetic activities' or 'developing a founda-tion for healthy living'[1] – happen over time, and a teacher must learn to wait.

Teachers need patience

Waiting for children to become fluent readers and writers, to develop a love of reading and so on may be why many people say that teachers need to be patient, and it's true. In a world that is enamoured with instant response, immediate results, constant deadlines and instant gratification, teaching and learning happen at a different pace. No matter what pressures of time are on a teacher, children need time to think, to savour, to investigate, to reflect and to pause. That takes patience.

A second kind of patience needed by teachers is to be able to react calmly to difficult situations: when a child fails to grasp a difficult idea after several attempts; or when children keep talking after being asked to work in silence; or when children make disparaging remarks about your clothes, your hair, your mannerisms or some other aspect of your person or appear-ance; or when a parent has taken issue with something you said to their son or daughter the previous day; or a colleague comments that none of the class you taught last year knows something they should have learned when in your class; or when the principal is planning for the following year and asks you to teach a class level you don't want to teach. Such situations may require you to take a deep breath and respond in a cool, composed, patient manner, even though your spontaneous response might be one of frustra-tion, annoyance, embarrassment, disappointment, hurt or anger.

And teachers need a third kind of patience. It is the patience you need to have with yourself. Teaching is a job that takes time to learn. No matter how good your initial teacher preparation programme is, it can never pre-pare you for the full range of predicaments, dilemmas, opportunities and problems you'll encounter in the classroom. Even after several years in the job, you'll still be learning. By acknowledging and accepting the trajectory of learning you're on, you can understand, manage and savour the journey on which you are about to embark.

Mind yourself

'Mind yourself' is a useful piece of advice for a beginning teacher. You need to look out for yourself, not in a selfish way but in a way that ensures you will last the pace. By nature, most teachers are conscientious about their responsibilities, interested in their work and dedicated to the development of the children they teach. But sometimes such characteristics can make you dissatisfied with your best efforts, or pressurise you into working unreasonably long hours, or convince you that the job is not for you. The gap between what you want to do and what you're able to do for and with the children may lead you to feeling stressed. Or after a couple of years you may feel that you are burned out – exhausted with little left to give.

For people who have never taught, or who have taught for only a short time, it is difficult to explain the toll that teaching and its responsibilities take on a person physically and mentally. Non-teachers may look in envy at the short school days and the long holidays but these features hide the demands on a person of teaching day in, day out over several years. The ongoing and intense emotional interactions of teaching leave you shattered at the end of each day. As well as the need to recover for the next day, you may have material to prepare or children's work to correct.

Despite the tiredness and the tensions, for many people teaching remains a most rewarding endeavour. Little can compensate for the breakthroughs you make with children who suddenly realise they have mastered something they couldn't do a short time ago, or for the enthusiastic welcome you get from a cheerful child on a dark, cold morning, or for the parent who writes an appreciative note about how you handled a difficult situation involving their son or daughter. But still, you must look after yourself.

Obstacles to minding yourself may be general or personal. Let's think of some general threats first. Although teachers are widely respected in some countries, collective morale can be affected by matters such as salary freezes or cuts, deterioration in conditions of employment, additional paperwork or increased class sizes. Alternatively, teachers or their unions may be criticised in the media. The criticism may be directed towards only a handful of teachers. Yet general public criticism of the profession affects teacher morale generally. Such barbs take little heed of the consistent commitment and sacrifices made by countless individual teachers whose efforts go beyond what is expected or required. It is easy to suggest ignoring critical remarks, but most of us won't.

In addition to trying to maintain a sunny disposition, teachers need to mind their physical health. Damage to the voice is a common occupational hazard for teachers.[2] Learning how to use your voice well can reduce the risk of damaging this key instrument of teaching. In addition, materials associated with teaching may trigger allergic reactions in some teachers. It is worth identifying allergies you may have to chalk, whiteboard markers, polish, air freshener or the like and taking steps to minimise their impact on your health. When you notice general or personal threats to your wellbeing, you can take steps to look after yourself. Staying healthy through lifestyle choices, diet, exercise, yoga, meditation and so on may help to set you up for years of healthy teaching and enable you to develop and refine your personal teaching style.

Minding yourself is not something you have to do alone. It is good to inform yourself about supports that are available and to draw on them as necessary. Possible sources of support include family, colleagues, a union, an induction service or employee assistance schemes.

Developing your teaching style

When I began teaching I modelled different aspects of what I did on teachers who taught me in school, at times even adopting some of their mannerisms. I tried to be as strict as Fr Dunphy. I wanted to be as caring as Sr Maria. I wanted my notes to be as apparently thorough as Miss Condon's were. I tried to quote lines of poetry like Mr Lyne had quoted them for us. I tried to remain calm amid chaos in the way that was modelled by Miss Church. But eventually, the mimicry dropped away as I began to integrate into myself all I learned about teaching, taking inspiration and ideas from anywhere I could get them. I am still refining how I teach. I have learned from many people in different ways – through reading, observation, discussion and analysis.

Over time our teaching style develops. Sometimes people talk about the key to genuine teaching as 'being yourself'. However, that phrase gives the impression that everyone teaches in their own way or that 'anything goes' in teaching. Although a personal style in teaching is important, it needs to be developed after fundamental practices have been acquired and established. Teaching is no more about 'just doing what feels right' than engineering, plumbing, nursing or policing are. Yes, it is true that sometimes you have to make a judgement call among several competing options but such judgements need to be informed by tradition, experience, knowledge and reflection.

Pam Grossman provides an analogy for how a teacher develops style and creativity in the work. She says that beginning teachers need to have mastered foundational practices of teaching but that in time these basic practices can be improvised upon. She compares this to culinary education where every apprentice chef must learn how to sauté. There are many ways to sauté and each chef will develop a signature approach to doing so, building on a basic skill that is mastered by every trainee chef. Similarly jazz musicians improvise their playing when they have mastered the basics.[3]

Initially your teaching style may be eclectic, though over time it is likely to become more personal to you. But how do you sustain interest in your teaching in order to take the time that is necessary to develop your own style? Your job is to inspire children but first as a teacher you must yourself be inspired.

Being inspired and inspiring children

Inspiration for a teacher may come from anywhere: it may be a person, an idea, a feeling, an artefact or a spark that guides and influences our work. Such inspiration may come from spiritual or worldly sources, such as family, an interest in or commitment to equality, justice, community, religious faith, the arts, sports and so on.

Sometimes teachers draw inspiration from the schools in which they teach. Most of my teaching was in schools that were relatively young (less than five years in existence when I began working there) and I felt inspired by the energy of like-minded people working towards a similar goal and the countless opportunities to innovate offered by such fledgling schools.

Some teachers are inspired by the arts – visual arts, theatre and drama, music, literature – and by seeing children perform and create. Artists respond to life in a myriad of ways and can enrich it through generating memories, images, characters or situations that help us see life differently. Introducing works of art to children for the first time is a privilege. I remember the parents of a girl I taught asking me for the name of a piece of music I played for the class – *The Moldau* by Smetana – because the girl liked it so much she wanted a recording of it as a birthday present. Inspiring children to create art in any medium is another aspect of teaching that is rewarding for many teachers. Given basic techniques and a suitable stimulus in fiction, the visual arts, music or drama, children can produce wonderful work which brings pride to them and to their parents.

Many teachers I know are inspired by the work they do in sports with children. They train children, prepare teams for league matches, travel to venues to play. Participation in sports from an early age helps children develop their physical skills, strength and fitness. Participation in team sports is great for building children's character as they experience collective effort and learn to deal with triumphs and defeats as well as delights and disappointments. Many teachers organise leagues for children in various sports at local level and beyond.

Others are inspired by opportunities to promote cultural and language activities. Those teachers bring second languages to life by performing plays in the classroom, entering language competitions and attending every professional development opportunity they can in the area. They are passionate about a subject and they go way beyond the call of duty to share that passion with children. Passion in any curriculum area is a great resource for teaching. Children sense the teacher's passion for the sport or for the language and they are inspired by it. The teacher opens up a world for the children beyond the one they have experienced to date. The children will forever remember that teacher for their interest in sports or language. The interest could be in other areas from computer coding to chess and from drama to poetry.

I think of a teacher in one school who taught the children in his class how to play a musical instrument. At least one boy in the class was so enthused by the lessons that he signed up for advanced lessons after school. He subsequently joined music groups and began to learn other musical instruments. He made several new friends through his involvement in music. He went on to represent his local area in music competitions and in turn got other members of his family involved in playing music. A substantial amount of the family's time is now spent in music-related activities – all because of one inspirational teacher.

Versions of that story are replicated in many schools year in year out. A good question to ask as you start out in teaching is: how you would like children to remember you? It might take a few years' experience before you are ready to inspire such passion, but you can do it.

In a job like teaching where so many members of the profession have talent for sports, acting, music, dancing, art, writing and language, it is easy for the rest of us to believe that we have nothing special to share with children. Many teachers are generalists and they do an excellent job introducing children to the vast range of human knowledge – in the disciplines, in the creative arts and in sports. Developing children's ability to think clearly and to act creatively is a passion too, and doing so enriches children's lives. It may be less visible immediately than the ceremony that goes with participation and achievements in sports and music but its value is immense. Furthermore, a lack of special talents does not preclude the cultivation of other interests.

Many teachers develop interests in areas like local history, gardening, knitting, chess, storytelling and languages, and such interests are valuable in themselves. Furthermore, skills in such areas can easily be shared with children. One environmental educator I know,[4] had his interest in flora and fauna awakened by a curious teacher who used a book or two in the classroom to identify and learn, with his students, the names and details of plants and birds that were observed in the local area. Such interests can be cultivated at any stage of your career and as well as enriching your own life, they can be shared with the children. Children can be inspired in different ways, and the fruits of inspiration may not be visible for many years. That is part of the mystery and the promise of teaching.

Opportunities to develop interests outside school may vary at different stages of your career. In your first year or two you might find that you are exhausted at the end of each day and much of your time is taken up correcting work and planning. Furthermore, demands on your time outside school will vary over the course of a career, as life unfolds through relationships, children, career opportunities, professional development, life crises, illnesses, and deaths of family members. Nevertheless, although a teaching day is intense, the part of it involving contact with children is relatively short compared to other jobs; this may provide some flexibility as to when you prepare the next day's work or engage in personal and professional development. In short, the benefits to be reaped from developing interests outside work are many and they can pay dividends both in teaching and in life.

When inspiration fades

Despite the inspiration and encouragement teachers receive from children, from the curriculum and from outside interests, there are times when teaching can become mundane or even tedious. This is one way that teaching as a career differs from school placement, or teaching a model lesson, or teaching that is short-term or observed for probationary or other purposes. In real-world teaching one day can merge into another, and the future can seem like an interminable path through a largely similar landscape. In that regard, teaching is not unique as a career. Even when you embark on a career with enthusiasm and anticipation, over time the work can become monotonous or routine.

Robert Pirsig noticed that and reflected on how people can make what is potentially tedious work more interesting:

[I]f he takes whatever dull job he's stuck with – and they are all sooner or later dull – and, just to keep himself amused, starts to look for options of Quality, and secretly pursues these options, just for their own sake, thus making an art out of what he is doing, he's likely to discover that he becomes a much more interesting person and much less of an object to the people around him because his Quality decisions change *him* too. And not only the job and him, but others too because the Quality tends to fan out like waves. The Quality job he didn't think anyone was going to see *is* seen, and the person who sees it feels a little better because of it, and is likely to pass that feeling on to others, and in that way the Quality tends to keep on going.[5]

Pirsig acknowledges that all jobs become dull in time. Teaching is similar to other jobs in that way. But Pirsig proposes a path by which to overcome the dullness. It is one that can be followed by an individual teacher regardless of whether or not the principal or colleagues cooperate with it, support it or even notice it. It also promises benefits to the children and to the profession more generally. Since I first read this passage, I have observed people in all walks of life who try to put quality into their work at the supermarket checkout, at the theatre, in insurance companies and in customer care offices. And others do notice.

A teacher can seek enlightenment and put quality into the work in many ways. It could be by taking extra time getting to know a student, or helping a student who is struggling with school work. It might be to develop expertise in an area of the curriculum by reading extensively or seeking professional development opportunities in that subject. It could be to put a little extra time into reading up about a topic that will be addressed in class shortly. A teacher may collect data on children's work, to try and understand the work of teaching better. What are the most common errors children make in spellings, or mathematics, or grammar, or science? What misconceptions do children have about phenomena? What can be done to help children grasp a concept more easily? Teachers can share ideas with other teachers through a journal for teachers, through a website or by maintaining a blog with observations about teaching.[6]

Atul Gawande identifies ways that an individual member of a system can become what he terms a 'positive deviant', a way to matter despite the fact that in our work each of us is replaceable. He identifies five ways to do this: ask a question that lets you make a human connection with a student, a parent, a colleague; when chatting with colleagues discuss successes, ideas and interesting problems rather than focusing on complaints; in your work count something – anything – that interests you in order to learn something interesting; write a poem, an article or a blog entry about your work to share with other teachers; and recognise inadequacies in what you do, seek solutions and be prepared to change.[7]

Responding to life's 'big questions'

Regardless of what inspires us in life, the very act of living presents us with many big questions: where do we come from? Why are we here? How big is the universe? Where did it come from? Why do bad things happen to good people? Why is there evil? Why do some people suffer more than others? What happens when we die? What is a good way to live? Religious people and non-religious people have grappled with such questions and will continue to do so.

From time to time children will pose such questions in school. Schools with a religious ethos have a rich, history and culture on which to draw. Notwithstanding some betrayals that have taken place in the name of some religions and under their watch, religions have inspired much of the art, music, stories, philosophy and culture that is experienced and enjoyed by people today. Religion has given meaning to people's lives for centuries.

Although the school's ethos may help a teacher answer life's tough questions, they can still be challenging for a teacher. When children ask big questions, they are 'moments of truth'. A teacher can deflect the questions, by saying 'I don't know' or by redirecting the children's questions towards the children's parents. Or a teacher could say 'Some people think this, but others think that'. Sooner or later one child will ask, 'What do *you* think teacher?'. Should a teacher answer such a question, or is it a question for parents?

I believe that a teacher should answer such a question for children. Big questions are not taboo, and children should be encouraged to ask them and seek answers to them throughout their lives. The teacher's response is not the last word on the question. But it is a view that children can hear and think about, consider and over time put it with other answers to the question. As they grow older, their questions may become more refined.

Some might disagree with a teacher answering such questions directly because of the influential role a teacher has on children. Parents can often be taken aback when their view on something is contradicted with a sentence beginning, 'But teacher says . . .'. Other parents may have strong or well-thought-out responses to such questions and they may not want their views undermined by a teacher whose view is different. Or parents may genuinely fear that a teacher may express views on such matters that are more liberal or conservative than they would wish or they may just worry because the teacher's view is unknown to them.

This dilemma places a teacher in a difficult predicament. One response is for the teacher to take a detached role and ignore such questions in the classroom. The teacher can stay on safe ground by serving an economic or functional role, where their main responsibility is to prepare children to be effective and conscientious participants in the economy. In such a scenario the teacher's priority is to ensure that children can do the 'three Rs' of reading, writing and arithmetic, and that will suffice.

But if schools only focus on fundamental skills, who will help create in children a sense of awe and wonder in the biodiversity of the earth, the expanse of the universe and the scale of time? The environmentalist John Feehan gives a useful analogy for time: imagine 30 large encyclopaedia-type volumes on a bookshelf, each of them 450 pages long. If each page represented a million years, the first page of the first volume would open with the 'Big Bang'. Mammals only appear in the last 65 pages of volume 30 and modern humans appear only at the bottom of the final page.

And despite their recent arrival on earth, the way humans have explored and shaped the world is an essential part of education. That is why children study science, the arts, history, geography, language, and physical education.

Becoming literate and numerate is essential for children; these skills open doors to a broader education. But if schools limit education to these skills, their education is a restricted one. Teachers need to resist having their roles narrowed to that of teaching only basic skills. Teachers can be trusted with the full education of children, which includes answering children's big questions about the world.

Of course, there are times when it is appropriate, even responsible, for a teacher to refuse to answer questions from children, mostly where they refer to matters in a teacher's private life. This includes personal questions that children may ask relating to sexual matters or substance use, for example. Such information is personal and not relevant to school. That is different to views on big questions about life where children are not seeking personal information but rather a personal view on a topic.

Providing a personal view on a topic may be problematic if your personal view conflicts with the ethos of the school. The dilemma is between being honest with the children and being committed to upholding the school's ethos. Although when you teach subjects such as religion, history, civics and morality, it may be difficult to be neutral, that does not mean the teacher can be partisan. Teachers can discuss with children criteria of reasonableness and of plausibility in these areas.[8]

When a child asks a question that seeks a personal opinion on a topic, a teacher can reply with an answer that is consistent with the school's ethos. If a child presses you for your personal view, you could explain that it is a complicated matter and then outline your view on it. Of course if you are teaching in a school where you could be censured for providing a personal view that is contrary to the ethos of the school, then you must comply with the school's wish and not undermine its ethos. However, I would say to the school that children appreciate the honest expression of sincerely held views and can take them for what they are, one person's view.

Sensitive topics

Some topics are particularly sensitive and arise in political and media discussions from time to time. I'm thinking of topics such as euthanasia, suicide, abortion or contraception. Children may raise them in class and the issues may be teased out. You need to make a judgement on whether or not to give a personal opinion on these matters. In making the judgement, you will need to consider how aligned your views are with the school's ethos, how sincerely the question is being asked by the child, the depth of the discussion on the topic and the range of views expressed in class, the age and maturity of the children, and the strength of your own views on the matter. The bottom line again is that teachers are a key part of a child's education; you need to support the ethos of the school, and while keeping personal information private, you need to be honest and sincere with the children when answering big questions about life.

Teachers occupy a trusted position in children's lives and the trust is retained as long as the teacher is sincere and credible. As in all walks of life, some teachers will have a strong stance on ethical, religious or political matters, such as abortion or suicide. Although the teacher is entitled to hold those views, school is not a place where the teacher can attempt to impose such views on children. An unequal relationship exists where the children are just beginning to learn about the world and the teacher has more experience of the world, so a teacher cannot discuss such matters with children as if discussing the matters with a colleague or a friend.

If such sensitive issues are being discussed, the teacher's job is to give a fair hearing to different perspectives on the topic. If a teacher is asked for their view, they may choose to share that view with the children in a balanced way, referring to the sensitivities involved in the matter. Advocating a particular viewpoint or promoting a particular viewpoint on such matters means that one has moved from the position of teacher to one of activist in the classroom. In short, an honest and voluntary expression of a thoughtful, honest and sincere position is teaching, seeking to convert children to a position is activism and is unlikely to have a lasting impact.

Any attempt to advocate a particular viewpoint in the classroom is unlikely to be effective unless the message is supported by the wider society in which the school exists.[9] Although teachers influence children, the influence is not a direct one and many other factors influence people's views and actions as they mature.

Teachers have always had a role in promoting behaviour among children that is moral, disciplined and respectful of others. However, attempting to force particular views on children about social or political issues, which are not currently relevant to them or which they can do little to influence, represents poor use of teaching time.

Notwithstanding that, teaching is a job where issues of social justice frequently emerge. Many teachers witness children coming to school hungry, poorly clothed, tired or anxious. They see children who are discriminated against because of poverty, where they live, ethnicity, or the language they speak. In light of observing such trauma teachers may be driven towards action for social justice. In addition to taking steps to address such difficulties at a local level in school, a teacher's impulse towards social justice can be further channelled into relevant activities outside the classroom, through politics, membership of a union or of other organisations working for justice in order to bring about a better life for more people.

What is teaching for?

Teaching cannot be detached from life – the children's lives create the need for education. At its most basic, teaching is about one human using their capacity to help other humans realise, awaken and achieve their potential. Helping children live the best lives they can live now and in the future is a goal of all teaching. Therefore what is happening in our country and in the world, socially, culturally, economically, politically, scientifically and technologically will impact on teaching.

However, a teacher needs to be able to discern the difference between developments that are sustained and continuous versus priorities that are given short-term prominence by various media only to be replaced when the next topic comes along. Some events are dramatic but may be one-off. Other events are part of an underlying pattern. It is good to be able to discern whether an incident is isolated or part of a pattern. For example, you need to think about what impact, if any, factors such as the following will have on how and what you teach: global warming, childhood obesity statistics, the availability of various new and old technologies, secularism, materialism and changing family structures.

On occasion you may find yourself thinking about what lies in store for the children you teach. However, such speculation serves little or no purpose. Multiple factors will influence children's future – some predictable, many not. Take the area of what work students may do. Many children will end up working at jobs that currently do not exist. Some children will be unemployed. The children you teach will likely occupy a range of roles in society, some paid, some not: scientists, engineers, mechanics, volunteers, politicians, astronomers, artists, parents, actors, builders, unemployed, butchers, shop assistants, truck drivers, hairdressers, musicians, nurses, medical doctors, painter/decorators, teachers or carers. The list is endless. What matters more than what career path children follow is how well they can survive in society, how satisfied they are with their position, how well they have fulfilled their potential, how conscientious they are about doing their work, how curious they are about improving what they do and how reliable and trustworthy they are.

The future of schools

Some may question the wisdom of writing a book about teaching at this time as various commentators envisage a day when technology may replace teaching.[10] Although opinions are far from unanimous about this, many claim that the days of schools as we know them are numbered and very soon children will be educated at home or in specialised centres supported by dedicated online resources. None of us knows how education may change in response to developments in technology and online learning. As a cautionary tale one need only look at what happened to music and book sales over the last two decades to see how seemingly invincible institutions can be dismantled in a short period of time. Even if schooling has remained largely constant over several centuries, it is not immune from change, possibly even radical change. That is why teachers need to be aware of what is possible with technology and to be open to adapting how they teach.

Children can learn some things from machines, or on their own, better than they can learn them from a teacher or in a class with twenty others. A vast range of information on any topic you can think of is available instantly with accompanying pictures, videos, diagrams and definitions to support computer-based or independent learning. Online learning can do video demonstrations very well. Computers don't get impatient if they have to present a demonstration repeatedly or if they pose a question and receive wrong answers several times.

Phone calls with pictures can be made to anyone around the world to ask them about their lives, their work, their environment. Experts from anywhere can be consulted on any topic. Records of observations in the environment can be shared simultaneously. Unlimited material in almost any language you imagine can be accessed to support language learners. Technology is becoming increasingly more accessible and portable. Teachers can share and discuss ideas with like-minded peers in their own country and around the world. It's easy to see why proponents of educational technology get excited at the opportunities and possibilities that are limited only by our imaginations.

Of course the potential contribution of technologies to the education of future generations is not just limited by our imaginations, but also by the technologies themselves and by the infrastructure in which they exist. A lot of material on the internet is reliable but some of it is not. Despite the growing availability of technologies, access to them is not universal and some children have little access to what is available. Because of existing funding models, many websites are accompanied by advertising, which has sometimes had a dubious, if not fully understood, relationship with schools.[11]

Some educators worry that children who are educated in television or online settings may have more mediated experiences with the world and fewer direct experiences. This is how one such educator expressed concern on this topic three decades ago, before the World Wide Web was developed:

> The sunset we see is the sunset on television, not the sunset we climb to the top of the hill and stand shivering in our duffle coats to watch. The dawn chorus is the birdsong we hear in ever-improved stereo in the carpeted comfort of our living room, not in the mist of the early May morning with tears in our eyes. The life at which we marvel is coming at us from the Wonderful World of Wildlife: it is not the life we touch with our own hands or sense with our own eyes and ears and nose and mouth. We are increasingly alienated from our experience, in the true sense of that word: *alienus*, belonging to another person, a stranger. Our mediated experience of sunset, dawn chorus, life, love, is the direct experience of another. It is not ours. Television is an invention of tremendous possibility. But we may be satisfied with it; it requires little or no effort of the senses. We learn a great deal from it we might not learn so well anywhere else, and we get a great deal of enjoyment from it. Yes, but alone it does not

draw out our *human potential,* does not make demands on our human capacities in all their potential richness and power. It does not ask us *to live for ourselves:* it tempts us to be satisfied with the living of others.[12]

This concern about living passively in the world can only have intensified with the advent of always-on broadband and various technologies that use the internet. More important than learning to use the technology is for children to learn how the technology shapes the society in which they live and their own lives. Children need to learn how to be discerning users rather than servants of technology.[13]

Technology and teaching

Other questions need to be asked about learners and about teaching in an era of evolving technology in education. How will learners be motivated to participate in online education? Just as some children love going to school, some will need no motivation; but others will. How will children learn values that are taught in school, such as citizenship, honesty, cooperation, persistence and respect? Which of the current educational principles we value will we be prepared to forgo? Which ones will be easier to implement? Finally, will technologies continue to exist alongside schools and to coexist with them or are they ultimately in competition with schools and seeking to replace them?

Teaching today can vary in its form and its quality, so it's difficult to give a generic answer as to how technology could trump it. One reason that teaching varies is because it is vulnerable to political interference and other cultural influences. Furthermore, little consensus exists about how teachers are prepared and assessed for practice, and therefore teacher education and requirements for teacher certification vary widely. And finally, teaching is a human activity; regardless of teacher education and other influences, like art, teaching is influenced by the person who is teaching.

If technology without teachers could solve the problem of making a good education accessible to all children, it probably could exert a more even and consistent effect than it currently has; but would it have a human touch? Consistency may be gained at the price of a few words of personal encouragement or the understanding that a child may be upset or tired or enthusiastic on a particular day.

Teachers must be mindful of the potential for technology to change, or even in time replace, the work teachers do. But rather than despairing of such a threat, teachers can look afresh at the work they do and the work they could do. Teachers need to know what they can do, which cannot be done by a device with sophisticated software. If what children experience in school could be replicated by viewing videos or playing educational games online, it is difficult to make the case for a specific contribution that teaching makes to children.

However, a live teacher can respond in the moment to children who look confused or engaged or distracted. The teacher can relate the content to contexts and interests that are familiar to these children in this locality. The teacher can judge when the level of challenge of a task needs to be raised or lowered. A teacher can decide which children would work productively together. A teacher can empathise with and respond to a child who is feeling sad, upset, angry or excited. It's difficult to envisage how technology can replace the direct person-to-person relationship that is at the heart of children's earliest experience of education.

The future of teaching

But just suppose the day came where technology could replace teaching. Then the expertise of teachers may be channelled in a different direction. No doubt people will still be needed who have expertise in knowing how people learn, in planning for such learning, in designing educational tasks for children, in managing discipline and safety among groups of learners, in responding to differences among children, in assessing student knowledge, and in reporting to parents about their children's progress and advising them on how to support their further learning. Greater specialisation may be needed in certain activities, but it is difficult to envisage a future where there will be no need for teaching competence.

Frequently the promise – or threat – of change in society, how we live and so on is used as a pretext for education to change.[14] No doubt a curriculum cannot stand still and it must respond to changing lives and circumstances. However, sometimes the extent to which our lives are different to those who lived in previous centuries can be exaggerated.

Many quotes from Shakespeare can apply to aspects of our lives today; for example 'neither a borrower nor a lender be' from *Hamlet* or 'how sharper than a serpent's tooth it is to have a thankless child' from *King Lear.* Such lines help us appreciate that even when technologies change, we humans have characteristics, traits and foibles that have endured, and the challenges we encounter are not as unique as we often think. An Irish novelist once expressed appreciation for 'gifts beyond the gifts of fairies [that] we [in different countries] can all see and hear what each other are doing and do and read the same things nearly at the same time'. The novelist, Maria Edgeworth, wasn't marvelling at the speed and power of the internet but at the 'printing press – the mail coach and the steam packet' in 1821.[15]

What may change, however, are the children in our classes. How they read, write and think is changed by technology; this doesn't happen instantly but slowly over time.[16] Their emotions, instincts and desires are similar to those of their ancestors but how they handle and respond to them changes with the instruments they use to express or act on them.

Conclusion

Teaching seems to be a commonplace activity; at one time or another we have all experienced it. Teaching happens every day all over the country in remote rural villages and bustling inner city areas. Teaching is so ubiquitous and widespread that it is easy to take for granted; sometimes it looks easy, as if anyone can do it. When we think of teaching, most of us can conjure up the image of an adult, textbook in hand or whiteboard behind, standing in front of twenty or thirty children in a classroom. We hardly question it. And yet, just the presence of an adult and children in a classroom is no guarantee that teaching is happening. The children's minds may be elsewhere, the subject matter may be banal and the adult may be speaking in a way that is abstract or distracted.

So as you embark on a career in teaching, remember that teaching is about the relationship between teacher, student and content. Each part of the relationship exists independent of and in interaction with the whole relationship. Students have friends and families with whom they interact and who influence them. Teachers have employers and colleagues to whom they are accountable and who have expectations of them. Both teachers and students are shaped by their friends and families and by the wider society in which they live.[17] The subject matter too is constantly evolving, in ways that are rarely captured by school textbooks.[18] The status of each curriculum subject is influenced by society – messages about the perceived importance of subjects for promoting health, happiness, economic development and cultural enrichment and so on are often matters for discussion through various media.

Mostly when teaching is discussed, it is done as if it is the same job everywhere. But although the stated goals, curriculum, textbooks and resources may be similar, teaching differs widely from place to place and from time to time. Teaching primary school children in a disadvantaged urban area where only a handful of parents and guardians have completed second-level education and even fewer have gone to third level is quite different to teaching children of the same age in a middle-class area where parents and guardians consider themselves to be well educated and they expect their children to attend university because they see it as a route to success and happiness in life. Different again is it to teach in a two-teacher rural school where each classroom has four grade levels and most children come from farming backgrounds and many are related to one another.

As a teacher you experience such differences in where you live, how you travel to school and what you see as you get there, all of which influence the pace and quality of your life. The children's background knowledge and experiences too differ; some children may have become good at 'staying safe',[19] by protecting themselves from threatening or dangerous situations; others are accomplished at appreciating the cycle of the seasons, and still others at knowing resources that will support their learning. What they need to learn in school and how they learn it is shaped, in part at least, by such life experiences. As a teacher you have a responsibility to try and understand the children's background, their values, dreams, challenges and aspirations so that you can use such information in your teaching.[20]

Teaching happens in the interactions of a teacher, students and subject matter. Although all three are essential for the relationship to work, the teacher is the lead partner in this relationship. The teacher can recognise and know something about the independent existence each element has but teaching only happens in the interaction among the teacher, the students and the subject matter. Teaching breaks down if the teacher or children are distracted or bored or if the subject matter is too difficult or too easy.

The student–teacher–subject matter interaction is fragile and never guaranteed. Nor is it confined only to the teacher, students and subject matter. Each one has their own complicated set of interactions with others that influence the relationship. The teacher is influenced by their own education, their family, their colleagues, their principal, inspectors, a union and the weight of such influences vary throughout a teacher's career. The children are influenced by their family, friends, classmates, life experiences, interests, media and self-perception, and each influence varies over the course of a life in school. The subject matter is influenced by its perceived political or historical status, its perceived economic value, its level of difficulty and its history as a discipline; these perceptions can vary over time. Similarly the interactions among these features further complicate teaching. A teacher may perceive themselves to possess or to lack competence in a particular subject; colleagues in a school may place a particular priority on a given subject or part of a subject; a child may like a particular subject or a particular teacher or may feel competent or incompetent in a particular subject and so on. All these interactions are happening constantly, affecting the work of teaching.[21] Yet they are rarely spoken about by teachers and policymakers or appreciated by those who do not teach.

So as you set out on a career in teaching, you are entrusted with an important responsibility. It is to be aware of the complex interactions that are going on around you and of which you are an integral part. The responsibility is daunting and could even seem overwhelming. But remember that at its heart, teaching is human – one human shares the wisdom of generations of humans with a new generation of humans. Although it can seem overwhelming at times, all you can do is your best; be patient with the mistakes you'll make and the difficult interactions that will occur from time to time. Mistakes made when a person is sincere in their efforts to do a good job are forgotten quickly; it's the effort that's remembered.

If you look on teaching as a job dedicated to constant learning – by your students and by you – it is a job that never becomes dull or mundane. You are engaged in discovering and passing on key parts of our inherited legacy to the next generation of children so that they are prepared to live their lives – however they develop – in ways that are happy, fulfilling and productive. Even though it can be tough at times, it is one of the most exciting, privileged and rewarding ways to live a life.

Key points of Chapter 9

1 As a teacher you need to learn patience, in waiting for learning to happen, in personal interactions with children and colleagues, and with yourself.

2 Inspiring children and being inspired are central to teaching and even if your own inspiration fades, it can be re-ignited.

3 Teaching is a responsible job that requires a teacher to show balance and respect when discussing big questions or sensitive topics with children.

4 Although technology may change where, when, and how teaching takes place, expertise in core practices of teaching will be needed for many years to come.

Notes

1 Government of Ireland (1999, p. 36).

2 See, for example, Smith, Lemke, Taylor, Kirchner & Hoffman (1998).

3 From an interview I conducted with Pamela Grossman, which is available here: http://insideeducation.podbean.com/2011/06/01/programme-96-pam-grossman-on-putting-practice-into-teacher-education-22-5-11/.

4 This is my colleague, Paddy Madden. You can hear him talk about it here: http://insideeducation.podbean.com/2009/12/14/programme-23-paddy-madden-on-environmental-education-pt-2-and-budget-analysis-13-12-09/.

5 From *Zen and the Art of Motorcycle Maintenance* by Robert M. Pirsig, published by Bodley Head. Reproduced by permission of The Random House Group Ltd (Pirsig, 1974, 1989, p. 362).

6 If you publish messages on a blog, you need to maintain confidentiality about children, parents, colleagues and others. If pictures or videos of children or their work are used, consent must be sought.

7 Adapted here for teachers based on recommendations for doctors in Gawande (2007, pp. 251–257).

8 This sentence and the one preceding it are based on an excerpt from Williams (2007, pp. 686–687).

9 Advocating a particular viewpoint resembles what Freire (1970, 1993) describes as a banking approach to teaching; preferable is one that promotes critical thinking and problem posing and in so doing acknowledges students as people who are "becoming."

10 See for example http://www.theguardian.com/teacher-network/2015/feb/24/computers-replace-teachers, http://www.edweek.org/ew/articles/2012/08/08/37replace_ep.h31.html, http://www.theatlantic.com/education/archive/2015/03/the-deconstruction-of-the-k-12-teacher/388631/ and http://content.thirdway.org/publications/714/Dancing-With-Robots.pdf.

11 Brent & Lunden (2009).

12 Feehan (1983, p. 16). Emphasis in original.

13 Postman (1999, p. 171).

14 Furedi (2009, p. 23).

15 Maria Edgeworth, 29 December 1821 (from *Maria Edgeworth: Letters from England, 1813–1844*).

16 For a full discussion of this phenomenon see Carr (2010), specifically around pages 199–200.

17 Lampert (2001).

18 Collingwood (1946, pp. 7–8).

19 This point was made to me by Lisa Delpit http://insideeducation.podbean.com/2012/05/06/programme-138-lisa-delpit-on-educating-minority-learners-6-5-12/.

20 Ken Zeichner elaborates on this point in http://insideeducation.podbean.
com/e/programme-238-ken-zeichner-on-teacher-education-pt-1-13-1-16/
and http://insideeducation.podbean.com/e/programme-239-ken-zeichner-
on-social-justice-20-1-16/.

21 These interactions are well described by Lampert (2001).

References

Brent, B. O. & Lunden, S. (2009). Much ado about very little: The benefits and
costs of school-based commercial activities. *Leadership and Policy in Schools, 8*(3),
307–336.

Carr, N. (2010). *The shallows.* New York: W.W. Norton & Company.

Collingwood, R. G. (1946). *The idea of history.* New York: Oxford University Press.

Feehan, J. (1983). *Laois: An environmental history.* Stradbally, Laois, Ireland: Ballykilcavan
Press.

Freire, P. (1970. 1993). *Pedagogy of the oppressed* (M. B. Ramos, Trans.). London:
Penguin Books.

Furedi, F. (2009). *Wasted: Why education isn't educating.* London: Continuum International Publishing Group.

Gawande, A. (2007). *Better: A surgeon's notes on performance.* New York: Metropolitan
Books.

Government of Ireland. (1999). *Primary school curriculum: Introduction.* Dublin: The
Stationery Office.

Lampert, M. (2001). *Teaching problems and the problems of teaching.* New Haven, CT:
Yale University Press.

Pirsig, R. M. (1974, 1989). *Zen and the art of motorcycle maintenance: An inquiry into
values.* London: Vintage.

Postman, N. (1999). *Building a bridge to the 18th century: How the past can improve our
future.* New York: Vintage Books.

Smith, E., Lemke, J., Taylor, M., Kirchner, H. L. & Hoffman, H. (1998). Frequency
of voice problems among teachers and other occupations. *Journal of Voice, 12*(4),
480–488.

Williams, K. (2007). Religious worldviews and the common school: The French
dilemma. *Journal of Philosophy of Education, 41*(4), 675–692.

Appendix I

Teaching reading to children

Many elements are necessary to teach reading to children. A major study conducted by the National Reading Panel in the United States[1] identified five elements that were shown to help children learn to read. They are phonemic awareness, phonics instruction, fluency instruction, vocabulary instruction and text comprehension instruction. Although all five elements are essential for teaching reading, the list is incomplete. For instance, one expert on reading, P. David Pearson, noted that the list does not include the reciprocal relationship of reading and writing, or the importance of talking about text, or ways of grouping children for instruction.[2]

Despite the incomplete nature of the list, it is the five components identified by the National Reading Panel that I have chosen to elaborate on in this appendix. This is because each is important in its own right and because I found some aspects of them difficult to implement when I began teaching.

Phonemic awareness[3]

Let's begin by looking inside the classroom of one teacher. Rebecca Grace has been using phonemic awareness activities for several years now to help the children's reading and spelling. 'To be honest, when I started teaching, I hardly knew what a phoneme was', she laughs, explaining:

> They are the smallest units of spoken language, the smallest sounds, and English has about 44 of them. A word such as 'last' has four letters and four

phonemes /l/ /ɑː/ /s/ /t/, whereas 'ship' has four letters and only three phonemes /ʃ/ /ɪ/ /p/ and 'box' has three letters and four phonemes /b/ /ɒ/ /k/ /s/.[4]

Rebecca started reading about phonemic awareness when some of the children in her class were having problems reading:[5]

> I learned what onset and rime are. Onset is the sound that precedes the first vowel in a syllable and the rime is the first vowel and the remaining consonants. For example, in the word 'mill' m– is the onset and –ill is the rime and in 'fold' f– is the onset and –old is the rime. We do lots of oral work on those, responding to prompts such as 'I'm thinking of a food that rhymes with lake' (cake, hake or steak, for example).

'I was told about oral activities I could get children to do in groups in the class' she says:

> They isolate phonemes (e.g. what is the first sound in the word 'bat'?), they identify common phonemes in words (e.g. what sound is the same in 'top,' 'tin,' 'tan'?), they categorise phonemes (e.g. which word does not share a phoneme the other words have such as 'cat,' 'can,' 'car,' 'bag'?), they blend phonemes (listen to these phonemes and tell me what word they make /b/ /ɛ/ /g/?), they segment words into their phonemes, they delete phonemes (what is flight without the /f/?) and they add phonemes (what do you get if you place an /s/ sound before car?).

Rebecca's former college lecturer[6] advised her to animate these questions by using a puppet to 'snatch' phonemes away from words and to add them to words.

This year Rebecca is teaching a class of four- and five-year-old children. Most children in the class are readers who are developing as expected; others, however, are deemed to be at risk of developing reading difficulties (possibly because they have low phonemic awareness knowledge, low reading performance, low socioeconomic status, language delays or cognitive disabilities); and a handful of children are already at least a year behind their class level, despite having at least average cognitive ability.

Over the years Rebecca has tried different ways of teaching phonemic awareness to the children – working with individual children, working with small groups and working with the whole class. The children do best on phonemic awareness, reading and spelling when she works with small groups.

She sometimes gets the children to complete phonemic awareness activities on a computer, such as breaking words into phonemes and blending phonemes to make words.[7] Although it works quite well in developing their phonemic awareness knowledge, it does not impact on their spellings as much.

She also says that she doesn't need to devote a huge amount of time to the activities; the children in her class receive around six hours of phonemic awareness activities during the school year. When she started out working explicitly on phonemic awareness with her classes she used to do all seven activities (isolation, identity, categorisation, blending, segmentation, deletion, and manipulation of onset–rime units). However, more recently she has found that focusing on one or two skills at a time does more for the children's phonemic awareness, their reading and their spelling than working on multiple phonemic awareness skills. In particular, she found that working on blending and segmenting improved the children's phonemic awareness.

Rebecca finds that working on phonemic awareness activities with the children improves their phonemic awareness, and it in turn helps their reading and spelling. This is particularly true when teaching four- and five-year-olds.

Rebecca says that when she does these activities, all children's phonemic awareness skills improve, especially those who are at risk and those who are progressing normally. She noticed improvements in the spelling of the normally progressing and the at-risk students but the phonemic awareness activities did not help the spellings of the children who were behind in their reading.

Getting the children to select plastic letters to represent the sounds is better for the children's reading and spelling than using speech alone, she finds. The letters seem to provide concrete symbols for the sounds that help the children grasp them. When she does this, Rebecca is moving away from focusing solely on phonological awareness and closer to sound–letter relationships as found in phonics.

Systematic phonics instruction[8]

Another central element of Rebecca's teaching of reading is the systematic use of phonics. The goal of teaching phonics is to help children read and spell words by equipping them with alphabetic knowledge, even though it has also been found to help with oral reading and comprehending text. Rebecca remembers hearing in college that systematic phonics teaching was a better help to children's reading than incidental or unsystematic phonics, (i.e. systematic phonics teaching is better than the kind of phonics teaching that is often associated with regular graded reading textbooks, and whole language and whole word approaches).

Sometimes she teaches the children how words consist of sounds which can be represented by letters (including letter blends such as fr and cl). When children encounter the word 'fat', they will be able to use their alphabetical knowledge of the sounds /f/ /a/ and /t/ to decode the word.[9]

Other times she takes words the children already know, like their own names and commonly used words (such as 'fill') and helps the children ana-lyse how the letters and sounds are related.[10] For instance, the children may look at the word 'fill' and decode it using their knowledge of the initial /f/ sound, the /ɪ/ sound and the /l/ sound. They will also learn that the rime 'ill' occurs in many words which can be represented in print by changing the onset letter f to b, h, m and so on.

Rebecca finds that teaching phonics as one element of teaching reading helps children decode previously unseen words, even after she has stopped formally teaching them and when the children move through more senior classes of the school. She typically starts teaching phonics to four-year-olds and continues it with five-year-olds and her colleague continues it with six- and seven-year-olds. Children tend to learn their phonics equally effectively whether they are taught one-to-one, to small groups or to the whole class.

Rebecca finds that children from homes which are disadvantaged educa-tionally benefit most from learning phonics. When she taught older classes Rebecca found that teaching phonics helped readers who were progressing normally and those with reading difficulties. They worked less well for improving the reading of readers who are low achieving. Nevertheless, she finds that the greatest benefits occur with younger children.

She finds commercial programmes can be good for helping to teaching sys-tematic phonics. When choosing a phonics programme to adopt for her class or to recommend to her colleagues she looks for features such as the following:

1 provision for learning letter sounds;
2 practice at blending sounds;
3 practice at letter formation;
4 inclusion of pictures, stories, actions and mnemonics (such as the handle of a cup looking like a 'c') for teaching letter–sound relations;
5 provision for identifying sounds in words;
6 learning high-frequency words that have irregular spellings;
7 opportunity for authentic reading and writing.[11]

Rebecca says that although systematic phonics works better than whole language approaches, such as big books or a language experience approach alone, she has integrated phonics instruction with whole language approaches rather than eliminating them altogether. She thinks children gain more when phonics is learned in context. Although phonics is effective for teaching reading, Rebecca finds that it needs to be combined with fluency and instruction in comprehension and vocabulary in order to give every child the best chance of learning to read.

Vocabulary[12]

Although Rebecca works on vocabulary instruction with her class, we may get a better idea of what is involved if we look into the classroom of her colleague, David Markham, who is teaching six- and seven-year-olds. David realises that most vocabulary is learned informally as children encounter and use language in interactions with family, friends and various media. Nevertheless, he knows that he can promote vocabulary learning informally by reading aloud to children – something he also did when he taught eleven- and twelve-year-olds – and by encouraging them to read widely themselves, especially at home. He is conscious too that children from low-income families may have heard much less spoken language in their early years than children from working-class families.

When David focuses on vocabulary as an element of teaching reading, he is particularly interested in children learning the meanings of words rather than just decoding them. Children's knowledge of a word may vary from none to: being somewhat familiar with it having seen or heard it before; being able to use it appropriately in some situations; knowing the word in a nuanced way, with multiple meanings and relationships to other words. David regularly uses various word maps[13] in his class to help children see how words are related to one another. Such maps may have the word being learned at the centre and a definition, synonyms, antonyms, examples and non-examples around it, as illustrated in Figure AI.1.

David likes to show children how words are related to one another. Sometimes he works with the children to place words on a continuum showing their relationship, such as big, huge, gigantic, enormous and vast. On David's classroom walls are charts containing lists of words organised in categories such as types of animal, food, feelings, jobs and means of transport.

Other times David focuses on the multiple meanings and uses of words. For example, children in his class know that a 'bat' can be a winged animal or something used in sports such as table tennis and that 'fine' can describe

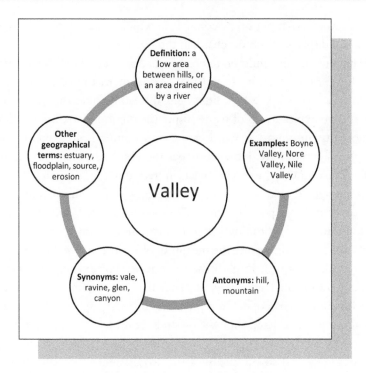

Figure AI.1 Word map for 'valley'

weather or small particles of sand, or refer to money paid as a penalty for an offence.

When choosing words to teach, David knows that children will develop many words through encountering them in daily use – person, look, different, under and would, for example – and he knows that others are too obscure or infrequent to spend time on – such as legislature, carcinogen, procrastinate. It is the words in between, those which are useful to have but which don't occur often enough in daily use for children to pick up indirectly, that he chooses to teach directly. In choosing vocabulary to teach directly, he also looks for words that are important for understanding texts being read in school. He gives priority too to idiomatic expressions – 'let the cat out of the bag' or 'at the drop of a hat' – and to words that are difficult because they have multiple meanings – turn, break, run, cross, score, for example.

David likes to directly teach about eight or ten new words each week. However, his experience has taught him the importance of returning to revise words repeatedly in order to help children really learn them:

> I used to find that at the end of a week most of the children would know most of the words taught that week. But if I checked again a few weeks later, lots of the words would be gone again.

Now he is always looking for new contexts in which to use words previously taught and he displays words on charts in the classroom.

David encourages the children to consult dictionaries when learning new word meanings. However, he found that asking them to copy definitions directly from a dictionary was of little help. Instead he likes the children to make their own explanations of words, using the dictionary definition along with synonyms, antonyms, a word category, a comparison, a picture and an example, as appropriate. He encourages the children to record the new words they learn in their own vocabulary notebooks.

He encourages children to learn the meanings of common prefixes – un-, re-, in- and dis- especially, and suffixes – such as -less and -ful. These help children understand the meanings of many new words.

David spends time discussing the meanings of Latin and Greek root words because so many words in English use these roots. For example the Greek word '*mikros*' means small and gives us words that have 'micro' in them such as microchip and microscope. He remembers introducing the Greek word '*log-*' meaning word, reason, thought or study and how the children spent time over several days compiling words ending in -ology – psychology, biology, sociology and so on; many of the words referred to the study of various aspects of life. In history class, he helped the children remember what an aqueduct is by telling them that the Latin word for water is '*aqua*' and he linked it to the word aquarium.

Fluency[14]

When David was in college, he never learned about teaching oral reading fluency; it was assumed that once children could decode words, fluent reading followed. However, Rebecca, who left college more recently, explicitly teaches fluency and has persuaded David to do the same with his class; he has noticed that it helps the children's reading a lot. He now expects children in his class to be able to read aloud, accurately and with expression,[15] at a rate of about 90 words per minute. Readers who have not yet developed fluency read slowly, and their reading can be described as 'choppy and plodding'.[16]

Both David and Rebecca agree that fluency instruction must have three essential features. First, it must be based around oral rather than silent reading. Second, children need to have repeated chances to read a text and sometimes have repeated chances to listen to the text. Rebecca tends to get the children to read the text three times, whereas David usually gets them to do it until they have read it with suitable accuracy, expression and speed, whether that is reading it once or five times. Third, children must receive either guidance or feedback on their oral reading; such support can be provided by the teacher, volunteer parents, a classroom assistant, or a peer.

David uses poetry, literature and expository (informative/factual) text when choosing texts for developing oral fluency. He doesn't want the chosen text to be too difficult or too easy so he uses a technique he learned from a teacher when he was on school placement in college.[17] He asks a child to raise their hand as a fist and to begin reading a typical page in a book. Each time the child comes to a word that they do not recognise, the child is asked to raise a finger of their clenched fist. If no fingers are raised by the end of the page, then the text is too easy; if all fingers are raised before the end of the page, the text is too difficult and if between one and five fingers have been raised by the end of the page, then David deems the difficulty level of the text to be about right for developing oral reading fluency.

The approach David uses in class varies depending on the supports available. When he has access to a classroom assistant or a parent volunteer, he asks the adult to read the text for the child to model fluent oral reading. Then the child reads the same piece with the assistant or parent providing encouragement and feedback. David suggests to the adult helper that the child be asked to repeat the passage until it is done fluently.

Other times David puts the children in pairs to work on a specific text. One child is designated as the reader and the other is a guide. The reader reads a short passage and the guide decides if the passage needs to be re-read based on the accuracy, expression or speed of the reading; the guide may also assist in decoding words or modelling fluent reading. Later the roles are reversed.

Technology can also be used; a recording is made of a text being read fluently, with no sound effects or music. A child can listen to the recording, using headphones if necessary, following the recording in a written text. Gradually over a number of times the child tries to read alongside the recording until the child can read the text fluently without the assistance of the recording.

Rebecca sometimes uses a big book or a class book, which every child can see, and reads it aloud modelling fluent reading for the children. Then she reads the book again, encouraging the children to join in with her when they see words they know. She would repeat this process one or two times on one day and read it again with the children later in the week.

When David himself was in primary school, his teacher used to get David and his classmates to read by going around the class asking each student, in turn, to read a section of the text aloud while everyone else followed. This approach, commonly known as 'round-robin', is considered to be a waste of time and will do little to promote oral reading fluency because the children 'spend most of their time waiting instead of learning'.[18]

Both David and Rebecca spend a good deal of reading time on developing students' reading fluency. 'It helps everyone in the class' Rebecca says, 'even those students for whom English is not their first language'. David agrees and says that even when he taught nine- and ten-year-olds, he encouraged the children to do more silent reading at home while he spent time in school developing their oral reading fluency. David knows one or two children who could read fluently but whose comprehension was poor. 'However, in the vast majority of cases, children who read fluently are well placed to develop good reading comprehension', he says.

Comprehension[19]

Both Rebecca and David include comprehension as a key element of teaching reading. Comprehension is about actively engaging with text in order to understand what you read, think about it, remember it and communicate with others about it. In his reading classes David works hard to help children use a range of comprehension strategies so that the children can interact more deeply with the texts they read. David encourages the children to deliberately combine some of these strategies when they are reading in order to be more aware of how they are engaging with the text.

He encourages the children to ask questions before they begin reading a text. If the text is fiction, the questions may be based on the cover of the book, the title, the pictures, the chapter titles or previous reading. For example, last week the children read a picture book called *Just Another Ordinary Day*.[20] The cover of the book featured a girl sitting on a sofa reading a book with a sleeping lion lying across her legs. 'Why is the lion in the picture?', 'Why does the title say it's an "ordinary day" when it is very unusual for a lion to be sleeping while lying on a girl?', 'Why does the girl not look scared?' and 'Does the lion eat the girl?' were some of the questions posed by children before they read the story, giving them a purpose for reading it.

A second strategy for improving comprehension is answering questions. The answers may be to questions posed by the children themselves or by the teacher. The questions help focus the children on the text and encourage them to think about what they are reading as they do so. Sometimes the information needed to answer a question is stated explicitly in the book, sometimes the answer may be implied – like if the text states that an event occurs in wintertime at the North Pole, we can infer that the weather is cold even if it is not directly stated. Other information may not be found in the text but is part of what a reader knows – so if a young girl is not afraid of a lion, she could be an extraordinary young girl, naïve perhaps; maybe there is an element of fantasy in the story; or maybe the lion is unusual in some way. Reading the text and using prior knowledge can help a child to resolve this apparent contradiction.

In addition to asking and answering questions, another strategy to promote comprehension is for children to monitor their reading. As children read, they can be encouraged to check how well they understand the content. When students realise that they do not understand something or need further clarification, they can try to find what section of the text they don't understand or what seems not to make sense, and they can identify what it is about this section they don't understand. They may try to paraphrase a section in their own words, or refer back to earlier in the text to seek information that would help clear up the confusion, such as the name or relevant trait of a character that they had missed when the character was introduced. The student may also ask for help.

For example, in *Just Another Ordinary Day*, one page in the book reads 'Her dad decided to cook a curry for dinner. As usual, it was just a little too hot'. The accompanying illustration has a picture of three plates of curry with fire and smoke emanating from them and a fire-fighter with a hose standing alongside the family members. A child who reads the text and sees the illustration may think that Dad's dinner somehow caught fire before or after it was placed on the table. However, if a child is monitoring their comprehension and asks for help, the child may learn about the additional meaning of hot as a synonym for very spicy; this adds an extra dimension of meaning for a child who has never tasted curry.

A fourth powerful comprehension strategy David teaches the children is how to summarise text. He regularly encourages the children to paraphrase text either after they have read a section of the text or else to do it a number of times while they are reading it. He finds that children who have success-fully learned to summarise text can identify the main ideas, connect the main ideas of a text to one another, eliminate less important details and remember what they read.

A fifth strategy used by David is to have the children represent information on some kind of a visual aid, such as a map, web, graph, chart, frame or cluster. These are called graphic organisers or semantic organisers and they usually include text in them. When they are used with non-fiction texts, children can use them to show how different ideas in the text are related to one another. David says that they are great for getting the children to focus on the structure of a text and that they help the children summarise the text.

A sixth comprehension strategy that David uses involves making the children aware of story structure. He encourages the children to look out for the setting, the main character, the character's ambitions, an initiating or crisis event, reactions to the event, complicating factors and outcome. These characters and events may be represented using a story map, which is one kind of graphic organiser. At the start of the year, David knows that the children find it hard to organise this information but as they do it with more and more stories during the year, they get better at it.

David finds that he has to work hard to help the children acquire these strategies and he needs to remind children regularly to apply them in their reading. Although he encourages the children to combine strategies when reading, when teaching them initially, he could spend several weeks on teaching a single strategy, giving children lots of practice using it until they are able to consciously apply it in their independent reading. When focusing on teaching comprehension strategies he deliberately chooses text where most students will know most words so that they don't have to spend too much effort on decoding words. He applies the strategies to texts which are both fiction and non-fiction.

Sometimes David explains a strategy to the children in detail, telling the children what it involves, how to use it, when it is useful and why. He frequently demonstrates the use of a strategy by modelling the reading of a text and saying out loud what he is thinking as he applies the comprehension strategy. As the children try to apply the strategies, David guides and assists the children in order to help them practise them and become more adept in using them.

The work done by Rebecca and David as outlined here illustrates features of reading deemed to be important by the National Reading Panel in the United States. However, reading is intrinsically linked to other dimensions of language learning and in addition to the strategies outlined, progress in reading is helped by developments in children's oral language and their understanding of the relationship between writing and reading.

Notes

1 Eunice Kennedy Shriver National Institute of Child Health and Human Development (2000).
2 http://insideeducation.podbean.com/2011/10/11/programme-110-p-david-pearson-on-reading-pt-2-9-10-11/
3 The ideas in this section are largely based on Ehri, Nunes, Willows, Schuster & Yaghoub-Zadeh (2001).

4 The phoneme symbols used here are those used in Oxford Dictionaries (n.d.).

5 Phonemic awareness is a key component of phonological awareness, children's knowledge of spoken sounds. Phonological awareness is children's knowledge of sentences, which are made up of words, which are made up of syllables, many of which are made up of onset and rimes, which are made up of phonemes. Although many children will develop phonological awareness before coming to school, specific activities can be used where necessary to direct children's attention to sentences, words, syllables, onset and rimes and phonemes. For example, children can be asked to substitute words in a sentence ('The dog/cat/bird is grey/sick/old'). Children can be asked to recognise words that rhyme (for word endings) and that have alliteration (for word beginnings). Children can also be asked to count the syllables in words.

6 I acknowledge my colleague, Gene Mehigan, for this suggestion.

7 Sherman, Kleiman & Peterson (2004).

8 The information in this section is largely based on Ehri, Nunes, Stahl & Willows (2001).

9 This is known as synthetic phonics (Ehri, Nunes, Stahl et al., 2001).

10 This is known as analytic phonics (Ehri, Nunes, Stahl et al., 2001).

11 These features were identified by Ehri, Nunes, Stahl et al. (2001) as being present in either the Jolly Phonics and/or the Letterland programme. However, some (e.g. no. 6) are not typically part of a phonics programme.

12 This section draws on the following work: Shanahan (2005); Armbruster, Lehr & Osborn (n.d.); Mehigan (2010).

13 See for instance Mehigan (2010).

14 In this section I draw on the following work: Armbruster et al. (n.d.); Mehigan (2012); Shanahan (2005).

15 Expression is also known as prosody and includes elements such as 'expression, intonation, pitch, tone, stress, pausing, rhythm and regularly occurring patterns in language (Allington, 1983; Harris & Hodges, 1995; Kuhn & Stahl, 2003; Mehigan, 2012).

16 Armbruster et al. (n.d., p. 19).

17 The class teacher used this approach to assess the comprehensibility of text for particular readers.

18 Shanahan (2005, p. 18).

19 In this section I draw on the following work: Armbruster et al. (n.d.); Shanahan (2005).

20 Clement (1995).

References

Armbruster, B. B., Lehr, F. & Osborn, J. (n.d.). *Put reading first: The research building blocks for teaching children to read*. National Institute for Literacy/The Partnership for Reading.

Clement, R. (1995). *Just another ordinary day*. Sydney, Australia: Angus & Robertson, an Imprint of HarperCollins Publishers.

Ehri, L. C., Nunes, S. R., Stahl, S. A. & Willows, D. M. (2001). Systematic phonics instruction helps students learn to read: Evidence from the National Reading Panel's meta-analysis. *Review of Educational Research, 71*(3), 393–447.

Ehri, L. C., Nunes, S. R., Willows, D. M., Schuster, B. V. & Yaghoub-Zadeh, Z. (2001). Phonemic awareness instruction helps children learn to read: Evidence from the National Reading Panel's meta-analysis. *Reading Research Quarterly, 36*(3), 250–287.

Eunice Kennedy Shriver National Institute of Child Health and Human Development, NIH., DHHS. (2000). *Report of the National Reading Panel: Teaching children to read: Reports of the Subgroups* (004754). Washington, DC: U.S. Government Printing Office.

Mehigan, G. (2010). Direct vocabulary instruction in the primary classroom. *Reading News, Reading Association of Ireland*, Autumn.

Mehigan, G. (2012). Oral reading fluency: A link from word reading efficiency to comprehension. Paper presented at the 2012 Annual Conference of the Reading Association of Ireland. From Literacy Research to Classroom Practice: Insights and Inspiration, Marino Institute of Education, Dublin.

Oxford Dictionaries. (n.d.). Key to pronunciations (British and World English dictionary). Retrieved 9 January 2016 from http://www.oxforddictionaries.com/words/key-to-pronunciation.

Shanahan, T. (2005). *The National Reading Panel Report: Practical advice for teachers*. Naperville, IL: Learning Point Associates.

Sherman, D., Kleiman, G. & Peterson, K. (2004). *Technology and teaching children to read*. Boston, MA: Education Development Center, Inc. & Northeast and the Islands Regional Technology in Education Consortium (NEIRTEC).

Appendix II
Beginning to teach mathematics[1]

In this appendix I want to write specifically about teaching mathematics. I begin by predicting some of the problems you may encounter in teaching mathematics, I then propose some ingredients of mathematics teaching that are worth acquiring and I conclude by identifying strategies I have found useful in my own mathematics teaching.

Problems in teaching mathematics

I'll begin with some problems you're likely to encounter in teaching mathematics. Of all the subjects you'll teach, mathematics is one where you'll probably find a substantial mismatch between what you were advised to do in college and how you were taught yourself.

The structure of mathematics lessons is quite predictable in many English-speaking countries. Lessons begin with revision of what was done the previous day – that may include checking homework or doing a warm-up activity. Next, the teacher demonstrates how to solve the problems for the day by doing examples on the board. Children then practise similar problems from the textbook. Finally, the teacher corrects class work and assigns homework.

With minor variations, that description summarises most daily mathematics lessons in this part of the world. Indeed it also describes most mathematics lessons in the United States. It is only when you look at what mathematics lessons are like in some other countries that you realise that teaching is largely a cultural activity – one you learn from growing up in and living in a country – rather than an activity that is learned as a student teacher in college.[2]

In Japan, for example, maths lessons begin with the teacher or the students presenting a brief recap of the previous lesson. Then one problem is presented for the lesson. Students work on the problem individually first and subsequently in groups. Next, the teacher selects students to discuss one or more solution methods and the lesson concludes by highlighting and summarising the major ideas. My point here is that learning to teach is not something that began when you entered college. It's something you've been doing since you played school with friends or siblings, possibly before you even started school.

Ideas you learned about mathematics teaching in college – such as discussing multiple solution methods, promoting student thinking and not relying too much on textbooks – may conflict with what usually happens in school and with what your colleagues and your students expect. You may be tempted, indeed, encouraged to revert to how you were taught mathematics in school, even if you know deep down that it doesn't work for all children.

Another problem you're likely to experience is the range of achievement levels among children in your class. Some children will finish the work you assign quickly and will be capable of greater challenges than other children in the class. Managing variations in work rate and prior achievement makes demands on you. Similarly, motivating children to study a subject is challenging. 'Why do we have to learn this?' is a question you need to be prepared to answer, whether it is asked or not. You may have great ideas about how to approach teaching a topic such as problem solving but if children don't like it or accept it, the approach won't work. The needs children want to satisfy and the values they hold may differ from your needs and values.[3] Or the approach you want to take may not be supported by other features in the class such as the textbook used[4] or the layout.

Finally, your own mathematical knowledge or your perception of your mathematical knowledge may constrain how you teach mathematics.[5] Of course you need knowledge to be able to do the maths the children need to do. But you also need maths to look across children's errors and to see patterns among them, or to figure out if an unfamiliar method used to do a calculation will work every time or if a student just got lucky. You need maths too to anticipate what kind of tasks or examples will be confusing, interesting or motivating for children and to make mathematical sense of their ideas as they try, sometimes hesitatingly, to express them. You also need to know maths in order to figure out which representations work best for teaching particular ideas and how to sequence material so that students can understand it.[6]

Priorities in teaching mathematics

So, I've anticipated some of the problems you'll encounter when teaching mathematics: a lack of experience with the kind of maths teaching you were encouraged to practise in college; the range of achievement among children; textbooks that favour drill and repeated practice over mathematical thinking and developing mathematical skills or practices; and the possibility of children not finding your approach helpful or motivating. Even though teaching maths, like teaching any subject, has particular difficulties, I want to identify some priorities for teaching the subject that are worth working on. The first relates to thinking about the kind of knowledge mathematics is, the second refers to how content areas in mathematics are related to one another and the third relates to the importance of children acquiring the skills or practices of mathematics.

Mathematical knowledge

When Constance Kamii talks about learning mathematics, she refers to Piaget's knowledge framework.[7] She categorises three kinds of knowledge according to the ultimate sources of the knowledge. The first is physical knowledge. This is knowledge that has a source in the external world. So, a rock may be rough or smooth. Fish may smell fresh or 'off'. A ball may roll or bounce. Such knowledge can be acquired through the senses.

The second kind of knowledge is social-conventional knowledge. This knowledge is sourced in conventions that are made up by people. Thus we know that in the United Kingdom cars are driven on the left-hand side of the road; it is impolite to speak with your mouth full; and we name our numbers one, two, three, and so on. These are conventions and once someone tells you the proper term or what to do, you know it.

The third kind of knowledge is logico-mathematical knowledge. This knowledge is different in that it is not sourced in either the physical world or in the social-conventional world. Rather its source is inside us, in the relationships we perceive among objects. So, we can look at a set of multilink cubes and see them as similar (e.g. made of plastic, same size) or different (e.g. colours) or similar in some ways and different in others. How we perceive their relationship is internal to us. Mathematical knowledge is similar. Children do not learn that what many sets of three objects have in common is their 'threeness' just by being told that or by experiencing the sets through the senses alone. It is something they must figure out for themselves internally through lots of suitable experiences.

Difficulties in teaching mathematics can arise when mathematical knowledge is treated as if it were physical knowledge or social-conventional knowledge. So telling children something in mathematics doesn't mean they have learned it; they must make the connection themselves. Similarly, manipulative materials such as multi-link cubes or base-ten materials may help make some ideas concrete for children, but if connections are not made by each child, the knowledge has not been learned. In other words, mathematics learning requires thinking, in addition to memorising facts.

Big ideas

When teaching mathematics it is easy to focus on a given topic in isolation without referring to other ideas to which the topic is related. Teachers are sometimes encouraged to link topics together for children so that the children come to view a given topic as 'dependent on, and supportive of, other mathematical ideas and concepts'.[8] Sometimes these ideas are referred to as 'big ideas' in mathematics teaching and such ideas provide unity and coherence for what students are expected to learn. This is different to the way content is usually presented in textbooks where each topic is given its own discrete chapter. One scholar names 21 statements that capture the big mathematical ideas that students learn in primary school.[9] Whatever the topic under consideration at a particular time, it should relate to one of the ideas listed in Box AII.1.

Box AII.1 Big ideas in primary school and lower secondary school mathematics[10]

1 *Numbers:* The set of real numbers is infinite, and each real number can be associated with a unique point on the number line.
2 *The base ten numeration system:* The base ten numeration system is a scheme for recording numbers using digits 0-9, groups of ten, and place value.
3 *Equivalence:* Any number, measure, numerical expression, algebraic expression, or equation can be represented in an infinite number of ways that have the same value.
4 *Comparison:* Numbers, expressions, and measures can be compared by their relative values.

---

5 *Operation meanings and relationships:* The same number sentence (e.g. $12 - 4 = 8$) can be associated with different concrete or real-world situations, and different number sentences can be associated with the same concrete or real-world situation.

6 *Properties:* For a given set of numbers there are relationships that are always true, and these are the rules that govern arithmetic and algebra.

7 *Basic facts and algorithms:* Basic facts and algorithms for operations with rational numbers use notions of equivalence to transform calculations into simpler ones.

8 *Estimation:* Numerical calculations can be approximated by replacing numbers with other numbers that are close and easy to compute with mentally. Measurements can be approximated using known referents as the unit in the measurement process.

9 *Patterns:* Relationships can be described and generalisations made for mathematical situations that have numbers or objects that repeat in predictable ways.

10 *Variable:* Mathematical situations and structures can be translated and represented abstractly using variables, expressions and equations.

11 *Proportionality:* If two quantities vary proportionally, that relationship can be represented as a linear function.

12 *Relations and functions:* Mathematical rules (relations) can be used to assign members of one set to members of another set. A special rule (function) assigns each member of one set to a unique member of the other set.

13 *Equations and inequalities:* Rules of arithmetic and algebra can be used together with notions of equivalence to transform equations and inequalities so solutions can be found.

14 *Shapes and solids:* Two- and three-dimensional objects with or without curved surfaces can be described, classified and analysed by their attributes.

15 *Orientation and location:* Objects in space can be oriented in an infinite number of ways, and an object's location in space can be described quantitatively.

16 *Transformations:* Objects in space can be transformed in an infinite number of ways, and those transformations can be described and analysed mathematically.

17 *Measurement:* Some attributes of objects are measurable and can be quantified using unit amounts.

(Continued)

(Continued)

18 *Data collection:* Some questions can be answered by collecting and analysing data, and the question to be answered determines the data that needs to be collected and how best to collect it.
19 *Data representation:* Data can be represented visually using tables, charts, and graphs. The type of data determines the best choice of visual representation.
20 *Data distribution:* There are special numerical measures that describe the centre and spread of numerical data sets.
21 *Chance:* The chance of an event occurring can be described numerically by a number between 0 and 1 inclusive and used to make predictions about other events.

Although this may seem like a long list, it summarises the mathematics students need to learn from birth to well into secondary school. Consider just one of the ideas on the list, that of equivalence. Students need to grasp this concept to appreciate the meaning of the equals sign; they need to know it to master ideas of place value (4 tens and 2 units is equivalent to 3 tens and 12 units); they need to understand equivalent fractions; they need to appreciate equivalence among fractions, decimals and percentages; and they must appreciate equivalent measurements. Typically such topics are presented as discrete topics in textbooks but the big idea of equivalence connects several such apparently discrete topics.

Equivalence is not a trivial topic for students. I recall one girl in third class telling me that two quarters is the same as one half. But although she could show where one half was on the number line, she hesitated to place two quarters on the same point, settling eventually to place it slightly to the left of a half. The possibility of each point on the number line having infinite possible (equivalent) representations had yet to become established for the girl.

The concept of equivalence underpins many commonly used algorithms or procedures in various number operations. By reinforcing the idea of equivalence in each of them, children are encouraged to appreciate connections across the algorithms rather than seeing them as discrete ideas. Take subtraction for instance. The following calculation requires renaming. Children can use their knowledge of equivalence and exchange to accompany the renaming algorithm.

Box AII.2 Subtraction question

$$\begin{array}{r} 345 \\ -169 \\ \hline \end{array}$$

A child might say:

> Five minus 9, I cannot do using whole numbers,[11] but I can exchange one ten for ten units because four tens and five units is equivalent to three tens and fifteen units. Fifteen units minus nine units equals six units. Three tens minus six tens I cannot do, but I can exchange one hundred for ten tens. I now have thirteen tens. Thirteen tens minus six tens is seven tens. Two hundreds minus one hundred is one hundred.

The completed algorithm would look as follows:

Box AII.3 Subtraction algorithm completed

$$\begin{array}{r} {}^{2}\!\!\not{3}\ {}^{13}\!\!4\ {}^{1}5 \\ -\ 1\ \ 6\ \ 9 \\ \hline 1\ \ 7\ \ 6 \end{array}$$

Similar language can be applied to operations with fractions. Take the following calculation as an example:

Box AII.4 Subtraction of fractions algorithm

$$\begin{array}{ccc} 4^{1}/_{2} & 4^{2}/_{4} & {}^{3}\!4\,{}^{6}/_{4} \\ -\ 1^{3}/_{4} & -\ 1^{3}/_{4} & -\ 1^{3}/_{4} \\ & & \hline \\ & & 2^{3}/_{4} \end{array}$$

A student might begin this calculation by saying, 'One half minus three quarters is easier to calculate if both denominators are the same. I know that ½ is equivalent to ¾ so I can rename 4½ as $4^{2}/_{4}$'. If applying the language of exchange consistently, the student may continue:

Two quarters minus three quarters cannot be done without using negative numbers. But I can rename four and two quarters as three and six quarters because I can exchange one unit for four quarters. Six quarters minus three quarters equals three quarters. Three minus one is two.

The language of exchange can be applied to the subtraction of time as well. So if I want to find the difference in the duration of two films, one lasting three hours and four minutes and the other lasting one hour and fifty-three minutes, I might use the following algorithm:

Box AII.5 Subtraction of time algorithm

Hours	Minutes
$^2\not{3}$	^{64}
− 1	53
1	9

In order to do this calculation a student might say:

Four minutes minus fifty-three minutes I cannot do. But I can exchange one hour for sixty minutes because three hours and four minutes is equivalent to two hours and sixty-four minutes. Sixty-four minutes minus fifty-three minutes equals nine minutes. Two hours minus one hour equals one hour. The difference between the duration of the films is one hour and nine minutes.

Not only can such language of exchange and equivalence be used consistently across operations requiring subtraction, it can also be applied to division calculations using the equal sharing algorithm. Take the example of $469 \div 9$:

Box AII.6 Division algorithm

$$9)\ \underline{4\,^46\,^19}$$
$$\quad\ 5\ \ 2\ \ r\,1$$

The language used could be as follows:

I want to share four hundred and sixty-nine objects equally among nine people. I begin by sharing the hundreds. If I try to share four hundreds equally among nine people, I cannot share the hundreds equally in their current form [try to imagine sharing four flats from a set of base ten materials among nine people]. But I can exchange four hundreds for forty tens. I now have forty-six tens. If I share forty-six tens equally among nine people, each person gets five tens and I have one ten left over that I cannot share equally among the nine people. However, I can exchange that ten for ten units. I now have nineteen units. If I share nineteen units equally among nine people, each person receives two units and I have one unit left over. I cannot share that unit among nine people without using fractions so that unit is my remainder.

Focus on skills or practices

In addition to mathematical knowledge for teaching and big ideas, the third priority I would suggest is to focus on developing mathematical skills or practices in children. These are the ways of thinking that mathematicians use and they include: understanding and recalling; implementing; applying and problem solving; reasoning; integrating and connecting; and communicating and expressing. Many of the textbooks currently available do not explicitly help develop such skills but children can be helped to develop them through the use of deliberate and careful questioning. Table AII.1 illustrates how this might happen.

Specific strategies for teaching mathematics

Choosing tasks for use in class

The tasks you choose for children to work on have an important bearing on the kind of mathematics they will learn. A task refers to what you ask the children to do, the way you expect them to do it and the conditions or resources available to the children for completing the task.[12] A good task will require children to think about how to complete it, allow them to do a small amount or a large amount of the problem depending on their knowledge of the topic, provide interesting material for subsequent discussion with the class, tap into more than one mathematical topic and prioritise the quality of children's engagement with the mathematics rather than having lots and lots of tasks.

TABLE AII.1 Questions that can help prompt the development of mathematical skills and practices

Mathematical skill or practice	Questions that might help promote use of the skill or practice
Understanding and recalling	■ How does the commutative property help us in adding/multiplying numbers? ■ How do you define a . . .? ■ How are adding and subtracting related?
Implementing	■ Can you estimate what the answer would be? ■ How would you explain that using base ten materials? ■ Describe how you solved that problem.
Applying and problem solving	■ Could you have done it another way? ■ How did you get that answer? ■ How can you be sure that your answer is correct? ■ Compare the way you and _____ solved the problem.
Reasoning	■ Why . . . would that give the correct answer? ■ Someone else got this (different) answer, how do you think they might have got that answer?
Integrating and connecting	■ Could you draw a picture to illustrate how you approached the problem? ■ Could you think of a faster or more efficient way of doing that? ■ How does that connect with what we were doing in fractions/decimals/3D shapes etc.?
Communicating and expressing	■ Do you agree or disagree with . . .? ■ Put into your own words . . . ■ Are you saying that . . .?

Here are some examples of the kind of problems I'm thinking of:

■ 'A fourth-grade class needs five leaves each day to feed its 2 caterpillars. How many leaves would they need each day for 12 caterpillars?'

(Stein, Engle, Smith & Hughes, 2008, p. 316)

■ A car is going 55 km per hour. Make a diagram to show where it will be

(a) After an hour

(b) After two hours

(c) After half an hour

(d) After 15 minutes

(Problem slightly modified from Lampert, 2001, p. 11)

■ 'Gold leaf is a sheet of very thin gold. It is expensive and used on special occasions. It comes in square sheets with a side length of 12 cm.

(i) How many sheets of gold leaf would be needed to cover your desk?

(ii) Explain your answer. Remember you can cut the gold leaf but you don't want to waste any of it because it is expensive.'

(PDST & Delaney, 2012, p. 6)

In order to begin any of these tasks, students need to think about what to do. No hint is given as to the operation that is required. Even if students are unable to complete any problem in its entirety, most should be able to do enough to have some interest in the subsequent discussion about the problem that takes place in class. The caterpillar problem taps into ideas of proportionality. The car problem draws on children's knowledge of distance, time, fractions, multiplication and division. The gold-leaf problem draws on children's knowledge of length, area, scale, shape, multiplication, division and fractions/decimals.

The tasks most widely available to you in your mathematics lessons are usually those in the mathematics textbook. However, sometimes those tasks are predictable and repetitive; they relate only to one topic and make little attempt to provide for differentiation. Many textbooks that are available present lots of tasks in formats such as those shown in Box AII.7.

Box AII.7 A typical set of 'tasks' from a conventional mathematics textbook

	(a)	(b)	(c)	(d)	(e)
1	764 ÷ 38	149 ÷ 27	371 ÷ 69	452 ÷ 37	874 ÷ 46
2	684 ÷ 75	957 ÷ 51	356 ÷ 72	587 ÷ 16	863 ÷ 47
3	978 ÷ 98	862 ÷ 34	739 ÷ 49	829 ÷ 76	738 ÷ 36
4	657 ÷ 73	739 ÷ 38	649 ÷ 43	287 ÷ 17	947 ÷ 67
5	382 ÷ 51	467 ÷ 48	523 ÷ 27	439 ÷ 82	176 ÷ 18

The problem with such tasks is that children know immediately what operation to use, with little or no thought. If they can already do the calculation, they are learning little. If they cannot do the calculation, they are unlikely to learn how to do so with such tasks. The best that can be said for the calculations is that they may help students be able to do the calculations more automatically. However, it would be relatively easy to improve the problems just a little by amending the task in ways such as the following: 'Write a word problem where 764 ÷ 38 is the answer'; 'What number do I have to multiply by 46 to give me 874?'; 'Find three ways to calculate 829 ÷ 76'.

Sometimes the task is made easier by specifying a particular method to use when doing a calculation (see Box AII.8). But when a student faces such problems in tests, such guidance may not be provided and the student may struggle to know how to attempt the calculation.

Box AII.8 Sample problems from a textbook where students are told which method to use

Use the fraction method to find:

	(a)	(b)	(c)	(d)	(e)
1	50% of 250	10% of 170	$33\frac{1}{3}$% of 156	1% of 32 g	25% of €68
2	20% of 60 kg	$12\frac{1}{2}$% of 24	30% of 425	60% of 320	10% of €32

The shortage of suitable problems that are readily available to teachers means that teachers need to do a lot of searching to find good problems. Websites such as NRICH[13] help but you would definitely need to supplement those problems with problems from other sources. This adds a lot to a beginning teacher's workload. But if you keep an eye out for such rich mathematics problems, and gather them together, you will build up a collection of them over time.

Conducting whole-class discussions

I referred a few times to the importance of having students talk about mathematics in class. Seeking multiple solutions to problems and asking students to explain their reasoning is central to what is considered good mathematics teaching in most contemporary research on mathematics education.[14] However, discussion alone will not suffice. The discussion must build toward important mathematical ideas. That means that you need to ensure that the discussion is helping students who get wrong answers, and that connections are being made among different solutions, and that attention is paid to the solution strategies that are most useful or efficient in particular circumstances.[15]

Sometimes when people observe my teaching, they comment on how I act as a 'facilitator'. However, I associate the role of facilitator as acting in a neutral way and allowing everyone to contribute. Teaching requires more deliberate action in order to direct the discussion towards student learning.

In recognising the need to make the teacher's role in conducting discussions more visible, five steps have been identified[16] which a beginning teacher can work towards in order to lead educationally effective discussions in mathematics lessons. The steps are the following:

1 Before the children begin working on a task, anticipate the likely responses children will give to the task.

2 When children are working on the task, monitor the responses for their learning potential during the exploratory phase of the lesson.

3 After students have completed substantial work on the task, select children who will present their responses.

4 During the discussion of the task, purposefully sequence the responses that will be shared.

5 Help the class make connections between one response and another and between responses and key mathematical ideas.

It's easy to write down such steps but putting them into practice takes time. Set yourself an achievable goal. Choose one at a time and get some practice doing that. As you gain confidence in doing it, you may decide to take on another one. Remember that teaching is all about learning, for you as well as for the children.

Teaching that tries to help every child develop 'conceptual understanding, procedural fluency, strategic competence, adaptive reasoning, and productive disposition' towards mathematics has been labelled as 'ambitious mathematics teaching'.[17] Although it has been called ambitious, Lampert and her colleagues believe that such teaching is learnable by novices. They describe some activities they believe offer a 'productive starting place'[18] for novices. Three of the activities are:

1 *Choral counting:* Lead the class in a count. You decide what number to start with and what to count by. It could be in 2s, 10s, 19s, 3/4s etc.

2 *Strategy sharing:* Elicit multiple ways of solving a computational problem and help the class understand the general logic underlying each solution.

3 *Strings:* Pose several related computational problems and build on each one to try a more difficult one. So, you could use 4 × 4, 4 × 40 and 4 × 39. Or you could use 1 ÷ ¼, 5 ÷ ¼, 5¾ ÷ ¼.

As I finish this appendix, I am conscious that you receive much advice from many sources. Although it is important, teaching mathematics is just one of the many aspects of teaching you have to work on. And teaching is just one part of your life. Take your time. Although beginning teachers cannot be expected to change the culture of mathematics teaching, your energy and enthusiasm may help you to discriminate between the aspects of the culture of teaching mathematics that are helpful for children's learning and the aspects that are not.

Notes

1 An earlier version of this appendix was presented at the 2014 annual conference of the Standing Conference on Teacher Education North and South.
2 Stigler & Hiebert (1999).
3 Cooney (1985); Lampert (2001).
4 Cooney (1985).
5 For example Ball (1988).
6 Ball, Thames & Phelps (2008).
7 For example Kamii, Rummelsburg & Kari (2005).
8 Government of Ireland (1999, p. 3).
9 Charles (2005).
10 These are taken from Charles (2005), either verbatim or slightly paraphrased.
11 In saying 'using whole numbers' I am trying to make explicit the assumption that it is only true to say that 9 cannot be taken from 5 in the world of whole numbers; if we were using integers, 9 can be taken from 5, it is −4.
12 Doyle (1983).
13 http://nrich.maths.org/frontpage.
14 For example Chapin, O'Connor & Anderson (2003); Stein et al. (2008).
15 Smith & Stein (2011); Stein et al. (2008).
16 Stein et al. (2008).
17 Lampert, Beasley, Ghousseini, Kazemi & Franke (2010, p. 129).
18 Lampert et al. (2010, p. 136).

References

Ball, D. L. (1988). Unlearning to teach mathematics. *For the Learning of Mathematics,* *8*(1), 40–48.

Ball, D. L., Thames, M. H. & Phelps, G. (2008). Content knowledge for teaching: What makes it special? *Journal of Teacher Education, 59*(5), 389–407.

Chapin, S. H., O'Connor, C. & Anderson, N. C. (2003). *Classroom discussions: Using math talk to help students learn, grades 1–6.* Sausalito, CA: Math Solutions Publications.

Charles, R. I. (2005). Big ideas and understandings as the foundation for elementary and middle school mathematics. *Journal of Mathematics Education Leadership, 8*(1), 9–24.

Cooney, T. J. (1985). A beginning teacher's view of problem solving. *Journal for Research in Mathematics Education, 16*(5), 324–336.

Doyle, W. (1983). Academic work. *Review of Educational Research, 53*(2), 159–199.

Government of Ireland. (1999). *Primary school curriculum: Mathematics.* Dublin: The Stationery Office.

Kamii, C., Rummelsburg, J. & Kari, A. (2005). Teaching arithmetic to low-performing, low-SES first graders. *Journal of Mathematical Behavior, 24*, 39–50.

Lampert, M. (2001). *Teaching problems and the problems of teaching.* New Haven, CT: Yale University Press.

Lampert, M., Beasley, H., Ghousseini, H., Kazemi, E. & Franke, M. L. (2010). Using designed instructional activities to enable novices to manage ambitious mathematics teaching. In M. K. Stein & L. Kucan (Eds), *Instructional explanations in the disciplines.* New York: Springer Science+Business Media.

PDST & Delaney, S. (2012). *Area 5: Replacement unit.* Dublin: PDST/Marino Institute of Education.

Smith, M. & Stein, M. K. (2011). *5 practices for orchestrating productive mathematics discussions.* Reston, VA: National Council of Teachers of Mathematics.

Stein, M. K., Engle, R. A., Smith, M. S. & Hughes, E. K. (2008). Orchestrating productive mathematical discussions: Five practices for helping teachers move beyond show and tell. *Mathematical Thinking and Learning, 10*(4), 313–340. doi: 10.1080/10986060802229675

Stigler, J. W. & Hiebert, J. (1999). *The teaching gap: Best ideas from the world's teachers for improving education in the classroom.* New York: The Free Press.

Appendix III

Setting up for teaching in early childhood education

Very often novice teachers begin their careers teaching children in younger classes. Although teaching early childhood classes requires particular expertise, the positivity of the children towards their teacher makes it all a worthwhile, if initially daunting and exhausting experience. One of my colleagues who spent a lot of time teaching children of this age describes junior and senior infants as 'natural philosophers' – asking 'why' comes naturally to them. Children at that age also have a keen sense of justice. Provided rules are explained to them, they will follow them and will report any of their peers who do not.

Most children will have attended at least one year of pre-school before they begin primary school. Although frameworks are available that detail guidelines for work in infant classes,[1] this appendix addresses some questions that novice teachers may have when setting up for working with early childhood classes. In order to answer the questions, I spoke to an experienced teacher of children in the early years, Sarah Lawrence,[2] and began by asking her to show me the timetable she uses. The timetable she showed me is one she used when teaching a combined class of junior and senior infants (four- to six-year-olds) in the Republic of Ireland (Figure AIII.1).

Sarah explained that although the timetable looks quite rigid, she uses it mainly as a guide and as a way of making sure that her time is distributed proportionally across all subjects. She said that it takes a few weeks before she even tries to apply the timetable with the reception class but that by having

TIME	MONDAY	TUESDAY	WEDNESDAY	THURSDAY	FRIDAY
9:20	Assembly/Settling in				
9:40	Language 1 (Focus on reading activities and oral language)				
10:05	Roll Call/Informal Conversation in Language 2				
10:15	Mathematics				
10:45	Arts Ed. (Music)				SESE (Science)
11:00	Short Break				
11:10	Mathematics*	SESE (Integrated)*	Language 1 (Focus on writing)*	Arts Ed (Drama)*	SPHE (30 mins) / Language 1 (Writing – 20 mins)*
12:00	Religious Education				
12:30	Lunch Break				
3:00	Arts Ed. (Visual Arts)	SESE (History)	PE	SESE (Geography)	PE
13:30–14:00		Language 2	Language 2	Language 2	Language 2

Figure AIII.1 Sample timetable for teaching junior infants and senior infants

* Each of these subjects is intended to be taught in an integrated manner through play-based activities

(Time allocation: Language 1 (3 h 15 min); Language 2 (2 h plus informal conversation at roll call); Maths (3 hours 20 min); Social, Environmental & Scientific Education – SESE (2 h 5 min); Social, Personal and Health Education – SPHE (30 min); PE (1 h); Arts Ed (2 h 50 min); Discretionary (0 h); Religious Education (2 h 30 min); Assembly (1 h 40 min); Roll call (50 min). Stories are incorporated into the teaching of all subjects to develop children's imaginations and their vocabulary.

it ready from the start of the year, it gives her guidance about where she wants to go with them.

She said that she also includes transition activities between subjects on the timetable. These are activities that provide an opportunity for the children to do some actions or revise some rhymes or poems between one lesson and another. For example, the children may chorally count backwards from ten to one and jump up at the end; they may sing 'if you're happy and you know it, clap your hands' and so on.

Some aspects of the timetable strike me as unusual. I notice, for example, that she doesn't allow any time for the children to eat their lunches or to put on their coats if the day is cold. Sarah explained that a lot of time at the start of the year goes into teaching the children how to put on and take off their coats and helping them to do so. The same applies to eating their lunches and tidying up afterwards. In practice, sometimes she shortens the morning assembly time and starts the formal teaching a bit earlier and moves back each subsequent slot on the timetable to allow time for the children to eat and put on their coats before break.

I also note that she allows no time for giving homework or for tidying up at the end of the day. Sarah says that getting the children to tidy up is important but that after a couple of weeks, the children become quite efficient at tidying up. When she gives homework, she has it written on a sheet which is handed to the children as they are collected by the responsible person. She is reluctant to timetable such matters because she finds that if you allow ten minutes here and five minutes there, such administrative matters can eat into your teaching time. She tries to make running the classroom as smooth as possible through the use of routines.

Routines

Sarah explained that at the start of the year she carefully thinks through the kinds of routines she will use in the classroom during the year. She spends the first few weeks explicitly teaching the children how the routines work. She has routines for arriving in the morning, putting away their lunches, lining up to leave the room (in pairs and with a length of tape stuck on the floor for guidance), distributing copies and books, borrowing pencils, calling the roll, using the bin, going to the toilet and tidying up. She finds that once these are introduced and followed consistently, the children are really good at following them, and at identifying peers who flout them!

Introducing such routines to junior infants is much easier with senior infants in the room. They model them on a daily basis, making it easy for the junior infants to emulate. Later in the year she assigns tasks to children to encourage them to be responsible and to promote independence.

Setting up the room

When I asked Sarah about setting up the room for teaching children in the early years, she identified things that were for her use and a long list of resources for children. But first she talked about some of the play spaces she likes to have in her classroom.

Types of play

When Sarah thinks about setting up play areas in her classroom, she thinks of different types of play such as exploratory; constructive; creative; pretend, fantasy and sociodramatic; physical locomotor; and language or word play.[3] Among the kinds of play areas she has set up are the following:

Box AIII.1 Play areas in one early years classroom

Exploratory play:	Sorting and matching activities, geometric shapes
Constructive play:	Blocks, playdough, materials for collage and junk art, jigsaws, sand and water
Creative play:	Open-ended materials such as lengths of fabric, off-cuts of wood, lengths of plastic tubing. Any items that are safe can be used and the children can use them to make different things every day
Pretend, fantasy and sociodramatic play:	Clothes for dressing up, objects such as cash register and stethoscope, home corner, small world play
Physical locomotor play:	Plasticine, writing activities
Language or word play:	Board games, listening activities, book area, word games

---

Teaching resources

When Sarah was asked to name the kinds of resources she has in her classroom, she laughed, 'where do I start?!' There is just so much material that is useful in infant classes. She named books – big and small, plasticine, letter magnets, puppets, toy animals, beads/buttons for threading, links, pegs and peg boards, straws and links, compare bears, cubes, jigsaws (up to 100 pieces), bingo games, playing cards, dominoes, various kinds of building blocks, clothes and accessories for dressing up (avoiding high heels and hats), items for sorting, mini whiteboards and markers, male and female dolls of different ethnicities, road mat (with vehicles), tea set, cash register and coins, coloured paper, scissors, crayons, glue sticks.

Many of these materials come in cardboard boxes and Sarah suggests storing them in plastic containers such as lunch boxes or even the containers that takeaways sometimes come in. In relation to the jigsaws, she says it is worth putting a number, letter or sticker on the back of each piece and on the box because it makes it easier to replace pieces that go missing. If she gets rid of the jigsaw box, she takes a photo of the completed jigsaw with her phone and includes the picture of it in the plastic box.[4]

Displays

Sarah also listed charts that are useful for displaying in an early years classroom. They include letters of the alphabet, number strips (first) and number lines (later) up to 10 for junior infants and up to 20 for senior infants; these may be on the wall and on the children's desks. Other displays for the wall include days of the week, months of the year, colours, nursery rhymes, opposites, shapes, height chart, weather chart, seasons chart, question words, pictures for developing children's oral language.

Personalised displays may also be used such as the children's names, and photographs and a list of the children's birthdays. Furthermore, as early as she can, she displays work done by the children on the classroom walls.

Sarah labels everything in the classroom to create what her college lecturers called a 'print-rich environment' to support children's development of sight vocabulary. The play area uses several signs such as 'waiting room', 'ticket office' and 'please queue here'. Sometimes she writes the labels out herself, as neatly as possible. She notices that a colleague in a nearby school now types out and prints such labels but had to download a special font to do so because most standard fonts do not provide the kind of letters that the children are expected to use.[5]

Other requirements for setting up an early years classroom

Finally, Sarah listed items that she uses herself. She mentioned the need for kitchen roll to mop up spills and tissues for cleaning eyes and noses.

Although children may have toilet accidents at any age, they are more likely to occur in early childhood classes. For this reason Sarah keeps at least one change of clothes handy for when this happens. It may include tracksuit bottoms, underwear and socks, along with a pair of rubber gloves. She also keeps plastic bags for sending home wet or soiled clothes so that parents can wash the spare set of classroom clothing and return them for use when the next accident happens.

She also noted how quickly the children accumulate pages of work during the year and how important it is to store them well. Several years ago she asked a dressmaker to sew up thirty-five fabric 'pouches', which were big enough to hold A4-sized pages. She hangs these on 'clothes-lines' around the walls of the classrooms and allocates one for each child to store their pages. Every so often they are emptied and brought home to parents. Her colleagues use magazine files or empty cereal boxes for the same purpose.

For art lessons the children wear aprons so that they won't get paint on their clothes. However, she notes that the school only bought these recently. Prior to that they used discarded long-sleeved adults' shirts with the ends of the sleeves cut off or tied up and they worked fine too.

Topics and themes

Sarah identified many themes and topics that she has used for integration over the years. They include:

- *People who help us:* Garda, fire fighter, butcher, doctor, vet, nurse, shop assistant, postal worker.
- *Services:* shop, hotel, restaurant, post office, jeweller, bank, hairdresser, optician, TV station.
- *Animals:* fish, birds, mini-beasts, dinosaurs, life cycles, pets.
- *Plants:* flowers, trees, vegetables, school garden, eco-systems, habitats.
- *Seasons and festivals:* spring, summer, autumn, winter, holidays, Hallowe'en, celebrations, birthdays.
- *Myself and others:* family, senses, feelings, clothes, food, how I've grown, babies, friends.
- *Places:* zoo, farm, city, garden, desert, space, other countries, traditions, seaside.
- *Sports, toys and games:* toys from the past, Lego.
- *Films and books:* Bible stories, nursery rhymes, fairy tales, picture books, poetry, fiction.
- *Houses and homes:* kinds of homes (e.g. terrace, semi-detached, apartment, temporary dwellings), animal homes, traditional homes in different countries.
- *Forms of transport:* bus, train, car, bicycle, tram, airplane, ship.
- *Maths and science:* pattern, water, weather, magnets, pictograms, shapes, height chart.
- *Other:* pirates, princesses, circus.

In selecting themes to develop, Sarah frequently offers choices to the children so that they have agency in their learning. Over the course of a year she aims to balance teacher-led and child-led topics and activities. She finds that offering choices is motivational for the children and helps promote their creativity. Many of the topics she has used are good for promoting dialogue in the classroom, both child–child dialogue and child–adult dialogue.

Parents as partners

Throughout the year Sarah communicates frequently with the children's parents and guardians. She sees them as partners in their children's education and keeps in touch through notes, phone-calls, e-mail and informal conversations. Similarly, she encourages parents to inform her of anything that may affect their children's learning and to raise any questions they have with her.

Work for early finishers

In the early years classroom, as in most other classrooms, children will finish work at different times. It is essential for the smooth running of the classroom that the children know what they can do if they finish early. The goal is to find activities that are worthwhile educationally, while not being so attractive that the children will rush the main task in order to engage in the early finishers' work.

Sarah places a basket of activities on each desk at the start of the day, which children can use if they finish work early. Each basket contains different items and the baskets are rotated around the desks during the week. One basket contains books, another contains marla (modelling clay) and A4 sheets of lino to prevent the desk from becoming 'sticky,' one contains beads to thread, one contains materials that can be sorted in different ways, one contains small jigsaw puzzles, and another contains paper, pencils and colours for writing. Occasionally Sarah will ask children who finish early to do a job in the classroom, such as tidy the library or tidy up some toys.

First day with junior infants

Like many teachers who have experience in teaching children in their early years, Sarah has very clear ideas about how to make the first day of school run smoothly:

There are no guarantees, each year it is unpredictable because you don't know how a particular child or parent will react on the first day. I find it easier now that I have the senior infants in the classroom as well because they can help the junior infants to settle in by showing them routines.

However, she has taught in schools where there were no senior infants in the room to help the junior infants settle in.

Sarah plans the day like clockwork. Every child's name is written on a sticker and given to the child as they enter the room. As the children arrive Sarah is prepared to receive books and notebooks that the parents bring with them. Sarah read an idea on a discussion board which she has now adopted for her own class. She has a paper bag for every child and as parents arrive with children's books, Sarah puts each child's books into a separate bag, with the child's name on it, for sorting out later.[6] Sarah knows that the day is an important, sometimes difficult, one for the parents as well. She also knows that the sooner the parents leave, the sooner she will be able to begin helping the children settle into school.

When the children enter the room, they hear some gentle music playing in the background and they see a selection of toys laid out on tables around the room. The children may choose where they want to sit and the activity they want to engage with. The activities chosen for the tables include construction toys such as straws or bricks, drawing and colouring, farm animals, jigsaws, pegboards and pegs, board games and small world play (such as a doll's house and tea set). She puts out nothing too messy (such as sand, water or play dough) on the first day because it makes tidying up more difficult.

When the time seems right, usually about twenty minutes after the children arrive, Sarah politely asks any lingering parents to leave and shortly afterwards she talks to the children about tidying up the toys they have been playing with. She then talks to them about some classroom rules and procedures – about the importance of tidying up after each activity, about going to the toilet, flushing the toilet and washing their hands. Then they begin to do some action rhymes together such as 'The wheels on the bus', 'Head, shoulders, knees and toes', and 'If you're happy and you know it', and number games such as 'Ten green bottles'. She also reads a story to the children at this time.

The next routine the children need to learn about is lunchtime and Sarah takes time to show the children how to get their lunch boxes, how to eat their lunch, how to clean up spills and how to put away their lunch boxes. She lets the children have their break time at a different time to the other children for the first few days. However, she does line the children up and bring them out to the playground so that they can play there for a while. She then brings them on a tour of the school, so that they get to see other classrooms, including other teachers and any brothers and sisters the children might have in older classes.

One piece of advice that Sarah passes on to any teacher is the value of a second adult in the room on the first day. This could be a resource teacher or a special needs assistant but she has found that it helps the day run more smoothly if there is a second person to help out, even just to make sure that no child goes missing on the first day.

Notes

1 For example, Aistear in the Republic of Ireland.
2 Sarah attributes her ideas to previous colleagues and to many sources, in print and online. In particular she attributes many of her ideas to web forums such as: http://forum.educationposts.ie/index.php and to websites such as http://siolta.ie/ and http://www.ncca.ie/en/Curriculum_and_Assessment/Early_Childhood_and_Primary_Education/Early_Childhood_Education/.
3 Kernan (2007).
4 This idea was taken from http://forum.educationposts.ie.
5 The best font on most standard word-processing packages is Comic Sans but the letter q and the number 4 are different to what is expected. Sassoon fonts are closer to what children are expected to use and can be downloaded, for a charge, from http://www.sassoonfont.co.uk/. An alternative font that is similar can be downloaded from http://www.cursivewriting.org/.
6 Idea taken from http://forum.educationposts.ie/thread-9801.html.

Reference

Kernan, M. (2007). *Play as a context for early learning and development: A research paper.* Dublin: National Council for Curriculum and Assessment.

Appendix IV

Independent study strategies for children to learn

The purpose of this appendix is to support teachers in having productive discussions with children about how they do homework. It outlines strategies that can help to develop children's study skills during their time in school and for learning through life. The appendix begins with different ways children can be taught to memorise content in spellings, tables, poetry and general information. This is followed by strategies for getting organised to study and ways to think about what needs to be learned. It concludes with questions children can ask themselves as they learn to become better at studying.

Spelling strategies

Initially, children benefit from learning spellings taken from a common list of words that arise frequently for children of a particular age group. In time, children can transition to learning spellings from a personal spelling list drawn up based on each student's spelling needs and previous spelling errors. Because spelling is primarily a visual skill, it is better for children to group words that look the same for learning (e.g. what, hat; ear, bear, beard, hear, heard) rather than simply words that sound the same (e.g. herd, heard, erred; foe, go, owe, though, throw).[1] A useful strategy for learning spellings is to follow this series of steps:

1 Pronounce each word carefully.

2 Look carefully at each part of the word as you pronounce it.

3 Say the letters in sequence.

4 Attempt to recall how the word looks, then spell the word.

5 Check this attempt to recall.

6 Write the word.

7 Check this spelling attempt.

8 Repeat the above steps if necessary.[2]

Teachers could teach children to use this strategy to help them learn spellings for homework. A condensed version of this list is the widely used 'Look, Cover, Write, Check' strategy.

Alternatively, children can be encouraged to try and connect a new word being learned to spellings they already know. For example, if they are learning the word 'mandate', it may help them if they already know how to spell 'ate', 'date', 'an' and 'man'.

Some words, whose spellings are easily confused, can be remembered using specific strategies such as identifying words within words or breaking down syllables.[3] 'A secretary may have to keep a secret' is an example of learning a word contained within the bigger word. Exaggerating the syllables in a word such as 'Wed-nes-day' may help children remember its spelling. Other strategies can be based on relating an aspect of the word to its meaning. For example, if you confuse 'desert' and 'dessert', it is helpful to remember that a dessert is 'so sweet' and thus contains two s's. Each strategy is a way of getting children to attend more closely to the words when learning them so that the children can recall the spellings later when they need them in their writing.

Tables/number facts strategies

Knowing basic number facts in addition, subtraction, multiplication and division is essential for progress in mathematics. However, many children find it hard to learn off tables in lists as they chant, $3 + 0 = 3$, $3 + 1 = 4$, $3 + 2 = 5$, $3 + 3 = 6$ and so on. In order to memorise tables or number facts effectively, children need to experience three phases of learning. The first involves counting strategies. Children need to begin with a good sense of the cardinality of numbers – that is, being able to recognise and label sets of objects. Many children who struggle at mathematics cannot do this even by eight years of age and that complicates the learning of tables for those children.

The second phase of learning is to use facts children already know about numbers to figure out answers to calculations. Children can study an addition table or a multiplication table and try to identify patterns among the numbers. Some of these patterns will help them memorise key number facts. For example, through experience with lots of examples, children may notice that adding one to a whole number results in the subsequent whole number every time, or multiplying any number by one produces the same number every time.

Other patterns and number facts that children may notice are listed in Table AIV.1. Patience is needed during this phase. Children will need to think about their answers and they may be hesitant or slow in doing so. The thinking phase helps children build connections between numbers. It is good for the children to be given opportunities to notice these facts for themselves (through repeated practice of calculations that illustrate the fact). For example, if a child does several problems where they have to multiply numbers by 0, they can be asked if they notice a pattern. If not, more practice may be needed.

When children have mastered the counting strategies and the reasoning strategies outlined in Table AIV.1, they are ready to move to the third

TABLE AIV.1 Reasoning strategies that children may use in preparation for producing number facts from memory

Addition number facts		Multiplication number facts	
Commutative pairs	(e.g. $5 + 3 = 3 + 5$)	Commutative pairs	(e.g. $5 \times 3 = 3 \times 5$)
Add zero	($0 + n = n$)	Times zero	($0 \times n = 0$)
Add one	(next number)	Times one	($1 \times n = n$)
Add two	(next number and the next number)	Times two	(same as doubling)
Add ten	(only the tens digit changes)	Times four	(double and double again)
Doubles	(e.g. $4 + 4$, $7 + 7$)	Times five	(can be linked to 5-minute intervals on the clock)
Near doubles	(e.g. $4 + 5 = 4 + (4 + 1) = (4 + 4) + 1$)	Times nine	(multiply by ten and subtract one set)
Through ten	(e.g. $7 + 4 = 7 + (3 + 1) = (7 + 3) + 1$)	Times ten	(digit(s) move(s) one place to right)

phase of learning, which is meaningful mastery of the facts, where they can produce the answers automatically from memory. They are supported in doing this by the previous phases where they developed their number sense. Some children grasp number facts quickly and may appear to skip the first two phases of learning. However, many children will benefit from such deliberate work. By connecting new facts to facts they already know, children's ability to memorise is strengthened.[4] Constance Kamii believes that playing suitable mathematical games can help children develop their number sense.[5]

In keeping with the principle of connecting facts to what children already know, when it is time to learn subtraction facts, they can be related to addition facts. Children can work on families of number facts such as noting that $3 + 5 = 8$ and $5 + 3 = 8$. This can provide the basis for them to figure out that $8 - 5 = 3$ and $8 - 3 = 5$. In a similar way, division facts can be linked to children's knowledge of multiplication facts. The work of learning number facts can be done both in class and at home.

Memorising poetry

Memorising poetry is not as common in schools as it was in the past.[6] Nevertheless, some poetry selected by the teacher is worth learning by heart because it expresses 'the thought and feeling of people who have thought and felt very deeply about our human situation and expressed their discoveries with exceptional fluency and power'.[7] Children can best learn a poem for homework when they have heard it being recited aloud several times beforehand. Although some believe that a poem is best learned as a whole, it can also be broken into 'thought groups rather than into stanzas' in order to learn it. However, the poem should be reassembled as a whole as soon as possible.[8]

It is difficult for children to memorise poetry if they try to do it passively. They need to do it in an intentional or purposeful way and to pay close attention to the poem. This includes listening to the words and not just looking at them. Children should understand as much of the poem as possible before they learn it. The poem should also have personal relevance for the learner.[9] The best way to learn poetry is by heart, with feeling. A teacher needs to realise that even when they make substantial effort, some children are still unable to memorise poetry; nevertheless they can be given opportunities to listen to it, to enjoy its rhythms, rhymes and imagery.[10]

Mnemonics

Mnemonics offer a way that children can be helped to memorise other information. Many of us use mnemonics to recall the colours of the rainbow, the names of the planets, or the order in which to do various operations in a mathematical calculation with brackets, fractions and multiple operations. The single-letter mnemonics used in such examples generally don't work so well because children seem to need more than just the letters for a mnemonic to be memorable.[11]

As an example of how mnemonics can let children down, I observed a teacher showing children how to convert a mixed number to an improper fraction using the mnemonic MAD. 'First Multiply the denominator by the whole number', she said. 'Then, Add the numerator to the product. Finally, remember that the Denominator stays the same'. However, when children tried to apply the mnemonic, those who did not understand the mathematics involved thought that the 'D' stood for Divide rather than Denominator.

More effective than single-letter mnemonics are illustrations that help to explain a word. For example, children may find it difficult to remember whether the Tropic of Cancer or the Tropic of Capricorn is north of the Equator. A teacher could point out that Cancer rhymes with Prancer. Prancer is one of Santa's reindeer. Tradition has it that Santa sets out on his journey from the North Pole so that fact could help children remember that the Tropic of Cancer is the circle of latitude to the north of the Equator. This could be accompanied by a picture like Figure AIV.1.

After children have been introduced to several image mnemonics like this, they can be encouraged to create their own mnemonics for remembering meanings of words, geographical terms, and lists. Those deemed by the class to be most helpful can be shared.

Another kind of mnemonic is the 'pegword' method,[12] which can be used to remember a list of items in order. The first step in this method is to link an image to each of the numbers from one to ten. For example, it could be bun, shoe, tree, door, hive, sticks, heaven, gate, line, hen. Then the list to be remembered is linked to each of the images (in order if necessary). For example, if a teacher wanted to teach the children about life in Britain after World War II, they might want the children to remember the following six facts: the Education Act of 1944 provided for the creation of secondary schools for children aged over 11; the Labour Party won a landslide victory in the General Election of 1945; the National Health Service was introduced in 1948; a family allowance was introduced for each child after the

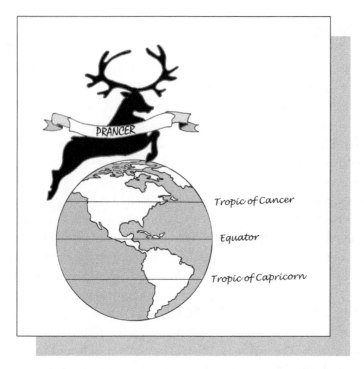

Figure AIV.1 When Prancer leaves the North Pole, he'll arrive at the Tropic of Cancer before he arrives at the Tropic of Capricorn

(Illustration by Emer O'Boyle)

first born; rationing continued until 1954; and damaged houses were rebuilt and new towns were planned.[13]

The six aspects could be remembered using images such as in Figure AIV.2.

Once the images have been established, they can be associated with different lists.

Mnemonic strategies work particularly well for children who struggle in school. However, it takes time for children to learn how mnemonics work and how to use them to help their learning. After children observe a teacher using mnemonics, the children can learn to use them and perhaps learn to create ones that work for them.[14]

Organisational strategies

Some children find it difficult just to get organised to do their homework. This may be why some children take longer to complete homework than

Figure AIV.2 Using the 'pegword' method to remember features of life in Britain after World War II: (a) bun; (b) shoe; (c) tree; (d) door; (e) hive; (f) sticks

(Illustrations by Emer O'Boyle)

teachers expect. If children discuss with their teacher and with each other how they go about doing their homework, they may share and learn strategies that help them to study better. Although each child will need to find what works best for themselves, some general guidelines may help: do difficult work when you are most alert – perhaps at the start of homework time; break up long tasks into shorter parts; alternate different kinds of work – such as writing and reading and learning; and be flexible about planning breaks or making up time if a friend calls or another interruption occurs. If children can establish and maintain a consistent routine for doing their homework, they are likely to succeed in doing it well,[15] even if it takes some time to help them develop these skills initially.[16]

Even when children have become better at time management and getting themselves organised, they need to learn strategies to help them understand and remember what they are expected to know. In order to do this, children need to discover how to make what they learn meaningful to themselves, to connect it to what they already know and to make connections among ideas they are learning.[17] From quite a young age, children can be taught how to understand and summarise text in their own words,[18] and represent ideas in a cognitive organiser like that in Figure AIV.3. However, it takes several weeks of instruction for children to become proficient at creating such cognitive maps.[19]

Monitoring the strategies used

Finally, children need to be able to stand back from the various strategies available to them and select the one that best suits the task being worked on. They need to learn to constantly monitor how effectively they are working. If what they are doing is ineffective, they need to find an alternative way to accomplish it. A teacher can initially ask the children such questions when they are working in class. What are you doing? Is it helping you? Could you do it another way?

Over time, children can be encouraged to ask themselves the questions. When they can ask the questions of themselves without being prompted, they are well on the way to becoming independent learners.[20] The kind of questions children might ask themselves include: Is the strategy I'm using working? Does this material make sense? Do I need to use another strategy? Such questions can be written on charts in the classroom or displayed in a workspace at home. Thus, even if its immediate benefits remain unsupported by research, homework may offer an opportunity for children to practise and develop a broad range of study skills.

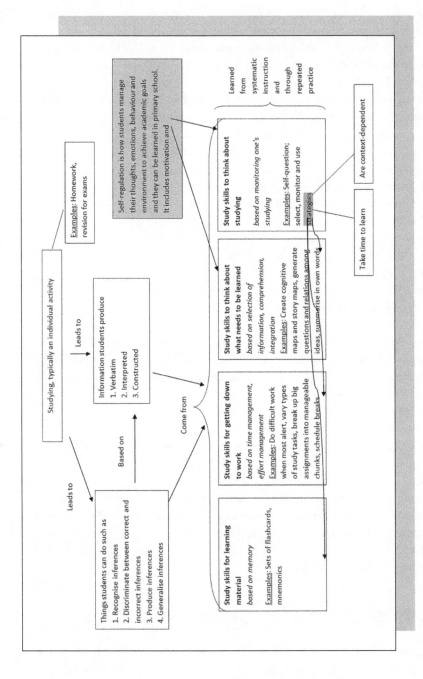

Figure AIV.3 Cognitive map summarising ideas about children developing studying skills to help them with their homework

(Compiled based on information in Baumann & Bergeron, 1993; Gettinger & Seibert, 2002; Ramdass & Zimmerman, 2011; Stoeger & Ziegler, 2008; Thomas & Rohwer, 1986; Wittrock, 1990)

Notes

1 This advice is from Brendan Culligan: http://insideeducation.podbean.com/2010/02/21/programme-33-spellings-and-news-21-2-10/.
2 Quoted in Allal (1997) and based on a method developed by Horn (1954) cited in Graham (1983).
3 Rudling (2011).
4 Although some of this material is widely available, I specifically referred to Baroody, Bajwa & Eiland (2009) when writing this section.
5 See for example Kamii & Anderson (2003), Kato, Honday & Kamii (2006) and https://sites.google.com/site/constancekamii/Kamii.
6 Robson (2012).
7 Blackburn (1966, p. 24).
8 Mackintosh (1927, p. 297).
9 Pullinger (2012).
10 Blackburn (1966).
11 Levin (1993).
12 Levin (1993).
13 These points were taken from http://archive.iwm.org.uk/upload/package/50/children/Exhibition/afterwar.htm.
14 Levin (1993).
15 From Gettinger & Seibert (2002). Gettinger and Seibert identify 'four clusters of study skills'. They are repetition- or rehearsal-based study strategies, procedural or organization-based study skills, cognitive-based study skills and metacognitive-based study skills.
16 Stoeger & Ziegler (2008).
17 Gettinger & Seibert (2002, p. 356).
18 For a research-based description of this see Wittrock (1990) or Baumann & Bergeron (1993); for a manual about helping teachers to develop self-regulated learners see Zimmerman, Bonner & Kovach (1996).
19 Typically six weeks according to Gettinger & Seibert (2002). Cognitive organisers are also referred to as cognitive or semantic maps. More detailed information about using them in primary school is contained in Government of Ireland (1999).
20 Gettinger & Seibert (2002).

References

Allal, L. (1997). Learning to spell in the classroom. In C. A. Perfetti, L. Rieben & M. Fayol (Eds), *Learning to spell* (pp. 129–150). Mahwah, NJ: Lawrence Erlbaum Associates.

Baroody, A. J., Bajwa, N. P. & Eiland, M. (2009). Why can't Johnny remember the basic facts? *Developmental Disabilities Research Reviews, 15*, 69–79.

Baumann, J. F. & Bergeron, B. S. (1993). Story map instruction using children's literature: Effects on first graders' comprehension of central narrative elements. *Journal of Literacy Research, 25*, 407–437.

Blackburn, T. (1966). Some rights and wrongs. In T. Blackburn (Ed.), *Presenting poetry: A handbook for English teachers*. London: Methuen & Co.

Gettinger, M. & Seibert, J. K. (2002). Contributions of study skills to academic competence. *School Psychology Review, 31*(3), 350–365.

Government of Ireland. (1999). *Geography (social, environmental and scientific education): Teacher guidelines*. Dublin: The Stationery Office.

Graham, S. (1983). Effective spelling instruction. *The Elementary School Journal, 83*, 560–567.

Kamii, C. & Anderson, C. (2003). Multiplication games: How we made them and used them. *Teaching Children Mathematics, 10*(3), 135–141.

Kato, Y., Honday, M. & Kamii, C. (2006). Kindergartners play 'Lining up the 5s': A card game to encourage logico-mathematical thinking. *Beyond the Journal, Young Children on the Web*, July, 1–6.

Levin, J. R. (1993). Mnemonic strategies and classroom learning: A twenty-year report card. *The Elementary School Journal, 94*(2), 235–244.

Mackintosh, H. K. (1927). Removing drudgery from the memorization of poetry. *The Elementary English Review, 4*(10), 297–300.

Pullinger, D. (2012). In living memory: The dying art of learning poetry and a case for revival. *Changing English: Studies in Culture and Education, 19*(4), 383–393.

Ramdass, D. & Zimmerman, B. J. (2011). Developing self-regulation skills: The important role of homework. *Journal of Advanced Academics, 22*(2), 194–218.

Robson, C. (2012). *Heart beats: Everyday life and the memorized poem*. Princeton, NJ: Princeton University Press.

Rudling, J. (2011). Spelling strategies and memory tricks for adults. Retrieved 1 April 2014, from http://www.slideshare.net/joannerudling/slideshare-spelling-strategies-memory-tricks

Stoeger, H. & Ziegler, A. (2008). Evaluation of a classroom based training to improve self-regulation in time management tasks during homework activities with fourth graders. *Metacognition Learning, 3*, 207–230.

Thomas, J. W. & Rohwer, W. D. (1986). Academic studying: The role of learning strategies. *Educational Psychologist, 21*(1&2), 19–41.

Wittrock, M. C. (1990). Generative processes of comprehension. *Educational Psychologist, 24*(4), 345–376.

Zimmerman, B. J., Bonner, S. & Kovach, R. (1996). *Developing self-regulated learners: Beyond achievement to self-efficacy*. Washington, DC: American Psychological Association.

Appendix V
Twenty sample tasks

When assigning tasks for children, I usually try to find tasks that will be of interest to me as well as to the children. I am thinking about tasks in a rather generic way here, it may constitute anything from a topic for discussion to a project the children work on over several weeks. Here are twenty tasks that have been used with children, by me or by teachers I know, arranged according to subject area.

Language

1　What are the advantages of wearing a school uniform?
2　What kind of books do eight-year-olds enjoy?
3　Compile stories that were told to you by your grandparents.

Mathematics

4　How many calculations can you make that result in the answer 12?
5　Identify as many 3-D shapes as you can in your school, locality. What shapes can you not classify?
6　How can you add all the numbers from 1 to 100?

History, geography, science

7　What legacy of the Vikings/Normans/Romans/Celts is evident in your country today?

8 How could you travel from City A to City B?

9 What's the difference between a moth and a butterfly?

10 Identify the names of the trees, plants and flowers in your school grounds, local park, home etc.

Physical education

11 How can you travel across the room without your feet touching the floor?

12 Make up a dance sequence to accompany this music.

The arts

13 Create a pattern for wallpaper.

14 Make a quilt using patches of fabric that have been tie-died.

15 What notes could you use to make up four beats?

16 Create a drama about someone who is happy, afraid, lonely, shy in school.

Social, personal and health education

17 How could you let someone know that you are angry?

18 What foods should be eaten in moderation?

19 How can you (encourage someone to) keep safe at the beach?

General

20 Write down a question that cannot be answered by reading a book, looking up an encyclopaedia or by doing a World Wide Web search. Now write down several more. Now choose which question you'd most like to answer.

Index